A LAWYER PRESENTS
THE EVIDENCE FOR
THE AFTERLIFE

A LAWYER PRESENTS THE EVIDENCE FOR THE AFTERLIFE

BY

VICTOR ZAMMIT
(Retired Lawyer)

AND

WENDY ZAMMIT

www.whitecrowbooks.com

A Lawyer Presents the Evidence for the Afterlife (1ˢᵗ Edition)

Published and printed in the United States of America and the United Kingdom by White Crow Books; an imprint of White Crow Productions Ltd.

White Crow Books
3 Merrow Grange
Horseshoe Lane East
Guildford
GU1 2QW
United Kingdom
e-mail: info@whitecrowbooks.com

Cover design: Caroline Sloneem
Production: essentialworks.co.uk
Design: Perseus-Design.com

Paperback ISBN   978-1-908733-22-1
eBook ISBN   978-1-908733-43-6

Non Fiction / Body, Mind & Spirit / Parapsychology

www.whitecrowbooks.com

To all those who are working to spread the light

CONTENTS

INTRODUCTION

Why read this book?

There could be many reasons why you picked up this book. Perhaps you are just curious about the afterlife. Or perhaps you have experienced the death of a loved one. It may be that you have had an out-of-body experience or a near-death experience or another mystical experience. Or you may be realizing that we all inevitably have to make the journey to the afterlife one day.

If you have been trained to respect scientific method, you will not accept tradition or wishful thinking. You want something that can be supported by evidence. You want highly reliable information as to whether or not we continue to live in the afterlife. And you want to know whether it is possible to get a message from your loved ones.

You want to know that the things people report about the afterlife are real and can be validated. You want hard, repeatable evidence that no one can rebut. You want witnesses – scientists, professionals and others with the highest credibility. You want to feel that the information you are receiving about the afterlife is the truth, the verifiable truth. And you may want something that you can share with friends and family members to show that there are good scientific reasons for accepting that there is more to life than the materialists claim.

This book presents highly convincing evidence amounting to proof for the existence of the afterlife. It shows that after investigating the evidence some of the most brilliant men and women – scientists and others – came to the conclusion that we all survive death.

The mediums and psychics studied by scientists were of course exceptional. They were the best of the best. People should be aware that not all psychics and mediums are developed to this degree and people need to take care in choosing a medium.

Over the last ten years an earlier book has been accessed on our website free of charge by more than a million people from all over the world. Readers who loved the earlier book translated it into Spanish, Italian, Portuguese, Dutch, German, French and Russian. Every day we receive emails from people who say that the material in this book has changed their lives.

After so many years we have decided that it is time to take the Evidence for the Afterlife to a wider audience. This new and expanded version includes important new research and the latest discoveries. But once again it concentrates on evidence that is credible, repeatable and admissible in a court of law.

The book gives an introduction to more than 20 different areas of evidence for the afterlife giving you the key facts and references. The chapters can be read in any order. We realize that many people reading it will not have English as their first language. We have tried to make it accessible to as many people as possible by writing in plain English, using short sentences and familiar vocabulary. Links to videos, audio interviews, pictures and excellent books for each chapter are contained on our website www.victorzammit.com. There you can also sign up for our free weekly Friday Afterlife Report. We are now in the thirteenth year of sending out these highly researched and informative weekly reports.

Victor and Wendy Zammit,
February 2013

ATTESTATIONS

The evidence for the survival of consciousness after death falls much more in the area of courtroom science than laboratory science. Who, then, more qualified to examine and weigh the evidence than Victor Zammit, a retired attorney. This book offers intriguing and convincing evidence that should meet the "beyond a reasonable doubt" standard of any open-minded reader.

MICHAEL TYMN, AUTHOR & EDITOR, HAWAII
VICE-PRESIDENT, ACADEMY OF SPIRITUALITY &
PARANORMAL STUDIES

Victor approaches the question of life after death as he would the key issues in a legal trial. He considers the arguments offered by the opposition in the light of the wide range of evidence. He leads the reader inexorably through his point-by-point analysis to his ultimate conclusion that there is an afterlife. He then proceeds to present a summary description of life in the hereafter. *A Lawyer Presents the Evidence for the Afterlife* is a must-read for anyone who has not made up his or her mind on whether the afterlife exists.

STEVE HEDGES
LAWYER, USA

As an attorney who has tried many jury cases to final verdict in California and Nevada and tried many nonjury trials to verdict, I can honestly state that the evidence Victor presents is very persuasive, and thanks to his work and my own independent review I now fully accept that the afterlife exists.

MICHAEL DANNER
LAWYER, CYPRESS CALIFORNIA, USA

A Lawyer Presents the Evidence for the Afterlife provided me with an informative, detailed launchpad for research into the afterlife. Being a scientist by profession, I was very skeptical of the paranormal phenomena that presents itself (ever more so) in our world. Fortunately I maintained an open-minded approach to the subject and upon reading the book I was compelled to research further. The more I read, the more overwhelming is the evidence that an everlasting afterlife awaits us once we leave this physical world. Thank you for changing my life for the better.

EDDIE DZENIS (BSc. SYD.)
SYDNEY, AUSTRALIA

Victor and Wendy your book on the afterlife is so full of information of the utmost importance and gives so complete a picture of the subject that anybody should be convinced of the truth it contains, even the very skeptical, on the condition that he or she is only open-minded. Being a lawyer, Victor, you wrote it bearing in mind the challenge of the acceptability of the proof. Thank you so much for the book and its extension through your weekly reports.

EDOUARD LE FEVRE
JENNINGS, USA
INDEPENDENT VETERINARY PROFESSIONAL, FRANCE

This may be the most important book that you will ever read! Without the need to 'believe' or 'to have faith' this book shows you through scientific method and first-person testimonies *exactly* what to expect after death. Logic and knowledge dispel fear and superstition and this book has it all! I cannot recommend this book highly enough.

GARY J MCCLEARY
MATHEMATICS TEACHER AND PARANORMAL AUTHOR, AUSTRALIA

Your fantastic book is packed with facts and evidence that no one can deny, and it's the first book I recommend to anyone interested. Alongside gaining personal evidence, reading it is by far the most comprehensive way of filling yourself with knowledge in all related areas, all in one place, in one great read.

CAROLINE SLONEEM
LONDON, U.K.

I thank you from the bottom of my heart for the information you are getting out to the world. This has saved my life. I now have hope where – after the first three months after my wife's passing – I had none!

TIM LEBLANC
JENNINGS, USA

Your book answered a lot of questions I had and I guess three quarters of the world's people have the same questions about the afterlife. The way you presented the information was excellent. You gave us all the information and like you said, here it is in black and white, here is all the data. You decide what to believe or not. You answered a lot of questions for me and my girlfriend. She finally started to understand what was happening to her and her gift.

JOHN TEDESCO
FLORIDA, USA

Chapter 1

OPENING STATEMENT BY VICTOR

Read not to contradict and confute, nor to believe
and take for granted, but to weigh and consider.

Sir Francis Bacon

There is undeniable scientific evidence today for the afterlife. I am a former practising attorney-at-law, formally qualified with a number of university degrees. I am also an open-minded skeptic.

The argument in this book is not just an abstract, theoretical, academic legal argument. As open-minded investigators, Wendy and I set out more than 22 years ago to investigate the existing evidence for life after death, and, with others, to test claims that communication with intelligences from the afterlife is possible.

After these many years of serious investigation I have come to the irreversible conclusion that there is a great body of evidence which absolutely proves the case for the afterlife. In fact I am stating that the evidence taken as a whole constitutes overwhelming and irrefutable proof for the existence of the afterlife.

To date, no materialist, no skeptic has been able to disprove this critically important evidence amounting to proof for the afterlife.

There have been millions of pages written about psychic phenomena and scientific research into the afterlife. Using my professional

1

background as an attorney and my university training in psychology, history and scientific method, I have very carefully selected aspects of psychic research and afterlife knowledge that would constitute objective evidence. This evidence would be technically admissible in the Supreme Court of the United States, the House of Lords in England, the High Court of Australia and in every civilized legal jurisdiction around the world.

When the evidence – from mediumship, near-death experiences, out-of-body experiences, after-death contacts, voices on tape, psychic laboratory experiments, the Cross-Correspondences, the Scole Experiment, proxy sittings, poltergeists and all of the other evidence contained in this work – is seen collectively, the case for survival after death is absolutely stunning and irrefutable. As a matter of fact, any judge would agree that this list of topics establishes a *prima facie* (on the face of it) case.

In absolute terms the evidence presented in this work will convince the rational and intelligent open-minded skeptic or the genuine searcher about the existence of the afterlife.

Why don't more people know about the evidence?

For many years there has been hostility towards psychic science in the mainstream media and in universities and in some of the churches. The discoveries of serious scientists working to prove psychic phenomena like telepathy and the afterlife have been misreported, distorted and ignored. High profile, closed-minded skeptics have been given unfair licence by the media to ridicule and misrepresent, with the result that members of the general public know very little about the great body of scientific research which has been accumulated.

Many people who are genuinely seeking to explore this fascinating area have not been able to access unbiased factual information. They may not have the time to read and analyze the huge number of technical books and articles available on this subject (*see* Bibliography). In some societies these books are still simply not available because of formal and informal censorship.

The emphasis in this book is primarily on the repeatable evidence. The afterlife has nothing to do with beliefs. It is a matter of scientific fact. Objective knowledge can be classed as scientific where the same results and the same cause-effect connection can be demonstrated over time and space. Science is regarded as 'objective' in that any person who follows the scientific formulas will get the same results.

Knowledge which is 'subjective' includes all information which cannot be independently substantiated. This includes personal beliefs – Christianity, Islam, Hinduism, Buddhism, Judaism and other religions. Subjective knowledge also includes closed-minded skepticism (in this context: a strongly held belief that the afterlife and 'paranormal' phenomena do not exist).

Originally, 'skepticism' meant to examine something critically without accepting or rejecting it. The original meaning had nothing to do with completely denying the afterlife or the validity of psychic phenomena. Genuine skepticism allows for acceptance once evidence is shown. Like religion, closed-minded skepticism is a personal, subjective belief which is subject to fundamental error and to complete invalidation.

The studies of mediumship, voices on tape, and instrumental transcommunication have clearly showed this element of repeatability. Investigators working independently in many different countries have been able to duplicate each other's work.

As well, in recent times there has been a huge increase in the number of people willing to talk about their personal experiences of direct afterlife contact. The common claim of people who experience these things is: "I don't care what science says, my dead loved one appeared to me one morning and no one on earth is going to take that away from me."

Lawyers and the afterlife

Much of the evidence for the afterlife depends on the testimony of witnesses who claim to have had direct experiences of it. Assessing

3

their credibility, examining their character, stability, reputations and motives is a standard task for attorneys.

When materialist scientists attack scientists and others who support the paranormal, the materialists do not allow their prejudices to be examined in public. Testing the credibility, the prejudices and the degree of expertise of an expert witness through cross-examination is another role for attorneys. They know that the outcome of many trials depends on the testimony of just one expert witness.

A word of caution

For the purpose of the record, it is not my intention to try to change anybody's beliefs or religion. This is not religious crusading. This is not a matter of faith or belief. This is a matter of either acceptance or non-acceptance of the evidence. You are being given access to some very important information about the afterlife. But ultimately, given all the information, you the reader will have to decide what you accept or reject.

Chapter 2

SCIENTISTS WHO INVESTIGATED THE AFTERLIFE

I am absolutely convinced of the fact that those who once lived on earth can and do communicate with us. It is hardly possible to convey to the inexperienced an adequate idea of the strength and cumulative force of the evidence.

Sir William Barrett FRS

It is quite true that a connection has been set up between this world and the next.

Sir William Crookes FRS

I have been talking with my [dead] father, my brother, my uncles... Whatever supernormal powers we may be pleased to attribute to [the medium] Mrs. Piper's secondary personalities, it would be difficult to make me believe that these secondary personalities could have thus completely reconstituted the mental personality of my dead relatives...

Professor James Hyslop

The eminent scientists mentioned above were among the first to scientifically investigate the afterlife. They were skeptical at first and it was only after thorough investigation that they accepted it. There were other famous scientists and thinkers around the world who also accepted the afterlife after years of investigation. Some of these were Sir Arthur Conan Doyle, Arthur Findlay, Camille Flammarion, Dr. Baraduc, Alfred Russel Wallace, Professor Robert Hare, Marconi, F. W. Myers, Professor William James and Dr. Carrington. From the middle of the 19th century until today there have been groups of prominent, well-respected scientists working to prove that the study of the afterlife is a branch of physics.

Eminent afterlife and paranormal investigators

Professor Robert Almeder, John Logie Baird, Dr. Peter Bander, Sir William Barrett, Dr. Julie Beichel, Professor John Bockris, Hereward Carrington, Edgar Cayce, Professor J. W. Crawford, Dr. Robert Crookall, Sir William Crookes, Andrew Jackson Davis, Dr. George T. Dexter, Lord Dowding, Sir Arthur Conan Doyle, Dr. C. J. Ducasse, Judge John W. Edmonds, Professor Arthur Ellison, Dr. Peter Fenwick, Professor Festa, Arthur Findlay, Dr. Edith Fiore, Professor Camille Flammarion, Professor David Fontana, Dr. Isaac K. Funk, Dr. Hamlin Garland, Professor Gustav Geley, Dr. Amit Goswami, Professor Ivor Grattan-Guinesss, Professor Stanislav Grof, Dr. Arthur Guirdham, Dr. T. Glen Hamilton, Professor Charles Hapgood, Emma Harding, Dr. Robert Hare, Professor Sylvia Hart Wright, Dr. Richard Hodgson, Professor James Hyslop, Professor William James, Dr. Raynor C. Johnson, Professor Brian Josephson, Allan Kardec Esq., Dr. John S. King, Dr. Jon Klimo, Dr. Elizabeth Kübler-Ross, Sir Oliver Lodge, Dr. Cesare Lombroso, Dr. Jeff and Jody Long, Dr. William McDougall, Joseph McMoneagle, Mark Macy, Maurice Maeterlinck, George Meek, Dr. Raymond Moody, Vice Admiral William Usborne Moore, Professor Augustus De Morgan, Dr. Melvin Morse, Rev. Stainton Moses, Dr. Gardner Murphy, Frederic W. H. Myers,

Dr. Morris Netherton, Professor William R. Newbold, Dr. Karlis Osis, Ron Pearson, Dr. Hal Puthoff, Dr. Dean Radin, Peter Ramster, Edward C. Randall, Dr. Konstantine Raudive, Drs. J. B. and Louisa Rhine, Professor Charles Richet, Dr. Kenneth Ring, Scott Rogo, Dr. Barbara R. Rommer, Aubrey Rose, Professor Archie Roy, Dr. Michael Sabom, Dr. Hans Schaer, Professor Marilyn Schlitz, Baron (Dr.) Albert von Schrenck-Notzing, Professor Ernst Senkowski, Dr. Rupert Sheldrake, Judge Dean Shuart, Dr. Bernie Siegel, Dr. Ian Stevenson, Dr. Claude Swanson, Emanuel Swedenborg, Governor Nathaniel P. Tallmadge, Professor Russell Targ, Professor Charles Tart, Rev. Charles Drayton Thomas, Professor Jessica Utts, Dr. Pim Van Lommel, Dr. Jan W. Vandersande, Dr. Alexander von Boutlerow, Professor Wadhams, Professor Alfred Russel Wallace, Dr. Helen Wambach, Dr. Brian Weiss, Dr. Carl Wickland, Dr. Carla Wills-Brandon and Professor Fred Alan Wolf.

Many of these were scientists and highly practical people whose major discoveries in other areas fundamentally changed the way people work and live. Many considered themselves to be Rationalists and Humanists and had to face intense opposition from both highly conservative Christian clergy and from materialist scientists. We are indeed standing on the shoulders of giants.

Emanuel Swedenborg and Spiritualism

One of the pioneers of modern afterlife research was Emanuel Swedenborg who was born in Sweden in 1688. A leading scientist of his day, he wrote 150 works in 17 sciences. Swedenborg was also a very highly gifted clairvoyant who spent more than 20 years investigating the afterlife in what today would be called out-of-body experiences. He claimed that he regularly spoke with practically everyone he ever knew after they had died (Swedenborg, 1758: 437).

Spirit communication began to attract the attention of scientifically educated professionals in America and Europe following events that took place in Hydesville, New York, in March 1848. Two young girls, Kate and Margaret Fox, began communicating with a spirit who claimed he had been murdered in the house they were living in five years before. They asked the spirit to use raps to spell out messages. This system of communication through raps, movement of tables, automatic writing and trance mediumship became known as physical mediumship, which was the basis of Spiritualism. Kate and Margaret Fox became professional mediums managed by their older sister Leah.

Scientists and other professionals who at first were highly skeptical about spirit contact began to investigate it. Many accepted that contact with the afterlife through physical mediums (those who could produce raps and movement of furniture) was real. These included a leading American scientist, Dr. Robert Hare. Another leading scientist was Professor James J. Mapes, Professor of Chemistry and Natural Philosophy at the National Academy of Design in New York and later at the American Institute. Dr. George T. Dexter was a New York physician who was totally opposed to Spiritualism when he first heard about it. He considered it an "outrageous deception". However, in 1851 he invited a leading medium to his home and was very impressed. Soon afterwards he himself became a writing and trance medium and began to transmit profound messages. The communicators claimed to be Emanuel Swedenborg and Francis Bacon who used him to write *Spiritualism* (Volume 1, 505 pages; and Volume 2, 543 pages). These books claimed to explain the nature of reality and set out a philosophical basis for Spiritualism (Tymn, 2012a: Chapter 4).

The greatest scientists of their time investigate mediums

In England, Sir William Crookes was a Fellow of the Royal Society – a most prestigious association of the leading learned scientists elected by their peers. Many people considered him to be the greatest scientist of his time. He decided to investigate mediums in his own house, under his own conditions and observed by his own friends. He worked with American medium Kate Fox, one of the Fox sisters whose mediumship had started the Spiritualist movement in the USA 24 years earlier. In 1872 Kate Fox was thoroughly tested in England by Sir William Crookes and in St Petersburg by Professor Boutlerow and found to be genuine. Crookes stated that he witnessed Kate Fox produce raps loud enough to be heard several rooms away simply by placing her hands on any substance. He also said that while he was holding both of her hands in his left hand, he had seen a luminous hand materialize, take a pencil from his right hand, write a message on a sheet of paper, throw the pencil down and then fade into darkness (Inglis, 1977: 264).

Sir William Crookes also conducted a number of carefully documented experiments, in good light and under tightly controlled conditions, with another famous physical medium. Daniel Dunglas Home was able to produce raps, movement of objects and levitation (floating in the air) in daylight. Professor Charles Tart cites them as the best research into macro-psychokinesis (large movement of objects with no apparent cause) even to this day (Tart, 2009: 151–58).

But Sir William's most famous and controversial work was with physical medium Florence Cooke. He was courageous enough to confirm that, through her mediumship, he and his friends had been able to repeatedly talk with, and photograph, fully materialized spirit people. That left him open to enormous criticism from both atheists and Christians.

His supporters, who also witnessed the materializations, included some of the greatest scientists of the time. In England there were the four great physicists: Sir William Barrett, Sir Oliver Lodge, Lord Rayleigh and Nobel Prize-winner Sir Joseph 'J. J.' Thompson, the discoverer of the electron. There was also Alfred Russel Wallace who developed the theory of evolution at the same time as Charles Darwin. Wallace carefully investigated Spiritualism over a number of years and claimed that its phenomena were proved quite as well as the facts of any other science.

The Society for Psychical Research (SPR) was founded in London in 1882 and, owing to the efforts of its founders, psychical research became a science. It established disciplined experimental methods and attracted some of the finest minds of the day (Broughton, 1992: 64). In the first century of its existence, 19 out of its 51 presidents were professors and other famous scientists.

The American Society for Psychical Research was founded in 1885 by a group of top intellectuals. These included Professor William James, renowned Harvard psychologist. It too attracted some of the most intelligent people in America who, after years of investigations, became convinced of survival after death. Professor James H. Hyslop who had been Professor of Logic and Ethics at Columbia University became involved in 1899 and spent 20 years investigating the evidence for the afterlife. In his 480-page book *Contact with the Other World,* he wrote:

> History shows that every intelligent man who has gone into this investigation, if he gave it adequate examination at all, has come out believing in spirits; this circumstance places the burden of proof on the shoulders of the skeptic (Hyslop, 1919: 480).

Spiritualism suffered a minor setback in its image with the public in 1888. The three Fox sisters, then in their fifties, were widows. They were heavy drinkers and needed money. Margaret Fox, with the support of Kate, accepted a bribe to say that the rappings which had started Spiritualism had been a hoax. She was given 1,500 dollars from the newspaper *The New York World* and R. Davenport. She withdrew her confession in full a few days later but by then the damage had been done. Davenport exploited the situation and wrote a book called *The Deathblow to Spiritualism,* and the myth that Spiritualism was based on fraudulent mediumship was created (Inglis, 1977: 370).

But balanced against this there were a number of scientists who continued to confirm the existence of the afterlife. In Europe from the early 1890s and through the 1920s there were other scientists studying and photographing physical mediums. These included Professor Cesare Lombroso, Professor Chiaia, Dr. Julian Ochorowicz,

Professor Camille Flammarion, Baron Dr. Albert von Schrenck-Notzing, Professor Charles Richet, Pierre and Marie Curie, Professor Eugene Osty and Professor Gustav Geley. All of them claimed that they had seen materializations of spirit people under controlled laboratory conditions. Their written reports showed that they had ruled out all possible sources of fraud. A hundred well known scientists, all skeptics, wrote that they were completely convinced of the genuineness of the materializations produced by medium Willy Schneider under the supervision of Dr. Schrenck-Notzing (Geley, 1927).

Leading scientists and inventors

Thomas Alva Edison, the American inventor of the phonograph and the first electric light bulb, was fascinated with the possibility of an afterlife. He experimented with mechanical means of contacting the "dead" (*Scientific American*, 30 October 1920). After Edison died, John Logie Baird claimed to have contacted him. Baird, the pioneer of television and inventor of the infrared camera, stated that he had contacted Edison through a medium. He said: "I have witnessed some very startling phenomena under circumstances which make trickery out of the question" (Logie Baird, 1988).

Robert Crookall (who died in 1981) was a geologist and botanist who was an early British authority on astral projection or out-of-body travel. He examined the evidence that people can leave their physical bodies and re-enter them after travelling unseen in an 'astral' body. He also undertook cross-cultural research into reports of after-death communication. Crookall concluded:

> The whole of the available evidence is explicable on the hypothesis of the survival of the human soul in a Soul Body. There is no longer a 'deadlock' or 'stalemate' on the question of survival. On the contrary, survival is as well established as the theory of evolution (Crookall, 1961).

George Meek

Another eminent scientist and inventor who became totally convinced of the existence of the afterlife was American George Meek. When he was 60 years old, Meek retired from his career as an inventor, designer and manufacturer. He devoted the next 20 years to researching the afterlife. Meek said that he was a "natural skeptic" and felt that what he had been told about the afterlife in his religion "just didn't make sense". So he began an extensive library and literature research programme and travelled all over the world to investigate mediums and healers and establish research projects. He worked with top mediums, doctors, psychiatrists, physicists, biochemists, psychics, healers, parapsychologists, hypnotherapists, ministers, priests and rabbis.

He established the Metascience Foundation in Franklin, North Carolina. There he worked with a psychic engineer named Bill O'Neill. In 1979, they developed an electronic device that allowed Bill to have real-time conversations with Dr. George J. Mueller, a man who had been dead at least 14 years. These recorded conversations went on for more than 20 hours (*see* Chapter 22, Instrumental Transcommunication).

His last book, *After We Die What Then* (1987), outlines the conclusions of his years of full-time research – that we do all survive death and that in the previous 25 years mankind has learned more about what happens when we die than was learned in all earlier periods of recorded history (Meek, 1987).

Modern research with mediums

Professor Archie Roy was professor emeritus of astronomy at the University of Glasgow, Scotland. He published 20 books, 70 scientific papers and scores of articles and directed advanced scientific institutes for NATO. For the best part of 30 years he was also passionately interested in psychical research. He worked with statistician Tricia Robertson, vice-president of the Scottish SPR, on research which proved some mediumship is genuine. Together they completed a five-year study of mediums in a project called PRISM (Psychic Research Involving Selected Mediums). This resulted in three peer-reviewed papers in the Society for Psychical Research *Journal*. The third paper showed that even in tightly controlled conditions a good medium can deliver relevant information to a sitter with the odds-against chance being a million to one.

In 1993, Professor Gary Schwartz, then Professor of Psychology, Medicine, Neurology, Psychiatry and Surgery at the University of Arizona, USA, and Director of its Human Energy Systems Laboratory, began his own personal search for evidence of the afterlife. He conducted a number of double-blind research studies with some of the top mediums in the United States. He writes:

> These mediums have been tested under experimental conditions that rule out the use of fraud and cold reading techniques commonly used by psychic entertainers and mental magicians (Schwartz *et al.*, 2002).

Dr. Julie Beischel, co-founder of the Windbridge Institute in the USA, has recently conducted many scientific tests on mental mediums. She has published peer-reviewed academic papers showing that they are getting very accurate results by means which are currently unknown to mainstream science. These scientific tests proved that the mediums were not cheating or guessing.

Recently it was announced that the Institute of Noetic Sciences will be working with Dr. Julie Beischel, the research team at The Windbridge Institute and a panel of Windbridge Certified Research Mediums to study the EEG patterns of mediums when they conduct readings. More specific information about the study and results will be available once the journal articles are published.

Summing up 150 years of afterlife research

In 2005 Professor David Fontana published a scholarly 500-page book called *Is There An Afterlife?* It reviews some of the evidence for the afterlife that has been collected during more than 150 years of systematic research.

Professor Archie Roy, in the introduction to the book, points out that the reason most mainstream scientists are hostile to the afterlife is that they are not aware of the evidence. They have never done afterlife research and don't know how much scientific study has been done. He says they are often hostile to the afterlife because they think it conflicts with their scientific worldview.

We have found that the materialist closed-minded skeptics who oppose the existence of psychic phenomena and the afterlife have not done their homework. They simply have not read, as we have, volume after volume of first-hand accounts by the greatest minds of science who were all initially highly skeptical before they started their own personal investigations.

Chapter 3

THE AUTHORS' MATERIALIZATION EXPERIENCES

The point is, if you want real conviction of life after death, physical mediumship is the answer.

LESLIE FLINT

DIRECT-VOICE MEDIUM

Physical mediumship of the kind investigated by Sir William Crookes and the other early researchers is incredibly rare in the world today – so rare that most people have never heard of it. Materialization mediumship is even rarer. David Thompson, an English medium now living in Sydney, Australia, is one of only a handful of mediums who has mastered the full range of mediumship: mental, trance and physical. He is able to go into deep trance and allow a team of spirit scientists working with him to take substances from his body to allow them to form temporary bodies. This is called materialization. They walk around the room, speak in their own voices and touch the people who sit in the Circle.

A session with a physical medium is called a 'sitting' because everyone sits in a circle around the medium who is usually seated in a curtained off enclosure called a 'cabinet'. The sittings have to take place in total darkness because the substance taken from the medium – called ectoplasm – is so sensitive that if lights are turned on before it is stabilized, it snaps back into the medium's body. Several materialization mediums have been injured and even killed in this way. The purpose of the cabinet is to allow the ectoplasm to be condensed in the one place. Very occasionally, when conditions are right, a red light can be turned on for a short time to allow people to see the ectoplasm or even photograph it.

For 15 months Wendy and I – and others – investigated David Thompson's mediumship in weekly 'sittings' which normally lasted about 90 minutes. After that time we continued to sit with David for five years as members of his Circle of the Silver Cord. We had full access to David before and after séances and travelled with him internationally. We examined tape recordings of David's sessions from ten years before we met. We confirmed that voices of the Spirit team had not changed over that time. We noted that David had exactly the same results whether he was sitting in England, America, Switzerland, Spain, Germany or Australia. He sat in many different places, in rooms which were prepared by others. The results were the same even when he had different people sitting with him. We checked the many different rooms we sat in before each session to make sure that there were no wires, trapdoors, cupboards where a person could hide etc. We tape recorded all sessions and analyzed the tapes afterwards. On no occasion did we ever see any hint of anything fraudulent.

Even though the sittings normally take place in total darkness, I am still convinced, by the precautions that we have taken, that genuine materializations are taking place. Occasionally a sitter is invited to feel the full body of the materialized spirit. Before every séance (a word that just means 'sitting') the medium, David, is thoroughly searched as are all the sitters. He is tightly gagged and bound hand and foot to a heavy wooden chair. His gag and binds are secured with one-way cable ties which have to be removed with wire cutters. We also put seals wherever we can – on the tags on each hand, on his gag, around the feet and thighs. Always we check windows and doors – even ceilings and floors.

During the séance all of the sitters hold hands and constantly talk to each other so they are aware of where each one is sitting. The session begins with a prayer for protection for the medium and the sitters and then music is turned on "to raise the vibrations". Soon the deep resonant voice of William, the leader of the Spirit team who claims to have died in 1897, is heard speaking slightly old fashioned British English. William welcomes everyone to the Circle and answers some questions about the afterlife. You can hear his footsteps as he walks around the room and claps his hands to show he is fully materialized. He moves from one side of the room to the other, greeting people in the pitch darkness by name. Sometimes he asks permission to touch people on the head and everyone comments on the size of his hand which is much bigger that the medium's hand.

The first time that we sat in the Circle, William stood directly in front of me. I could hear his voice coming from very close in front of me – I would estimate his height at over six feet. He leaned forward and patted me on the shoulder. At this time the medium was tied into the chair and gagged and all the sitters were holding hands; we could locate every other person present by their voices. During the session we heard seven completely different voices which were clear, loud and distinctive with different pitch, rhythm, pace, intonation and modulation. All of the voices answered questions intelligently and moved around the room. The sitters could constantly hear each other asking questions from their original positions.

To confirm that the voices are not David's, I have been allowed to hold onto David's gag and feel his mouth while a spirit voice was speaking on the other side of me. On two occasions I was allowed to hold the medium's right ankle while one of the spirit team was materialized on the other side of the room.

Often the entities begin speaking, using 'Independent Voice'. This is a normal voice coming from somewhere in the room – sometimes from high up near the ceiling. Then the spirits materialize with a distinctive sound and in an instant can be on the other side of the room in far less time than it would take a person to move there, especially in total darkness.

On one occasion a spirit energy claiming to be Sir Arthur Conan Doyle gave an eloquent speech on the topic of survival after death and how one's state of mind on crossing over determines what one experiences. During his talk he approached me and shook my hand. It was a real, moving hand which felt warm and solid and was huge. It was at least twice as large as the hand of the medium David Thompson and significantly bigger than the hand of anyone else in the room.

At the end of each meeting when the lights go on, the medium is still gagged and bound and in his chair. However, the heavy chair is usually moved without a sound into the middle of the Circle – sometimes several metres from its original position. The medium's cardigan is still on, with the plastic ties still unbroken; but now the heavy chair is reversed so that the buttons are up the chair's back.

On two occasions the conditions were right for low red light to be turned on so that we could see ectoplasm – the substance taken from the medium which allows the spirit people to become solid. It actively flowed down from David's mouth and over his lap. It was like very heavy living and moving smoke.

On several other occasions we witnessed David levitating (lifted high in the air) in his chair for three to four minutes. I could feel the four legs of the chair at my head's level and hear David's voice as he floated around near the ceiling. He was awake and conscious and he and William were talking at the same time. Indeed, we recorded them counting simultaneously.

Reunions

When conditions are right in David's séances, two or three spirits – friends and relatives of visitors – are helped by the spirit team to step into the ectoplasm and temporarily become solid. For a few minutes these materialized spirits can walk across the room and talk to their loved ones, sharing personal messages.

Wendy and I have been present at more than 100 of these reunions between a visitor to the Circle and a loved one who has "died". The kind of evidence that comes through in a personal reunion is not the kind of thing that can be researched in advance. Spirits say things like what was put into the coffin, thank their loved one for looking after them towards the end, apologize for not being more loving, tell their loved one to be happy and to go on with life or admit they were wrong about the afterlife. What is totally convincing is the extreme emotion of these reunions.

People materialize with the features they had while alive – they are recognized by their loved ones by voice and by touch. One young lady touched the face of her materialized brother. She could feel his usual unshaven face. All the men in the room that night were clean shaven. Another person recognized that his grandfather's materialized hand was missing the finger that had been amputated in life.

On two occasions Wendy's father materialized announcing his name. He was 'in the flesh'. He was speaking as when a loved one talks to you. It was his voice. It was his mannerisms. No one knew about the intimate circumstances raised by Wendy's father about their early life. He walked across the room and kissed Wendy on the forehead. Further, he wrote his full name on a piece of paper. No one in the experiment knew that name. On another two occasions my own younger sister, Carmen, materialized. She talked about very intimate circumstances no one else in the room knew.

Testimonials by many people who have experienced reunions with loved ones can be found on the Circle of the Silver Cord website:

http://circleofthesilvercord.net

People often ask why the séances cannot be held in light or videoed. William, the leader of David's spirit team, explained to us that while some physical mediums in the past had been able to materialize hands in red light, it usually means that there are no full materializations or spirits being able to talk in their own voices. Asking for materialization to take place in light is a bit like asking for snow in the tropics – it may happen rarely, but it is not the natural order of things.

We have also been fortunate enough to sit in séances with four other physical mediums and to interview many people who have spent years investigating physical mediumship. We spoke to several people who had reunions with David confirmed by the same spirit materializing through a different physical medium. Ron Gilkes of Jenny's Sanctuary, a centre for physical mediumship in England, told us that his daughter had materialized through five different physical mediums, each time confirming the reality of previous materializations.

The importance of harmony

Most people don't understand that in physical mediumship the harmony of the energy between the sitters is absolutely vital. We have seen sittings, where there is a large group of very positive and joyful people, produce stunning results. The next night if there are only a couple of people who are depressed, skeptical or anxious, the energy will be dramatically weakened. This seems to be the same through all forms of spirit contact.

In Germany, we visited the Felix Experimental Group in their Home Circle, where we were able to witness much physical phenomena and feel touches from spirit hands. Most impressively, we clearly saw in clear red light large amounts of ectoplasm produced from the mouth of the medium, Kai Müegge. We again sat with Kai and his wife Julia in Australia in 2012 where everyone present clearly saw ectoplasm produced in red light. There was no doubt that it was real. This time we saw a hand emerging from the ectoplasm in the middle of the floor. At first it was quite distorted and imperfect, but gradually it took form and became very realistic.

These are stunning and unforgettable personal experiences which caused us to go from 'believing' in the afterlife to knowing without any doubt that the afterlife exists.

Chapter 4

NEAR-DEATH EXPERIENCES (NDEs)

So much rubbish is talked about Near-Death Experiences by people who don't have to deal with these things on a daily basis. So I'm absolutely sure that such experiences are not caused by oxygen shortages, endorphins or anything of that kind. And certainly none of these things would account for the transcendental quality of many of these experiences, the fact that people feel an infinite sense of loss when they leave them behind.

DR. PETER FENWICK

As medical techniques are being improved, many people are being brought back from near-death. Some of them talk about their spirit body floating near the ceiling and seeing everything that happens around their physical body below them. They go through a tunnel and meet a 'being of light' and feel enormous love and peace. Sometimes they see a review of their entire life and meet relatives who have died. Some are given a choice to stay or go back, but most are told that it is not their time. They find themselves hurled back into their bodies with a deep sense of loss and regret. These experiences have been happening throughout human history and are one of the reasons that every culture on earth teaches that there is an afterlife.

The systematic study of NDEs began in the 1970s. Psychiatrists Dr. Elisabeth Kübler-Ross, Dr. Raymond Moody, Jr., and Dr. George Ritchie brought near-death experiences to public attention. Other studies by Dr. Michael Sabom and Dr. Sarah Kreutziger (1976), Dr. Karlis Osis and Dr. Erlendur Haraldsson (1977), Dr. Kenneth Ring (1980 and 1984), Dr. Michael Sabom MD (1980), Dr. Bruce Greyson MD (1980, 1989), P. M. H. Atwater (1988) and Dr. Melvin Morse (1990) extended the early findings.

Dr. Kenneth Ring, who produced a scientific study of near-death experiences in 1980, confirmed Dr. Moody's findings but found that people went through the experience in stages and a large number of people experienced only the first ones.

Evidence that Near-Death Experiences (NDEs) are real

1. NDE survivors have clear and structured memories of what happened to them

Patients who did not have a NDE during similar treatment were confused or could not remember anything. Dr. Jeffrey Long writes:

> When you talk to the patients who have actually survived CPR (resuscitation treatment for heart attack) one thing that is very, very obvious is that the substantial majority of them are confused or amnesiac when they're recovered. If you read even a few near-death experiences, you immediately realize essentially none of them talk about episodes of confusion when they just don't understand what's going on. You really don't see that at all. In fact, our research found that 76 per cent of people having a near-death experience said their level of consciousness and alertness during the NDE was actually greater than their earthly, everyday life (Long and Perry, 2010).

2. Whereas hallucinations are all different, near-death experiences are very similar in different cultures and throughout history

Near-death experiences have been reported in all cultures, and from as far back as 1760 BC (Zaleski, 1987). Whereas no two hallucinations are alike, NDEs all follow the same general pattern and have the same after-effects.

3. People see and hear things while they are unconscious that would be impossible for normal sensing

A huge percentage of near-death experiencers are able to describe exactly what happened to them while they were unconscious. They know who was present, what people were talking about even at a distance. Researchers call these 'veridical experiences'. Many of the patients who have been revived have been able to describe in great technical detail exactly what went on in the operating room.

Dr. Michael Sabom found that 80 per cent of his patients who had a heart attack without having a NDE could not describe how they were revived. But not one person in the group which witnessed what happened while out of their bodies made a mistake in describing the procedure (Sabom, 1980).

Dr. Lloyd Rudy was astounded when a patient described the post-it notes which were left on the monitor of the doctor's computer in the operating room. These were put up every time someone left a message for Dr. Rudy. But there had been no messages and no post-it notes before the patient's operation had started. There was no way the patient could have seen the computer from where he was (Rudy, 2011).

Dr. Pim van Lommel tells the case of a patient who, although unconscious at the time, later claimed he saw where a nurse put his dentures. A week later, the patient recognized the nurse and asked for his dentures back (van Lommel *et al.*, 2001).

4. People come back from a NDE with accurate facts they did not know before

There are many accounts of people having near-death experiences and returning with facts they did not know before. Emily Kelly reported a case in which a man became excited when he first saw photographs of his wife's dead father. He claimed that he had seen the man in his NDE before he had even met his wife (Greyson, 1998).

During his NDE, Dr. Eben Alexander met a beautiful girl he did not know. He had been adopted at a young age and it was only after his NDE that he received a photo of a biological sister he never knew he had. She had died as a young adult and he recognized her as the girl he had met in the afterlife (Alexander, 2012).

Dutch cardiologist Dr. Pim van Lommel says a five-year-old girl told him that she had been with a brother she did not know she had. The boy died before she was born (Greyson, 2010). Vi Horton claims that she met a boy in the afterlife who told her that he was her baby brother. Her father later confirmed that he was the only living person who knew that she had a brother who died (*Extra Dimensions* TV show, episode 5 aired 1987).

Russian George Rodonaia found himself out of his body while unconscious as a result of an accident. He went to the hospital next door where a friend's wife had just given birth to a daughter. The baby was crying and he was able to see that her hip was broken. He mentally communicated with her and she told him that her hip had been broken shortly after her birth when a nurse had dropped the child. Several days later, when he recovered enough to speak, his first words warned the doctors about the child with the broken hip. The doctors took X-rays of the child and all the facts were confirmed (Atwater, 2007: 165).

5. People report meeting with relatives they did not know were dead. In all cases they are correct

Maggie Callanan and Patrica Kelley in their book *Final Gifts* tell of an elderly Chinese woman who had a NDE in which she saw her sister. The sister had died but her family had not told her (Callanan and Kelley, 1997).

Dr. Kübler-Ross talked of a girl who was injured in a car accident. No one had told her that her mother and brother had died in the same accident. When the girl was having her NDE, she saw them in the afterlife. Even Dr. Kübler-Ross didn't know that the brother had died only ten minutes before the girl had her NDE (Kübler-Ross, 1997). Ian Stevenson published a similar case. A man's cousin in England had died without anyone in the United States knowing about it. During this man's NDE, he saw his cousin. It was some time before he received a telegram announcing his cousin's death (Stevenson, 1959).

P. M. H. Atwater reports a case of a woman who talked with her father during her NDE. Neither she nor anyone in her family was aware that the father had died only five minutes before the woman had her car/truck accident (Atwater, 2007: 164).

6. Some people come back with knowledge of the future

In some cases people are shown their family in two possible futures: one where the person stays in the afterlife and one where they return to their life (Atwater, 2007). Some see the children that they are going to have (Eadie, 1992).

Others have visions about world events but do say that they are told that they are only possible futures. Dannion Brinkley wrote in advance about: the defeat of the USA in the Vietnam War; the election of an American president with the initials R. R. (Ronald Reagan); turmoil in the Middle East; the 1986 Chernobyl disaster; the Desert Storm war against Iraq in 1990 (Brinkley and Perry, 1994).

7. Some people come back with advanced knowledge consistent with quantum physics

Almost all survivors say that they entered a dimension where there was no time and many were able to go back and forward through time. Olaf Swenson says it was because of the knowledge he gained during his NDE that he later went on to develop over 100 patents in sub-atomic chemistry (Morse, undated). Mellen-Thomas Benedict brought back from his NDE a great deal of scientific information. He says this knowledge was the basis of the six US patents he holds (Benedict, 1996).

8. Some people are cured of fatal illnesses during a NDE or have miraculous recoveries from serious injuries

Mellen-Thomas Benedict was in the last stages of dying from terminal cancer in 1982. He died and for an hour and a half his body was monitored showing no vital signs. Miraculously, he returned to his body after having a full NDE. Three months later there was no sign of the cancer in his body (Benedict, 1996).

Anita Moorjani was dying from cancer. When she returned from her NDE she had a total recovery of her health (Moorjani, 2012).

Elisabeth Kübler-Ross tells a dramatic story of a man whose whole family were killed in a terrible accident. He became an alcoholic and drug abuser until he was hit by a car and in a NDE saw his whole family well and happy in the afterlife. She writes:

> He finally re-entered his physical body, tore off the straps that were tied around him and literally walked out of the emergency room. He never had *delirium tremens* or any after-effects from the heavy abuse of drugs and alcohol (Kübler-Ross, 1991).

9. The blind can see during a NDE

In their book *Mindsight*, Dr. Kenneth Ring and Sharon Cooper report on in-depth interviews with 31 people who were fully or partially blind and had a near-death experience where they could see. One of their subjects was Vicki Noratuk who had been blind from birth. She could not even see black. During her NDE, she found she could see for the first time; she recognized her wedding ring and her hair. She also saw people made out of light – but she had never seen light before (Ring and Cooper, 1999).

Elisabeth Kübler-Ross also interviewed blind patients who were able to see perfectly while 'dead' and out-of-body (Kübler-Ross, 2005).

10. Some people have a group near-death experience

A group of fire fighters claimed that when they were overcome with smoke they all went out of their bodies. They communicated with each other and could all see the lifeless bodies below them. All survived and they agreed with each other afterwards that the experience actually happened (Gibson, 1999).

11. Some people have near-death-like experiences when there is nothing physically wrong with them

Researchers have found that deep meditation, deathbed visions, relaxation, psychic vision, astral projection, trance, mirror-gazing and eye movements can trigger elements of the NDE (see Kevin Williams' website: www.near-death.com).

12. Some people have a near-death experience when they are completely brain dead

Hallucinations can only occur when people have a functioning brain which shows an active EEG reading. But vivid near-death experiences have taken place during periods when brains have showed no electrical activity. At these times people should have no memory but the vivid NDEs are remembered by people years later.

Pam Reynolds needed a risky operation to correct a weak point in the wall of a blood vessel in her brain. For over an hour she was clinically dead. Her temperature was lowered to 60 degrees, her heartbeat and brain activity were stopped and her blood was circulated through a machine. There was no way that she could see anything as her eyes were taped shut. She could not hear anything as her ears were covered with plastic caps and sounds measuring 90 decibels were continually fed into them.

Yet after her heart was restarted and her body heated up, she reported that she had been able to see, hear, and feel what was going on. She said that it was like sitting on the shoulder of the doctor. She described details of her surgery which were later verified. She was able to remember this long and complex near-death experience from a time when she had had no brain activity (Sabom, 1998).

George Rodonaia's body was stored in the freezer in a hospital morgue for three days. He was revived when his body was being split open for an autopsy. But while he was 'dead' he had seen his wife outside the hospital selecting his gravesite and considering marrying again (Atwater, 2007: 166).

Eben Alexander is an academic neurosurgeon who had a near-death experience. He was unconscious from severe meningitis which wipes out all except the most basic human brain functions. He says that for over a week he was virtually brain dead, yet had a complex NDE that could not have been created by his brain activity (Alexander, 2012).

13. Many people experience a 'life review' during which they see their lives from the perspective of other people

Dr. Kenneth Ring and other researchers show that a key feature of the life review is that people do not see their lives from their own point of view. It is not like replaying a video recording. Instead they see them from the perspective of everyone else they interacted with. They access the feelings and memories of the other people involved. These are things that they would have no normal way of knowing (Ring and Valarino, 1998).

14. The after-effects of a NDE are unique and long lasting

The most common psychological effects (experienced by 80–90 per cent of adult survivors) are very recognizable. Cherie Sutherland, an Australian researcher, interviewed 50 NDE survivors in depth. She found that the effects on the lives of survivors had been remarkably consistent and quite different from the effects of drug or chemically induced hallucinations.

In *Transformed by the Light* (1992), she identified many effects which have been substantiated by other studies, e.g., Ring (1980 and 1984) and Atwater (1988). These included:

- a universal belief in life after death
- a high proportion (80 per cent) now believed in re-incarnation
- a total absence of fear of death
- a large shift from organized religion to personal spiritual practice

- a statistically significant increase in psychic sensitivity
- a more positive view of self and of others
- an increased desire for solitude
- an increased sense of purpose
- a lack of interest in material success coupled with a marked increase in interest in spiritual development
- fifty per cent experienced major difficulties in close relationships as a result of their changed priorities
- an increase in health consciousness
- most drank less alcohol
- almost all gave up smoking
- most gave up prescription drugs
- most watched less television
- most read fewer newspapers
- an increased interest in alternative healing
- an increased interest in learning and self-development
- seventy-five per cent experienced a major career change in which they moved towards areas of helping others.

P. M. H. Atwater adds another interesting fact. She claims that most researchers have found that at least 75–78 per cent of adult experiencers divorced within seven to ten years of their experience (Atwater, 2007: 89).

An independent American study by Dr. Melvin Morse found that NDE survivors have three times the number of verifiable psychic experiences as the general population. They are often unable to wear a watch. Many have problems using electrical appliances such as computers. Often their credit cards do not work. (Morse and Perry, 1992).

Alternative explanations don't account for the whole package

There have been many attempts to explain away the near-death experience. Some claim they are caused by oxygen deprivation. Others claim it is a natural effect of the dying brain or some accident of brain chemistry. Most of these theories are based on observations of a small number of cases. They may produce elements of the near-death experience but not the whole experience. And, most important, they do not have the same impact or after-effects.

Dr. Elizabeth Fenwick, co-writer of the book *The Truth in the Light: An Investigation of Over 300 Near-Death Experiences*, actually began her research thinking that all could be explained in scientific terms. But, after investigating, she concluded:

> While you may be able to find scientific reasons for bits of the Near-Death Experience, I can't find any explanation which covers the whole thing. You have to account for it as a package and skeptics... simply don't do that. None of the purely physical explanations will do. They [skeptics] vastly underestimate the extent to which Near-Death Experiences are not just a set of random things happening, but a highly organized and detailed affair (Fenwick, 1995: 47).

Dr. Pim van Lommel agrees:

> Our most striking finding was that Near-Death Experiences do not have a physical or medical root. After all, 100 per cent of the patients suffered a shortage of oxygen, 100 per cent were given morphine-like medications, 100 per cent were victims of severe stress, so those are plainly not the reasons why 18 per cent had Near-Death Experiences and 82 per cent didn't. If they had been triggered by any one of those things, everyone would have had Near-Death Experiences (van Lommel, 1995).

How can I share the benefits of Near-Death Experiences?

Learning about NDEs has helped many people to overcome the fear of death and share many of the positive changes experienced by people who have had one. We highly recommend *Lessons From the Light: What We Can Learn from the Near-Death Experience,* a wonderful book by Kenneth Ring and Evelyn Elsaesser-Valarino (1998). Kenneth Ring found that his college students who read the book and listened to talks by near-death experiencers became much less fearful of death. Many people have reported to us that they gained enormously from reading popular books about near-death experiences and from watching video accounts by NDE survivors (there are many on YouTube). Some found it helpful to join their local branch of the International Association for Near-Death Studies (IANDS) and attend meetings to hear NDE stories first-hand.

One word of warning is that some NDE experiencers tend to interpret their experience of 'a being of light' in terms of their existing religious training. Mellen-Thomas Benedict experienced the light changing into different figures like Jesus, Buddha and Krishna and was told that "the light" is really a "Higher Self matrix" (an aspect of God) which you experience according to your beliefs (Benedict, 1996).

Chapter 5

OUT-OF-BODY
EXPERIENCES

The greatest illusion is that man has limitations.

ROBERT A. MONROE
OUT-OF-BODY INVESTIGATOR

Out-of-body experiences (OBEs) are also called astral projections, astral travel or bi-location. They were recorded in ancient times in Greece, Rome, India, China and Tibet. Anthropologist Erika Bourguignon conducted a cross-cultural survey from 488 societies around the world in the early 1970s. She found that 89 per cent of cultures experienced them and had names for the part of us that separates from the physical body. The most common names for this in Western culture are the 'spirit body', 'astral body' or 'etheric body' (Bourguignon, 1972: 418).

Indigenous cultures in Australia, Peru, other parts of South America – as well as American Indians – all report people travelling out of the body and seeing things that are later confirmed. Early missionaries to Africa and America were surprised at how native tribes could have a detailed knowledge of everything that was happening within a radius of hundreds of miles (Inglis, 1977).

A Common Experience

Spontaneous out-of-body experiences are quite common. A 1954 survey at Duke University's Sociology department showed that 27.1 per cent of students reported having experienced OBEs. Two surveys conducted by Celia Green in British universities in 1967 showed that 19 per cent and 34 per cent had OBEs (Green, 1967 and 1973).

Studies by John Palmer and M. Dennis in 1975 showed that 25 per cent of the students and 14 per cent of the residents from Charlottesville, Virginia, claimed to have had OBEs (Palmer, 1975). The Out-of-Body Experience Research Foundation run by Dr. Jeff and Jody Long has a webpage replete with recent examples of spontaneous out-of-body experiences. Some of them happened as a result of meditation. A respected scientist, Dr. Robert Crookall, analyzed over 700 reports of OBEs. He found that 81 per cent of those who experienced them had a firm belief in life after death because of their personal experience. What astounded Crookall, a meticulous scientist, was the consistency of the reports of OBEs coming from all over the world. He also found that they were consistent with near-death experiences and with the communications coming from high-level mediums (Crookall, 1970).

William Buhlman stated that he conducted an online survey of more than 16,000 people from over 30 countries who had had OBEs. Twenty-four per cent of his sample (3,840 people) reported having fully conscious meetings with a loved one who had passed on. Twenty-two per cent saw or felt the presence of a non-physical being (a spirit). He writes:

> The reported contact can take almost any form: a child, a recently passed wife or husband, a cloud or sphere of intelligence, or a gentle grandparent. Sometimes the contact is with someone known; at other times it may be with someone who appears as a guide or teacher (Buhlman, 2001: 3).

Experiences which are confirmed

There are a number of books on out-of-body experiences in which writers give personal examples of seeing things while out of the body which were later verified. These include:

- Yram, *Practical Astral Travel* [or Projection] (1935 and 1974)
- Sylvan Muldoon, *The Projection of the Astral Body* (1919)
- Oliver Fox, *Astral Projection* (1920)
- J. H. M. Whiteman, *The Mystical Life* (1961)
- Robert Monroe, *Journeys Out of the Body* (1971), *Far Journeys* (1985), *Ultimate Journey* (1994)
- Robert Peterson, *Out-of-Body Experiences: How to Have Them and What to Expect* (1997)
- William Buhlman, *The Secret of the Soul* (2001)
- Thomas Campbell, *My Big TOE* (2007)
- Dr. Waldo Vieira, *Projections of the Consciousness* (2007)
- Jurgen Ziewe, *Multidimensional Man* (2008)

Robert Bushman (2009) has compiled a list of 2,000 books, videos and journal articles on out-of-body experiences which is available online. Virtually all of these give accounts of verified experiences.

Scientific documentation

The Society for Psychical Research has a number of cases of OBEs where the person was seeing things which were later confirmed. In one case, the subject actually saw his future wife's astral body moving across the room (Landau, 1963).

In the United States, Karlis Osis and Boneita Perskari spent several years doing scientific research with an excellent OBE subject, Alex Tanous (Williams, 1989: 35–36). One particular test involved Tanous travelling astrally to a different place miles away to visit a particular office. He was asked to see what was on the table then report back. Alex Tanous did not know that at this office a psychic,

Christine Whiting, was waiting to see if she could discern any-one coming to visit. With her clairvoyant sight she was able to see Tanous come into the office. She described in detail his position and the shirt with rolled-up sleeves and the corduroy trousers he was wearing (Greenhouse, 1976: 279–93; Williams, 1989).

Because of the co-operation of some gifted OBE experiencers, the phenomenon has come within the ambit of science.

- Dutch scientists succeeded in weighing the physical body before, during and after exteriorization (OBE). They found a weight loss of 2¼ ounces during exteriorization (Carrington, 1973)
- French researchers, including Professor Richet, spent many years having the exteriorized body move material objects, produce raps at a distance and affect photographic plates and calcium screens. They photographed exteriorization (Richet, 1923)
- Other experimenters, including Robert Lyle Morris at the Psychical Foundation of North Carolina, spent two years investigating OBEs. They worked with Keith 'Blue' Harary, who claimed to have been having out-of-body experiences since childhood. He was able to lie down in a sealed laboratory room and project himself to another house 20 yards away. He was able to read letters in the other house and accurately report which experimenters were sitting there and where they were sitting (Morris, 1976)
- George Meek was able to photograph his exteriorized body attached to his physical body by a cord. The photos can be seen on Mark Macy's World ITC website: http://www.worlditc.org/h_07_meek_by_macy.htm
- Dr. Karlis Osis and Dr. Carole Silfen conducted successful experiments on behalf of the American Society for Psychical Research in 1972. They worked with gifted out-of-body traveller, Ingo Swann. Dr. Janet Lee Mitchell (1981 and 2011) gives details of experiments which resulted in eight out of eight correct target observations. The way Swann described the targets suggested an out-of-body perspective

- In 1973, Karlis Osis sent an open invitation throughout the United States to any individuals who could project themselves out-of-body. He asked them to 'go' into the premises of the American Society for Psychical Research in New York and view four target objects. Fifteen per cent of the participants produced clear evidence of having visited the office (Mitchell, 1981 and 2011)
- Dr. Charles Tart conducted a sleep study with a young woman he called Miss Z. He attached electrodes to her which recorded her every movement. She was able to go out of her body and observe a five-digit random number placed on a shelf above reaching distance (Tart, 1968).

Robert Monroe

Robert Monroe was president of two corporations active in cable-vision and electronics. He produced over 600 television programmes.

While experimenting with sleep-learning in 1958, Monroe experienced an unusual phenomenon. He felt unable to move and felt extreme vibrations and noise. He described a bright light that appeared to be shining on him. This occurred another nine times over the next six weeks and resulted in his first out-of-body experience. Monroe recorded this in his 1971 book *Journeys Out of the Body* and went on to become a prominent researcher in the field of human consciousness. Later he wrote two more books, *Far Journeys* (1985) and *Ultimate Journey* (1994) which describe his explorations of other dimensions including the afterlife.

Monroe found that for many people the out-of-body experience begins with unusual sounds, vibrations and paralysis which can be frightening. He developed a method called Hemi-Sync that could allow people to project their consciousness more easily. This became the basis of 'remote viewing' which was found to be so useful in gathering accurate data that it was adopted by the US intelligence and military services.

In his book *Far Journeys,* he describes years of experiments with a core group of eight volunteers who spent time having out-of-body experiences together. They learned to speak aloud while in deep states of meditation. They reported talking with guides, meeting passed relatives, entering the light and receiving revelations and messages for themselves and others. They also described souls who died, but did not realize they were dead. His non-profit Monroe Institute based in Faber, Virginia, has taught tens of thousands of people both in residence and through distance learning to undertake out-of-body journeys.

Thomas Campbell

Tom Campbell is a professional physicist. For 20 years he was at the heart of developing US missile defence systems. He began researching altered states of consciousness with Bob Monroe at Monroe Laboratories in the early 1970s. Campbell claims that he knew his out-of-body journeys were real when he met up with another explorer while they were out-of-body on many occasions. When they met afterwards, they found they had experienced the same things. Campbell's three books that make up *My Big TOE* [Theory of Everything] (2007) present a model of existence and reality that is based directly on his out-of-body experiences. Some of Dr. Campbell's numerous public seminars are available free of charge on YouTube.

William Buhlman

William Buhlman states he has been having out-of-body experiences for more than 40 years. He has been teaching courses on how to have an out-of-body experience, in Europe and at the Monroe Institute, for a number of years. His book *The Secret of the Soul: Using Out-of-Body Experiences to Understand Our True Nature* (2001) deals with some of the different kinds of OBEs both positive and unwelcome. He talks about OBEs in children, OBEs caused by combat and trauma, meeting loved ones in the afterlife and transformational experiences. His book has excellent chapters on the history of OBEs and on how to have an OBE. He also discusses what can be expected from an OBE and what the benefits are.

Jurgen Ziewe

Thirty-five years ago, Jurgen Ziewe began having out-of-body experiences as a result of deep meditation. A commercial artist, he has drawn stunning pictures of the different levels in the afterlife that he has repeatedly visited. These can be viewed in his videoed talk which is on the internet and on his webpage. His book *Multidimensional Man* (2008) describes some of the alternate realities he visited from the lowest to the highest.

The International Academy of Consciousness

The International Academy of Consciousness is a non-profit research and education organization with a presence in nine countries and 13 cities around the world. Courses on how to have an out-of-body experience and on the nature of consciousness are run in many countries. It has a research centre located in southern Portugal for practice and research on out-of-body experience.

Its founder, Dr. Waldo Vieira, began having out-of-body experiences at the age of nine and has been studying them for more than 50 years. His book *Projections of the Consciousness* (2007) recounts 60 out-of-body experiences from a six-month period in 1979. He describes visits to non-physical educational communities, assistance to those who have recently passed away, and encounters with highly evolved consciousnesses. The IAC publishes articles, books, and various educational materials, and stocks works written by researchers. Many of these resources are available on its website.

Out-of-body experiences and the afterlife

The experiences reported by regular out-of-body explorers and their students are consistent with each other. They all claim that we existed before birth and will continue to exist after death. They report on many different worlds where thought creates reality. Many people report face-to-face meetings with loved ones, non-physical beings, guides and helpers (Twemlow *et al.*, 1980).

In addition, a number of researchers report that people who have had out-of-body experiences find themselves changed. The effects are similar to those reported by people who have had near-death experiences. Some of the many benefits reported include decreased fear of death and increased psychic abilities. Many report spontaneous healing, increased spirituality, increased intelligence and memory recall and a greater awareness of reality (Buhlman, 1996: 130–141).

How to have an out-of-body experience

There are a number of websites, books, videos and courses which claim to be able to teach anyone who is persistent enough to have their own out-of-body experiences. One of the easiest for beginners is *The Secret of the Soul: Using Out-of-Body Experiences to Understand Our True Nature* (2001) by William Buhlman.

Chapter 6

SCIENCE PROVES PSYCHIC ABILITIES

The experimental evidence for ESP [extra sensory perception] from a century of research is so strong and overwhelming that reasonable people should no longer doubt its reality.

Professor Russell Targ

According to Dr. Charles Tart, in his book *The End of Materialism*, there are five areas of psychic phenomena for which there is impressive experimental evidence. These are:

- telepathy – receiving messages from someone else's mind
- clairvoyance or remote viewing – knowing things without the use of the five senses
- precognition – knowing things before they happen
- micro-psychokinesis – minds affecting machines in ways that cannot be detected except by statistics
- psychic healing.

This chapter deals only with the evidence for the first three – telepathy, clairvoyance and precognition. It is a little technical and can be omitted by those not interested in the laboratory studies that prove that psychic skills do exist.

Psychic abilities and the afterlife

Psychic abilities are strongly associated with the afterlife. Those who communicate with the afterlife (mediums) say that they do so using a more developed version of telepathy and clairvoyance. Instead of communicating mentally with people in the physical world, they communicate with people in the spirit world. People who have near-death experiences and out-of-body experiences also claim that they experience communicating with non-physical beings using telepathy. An increase in psychic abilities including precognition is one of the strongest effects of a near-death experience and some out-of-body experiences.

Proving scientifically that psychic abilities do exist shows that these experiences can be real and helps us understand that the mind is greater than the physical brain. It also shows how materialist scientists have allowed prejudice and fear of ridicule to suppress an area of research which, like research into the afterlife, is of great interest to ordinary people.

Psychic abilities can be easily tested in a laboratory, and scientists in Europe and America have been investigating them using scientific methods for more than 150 years. Investigating telepathy along with mediumship was one of the primary aims of the Society for Psychical Research when it was set up in 1882. The word 'psychic' was created by William Crookes when he was conducting experiments with medium D. D. Home. Since 1942 the term PSI (from the 23rd letter of the Greek alphabet meaning 'mind' or 'soul') has often been used to describe those abilities which have been investigated in the laboratory.

The conscious universe

In 1997, Dr. Dean Radin, director of the Consciousness Research Laboratory at the University of Nevada, published an important new book. Called *The Conscious Universe: The Scientific Truth of Psychic Phenomena,* it analyzes the overwhelming scientific evidence for psychic abilities.

He shows how Edwin May and his associates combined the results of all experiments with psychic phenomena done at Stanford Research Institute from 1973 to 1988. There were more than 26,000 separate trials in experiments conducted over 16 years. The statistical analysis of these results showed that psychic phenomena had been demonstrated to exist with an odds-against chance of more than a billion billion to one.

Dr. Radin claims that as yet few scientists and science journalists are aware of "this dramatic shift in informed opinion". He claims that this shift in opinion can be seen in the change of mind by leading skeptic Dr. Carl Sagan who, before he died, admitted that he felt three claims in the ESP field "deserve serious study".

It can also be seen in the publication of favourable reviews for the evidence of psychic phenomena in well-known scientific journals – like *Foundations of Physics, American Psychologist,* and *Statistical Science* – which began in the 1980s. Then in the 1990s, there were invitations to parapsychologists to present papers on psi research at important scientific conferences. There were also government sponsored review committees of funding for psychic research (*see* chapter on Remote Viewing). As well, popular college textbooks are starting to include chapters on psi research (Radin, 1997: 1–21).

Telepathy and clairvoyance

Materialists continue to deny the existence of telepathy even though it has been tested and proved in controlled scientific experiments for almost 130 years. Sir William Barrett conducted successful thought-transference experiments between distant hypnotized subjects in 1883. In 1886, Edmund Gurney, Frederick Myers and Frank Podmore published *Phantasms of the Living,* a massive two-volume study of spontaneous cases of telepathy with a special focus on communications shortly after death.

The best known experiments are those conducted by Dr. Joseph Rhine and his wife Louisa at Duke University. From the late 1920s to 1965, most of their experiments involved Zener cards which had one of five different designs. A 'sender' would focus on a card and the subject – usually a volunteer student – would try to receive what card had been chosen. Note that these experiments were not done with gifted psychics but with ordinary people – 'volunteer' psychology students.

In their book *Extra-Sensory Perception After Sixty Years* (Rhine *et al.*, 1940), the Rhines claim that by 1940, 33 experiments had been done involving almost a million trials. Their experimental methods were very strict. They rigorously excluded possible sensory clues, e.g., by introducing distance and/or barriers between sender and receiver. Of the 33 studies, 27 produced statistically significant results. These studies were replicated in 33 independent experiments in different laboratories in the five years following the first publication of Rhine's results. Twenty of these or 61 per cent were statistically significant where five per cent would have been expected by chance alone.

Dream research

Psychic researchers have been able to show that it is possible to pick up telepathic messages in dreams. This is important as many people report that they have vivid dreams about loved ones who have died. Sometimes they feel that they are receiving messages from them.

From 1966 to 1972, psychiatrist Montague Ullman and psychologist Professor Stanley Krippner conducted experiments on telepathy. This was in a dream research laboratory at the Maimonides Medical Center in New York. An experimenter would note when a subject was experiencing the rapid eye movements that signal dreaming. At that time, another experimenter in an adjoining room would be notified. He/she would focus on sending a picture telepathically to the sleeping subject. When the subject's rapid eye movements stopped, he/she would be woken up and asked to describe any dreams. The judges would compare a transcript of the dream with a pool of pictures to try to locate which one was being transmitted. Between

1966 and 1973, a total of 450 dream telepathy sessions were reported. When all the trials were combined, the odds of getting the same result by chance were one in 75 million (Radin, 1995: 72).

Altered states of consciousness

Research shows that people are better at telepathy when they are in an altered state of consciousness. Honorton, Braud and Parker placed their subjects in a relaxed state (called the Ganzfeld state by the experimenters). The subjects were asked to choose which of four pictures had been sent telepathically by an experimenter in the next room. The success rate was 37 per cent, whereas 25 per cent would be expected by chance. The odds of this success rate occurring by chance were one in a trillion.

Other experiments were conducted over 30 years at five different laboratories. The experimenters asked the subjects in the Ganzfeld state to describe a video that a friend was watching in a separate room. Many were able to do so. Seventy-nine studies comprising hundreds of individual trials were put together and analyzed. The odds that the results had come by chance were almost one in a billion.

Precognition (seeing the future)

Many times those living in the afterlife are able to warn their loved ones of things that are about to happen. They say that time is different in the afterlife and they are able to see probable futures. Science has now demonstrated that we all have an unconscious awareness of the future.

In early precognition experiments, subjects had to guess which card would come up next from a shuffled deck of cards. In their book *Extra-Sensory Perception After Sixty Years* (Rhine et al., 1966), Joseph and Louisa Rhine claim that by 1940, 33 experiments had been carried out in all. These involved a total of almost a million trials. As seen earlier, of the 33 studies, 27 produced statistically significant results.

Between 1935 and 1987, more than 309 laboratory studies were conducted by 62 different experimenters. The subjects were asked to guess which one of a fixed number of possible targets would be randomly selected at a future date. The time intervals between the guess and the time the target was selected varied between a fraction of a second and a year.

An overall analysis of the experiments was conducted by Honorton and Ferrari. They found that 37 per cent of the studies had positive results and calculated that the odds of such a result occurring by chance would be one in a billion billion (Honorton and Ferrari, 1989).

The conductance of our skin changes as we sweat and is a good measure of heightened emotions. Dean Radin measured the skin conductance of subjects while they watched a computer monitor that randomly displayed images associated with various emotions – calm, erotic or violent. He found that around three seconds before the subject saw each image (which was selected at random) the subjects' skin conductance changed significantly in the direction of the content of the next picture. The odds of his results occurring by chance were one in 125,000. Since then his results have been duplicated by Spottiswoode and May (2003) using either a very loud sound or silence.

Sally Rhine Feather, Director of the Rhine Research Laboratory, writes:

> Laboratory experiments are necessary to prove ESP is real, but ESP usually happens outside the laboratory. Confining our study of ESP to the laboratory is like studying lions in a zoo instead of in the wild (Rhine Feather and Schmicker, 2005).

She claims that the files of the Rhine Research Laboratory contain 15,000 cases of spontaneously occurring ESP cases. Many of them are described in her highly recommended book, *The Gift* (Rhine Feather and Schmicker, 2005).

One of the questions she is asked most frequently is whether a negative event which is predicted can be avoided. She did a study of 433 cases of warnings of danger. In nearly two-thirds, the person took no action to avoid the danger and the negative outcome occurred. In those cases where action was taken to avoid the event, two-thirds were successful. One of the most dramatic of these cases was that of a streetcar conductor who had a dream of a terrible accident with a bright red truck. He awoke soaked in perspiration. Later that day a sequence of specific events began that triggered his memory of the dream. He slammed on the brakes of his streetcar and shut off the power. A truck shot directly in his path which his streetcar would certainly have hit had he not put on the brakes. He saw in the truck the same three people that in his dream he had seen dead and injured (Rhine Feather and Schmicker, 2005: 199).

The significance of psychic research

Laboratory studies have been necessary to prove to the satisfaction of the scientifically minded that psychic abilities exist. They have now done that over and over in experiments under controlled conditions which have met all the objections of skeptics. These experiments have been replicated by many researchers in different countries.

From the laboratory experiments, we now know that everyone possesses some degree of psychic ability which can be increased with training. But laboratory experiments under-represent the conditions in which psychic abilities operate in the real world. Laboratory experiments usually use untrained volunteer psychology students who are not selected for psychic abilities.

Testing your own psychic abilities

Dr. Rupert Sheldrake has compiled some practical experiments in telepathy that can be done by anyone using the internet in less than 20 minutes. The audio anticipation test, the telephone telepathy test, the joint attention test and photo telepathy test and the online staring test are available on his website http://www.sheldrake.

org/Onlineexp/portal/ along with instructions and results. They have been completed by hundreds of thousands of participants with highly significant results.

Chapter 7

REMOTE VIEWING

She went into a trance. And while she was in the trance, she gave us some latitude and longitude figures. We focused our satellite cameras on that point, and the lost plane was there.

FORMER US PRESIDENT *JIMMY CARTER*

The psychic researcher Ingo Swann coined the term 'remote viewing' as a neutral scientific term for clairvoyance. Initially, it referred only to situations in which a disciplined research protocol was used by the US military, but gradually the term has come into general use for the ability to perceive without the use of the five senses.

Although not direct evidence of the afterlife, remote viewing is included here because of its validation by extensive testing and practical application in highly controlled tests over more than 20 years. It is evidence of 'the sixth sense', the same ability which psychic detectives and mediums call upon to go forward or back in time and to solve crimes.

Different to OBEs

Researchers who intentionally practise both remote viewing and out-of-body experiences claim that there is a difference between the two kinds of experience. They say that in an out-of-body experience, the viewer perceives as if physically present, whereas in remote viewing, the viewer is able to clairvoyantly tune into all sorts of information about the target which would not be physically observable.

Military research

For more than 20 years, the United States military had a budget of 70 million dollars a year for the purpose of psychic research with special emphasis on 'remote viewing'. This research was confirmed by independent experiments at the Princeton Engineering Anomalies Research Laboratory (Radin, 1997: 103–105).

Stunning as it may sound to those who are unfamiliar with psychic phenomena, these and greater things have been done and are being done today in the United States and Russia. China has kept quiet about it but they do have the population and the advanced psychic knowledge to participate in remote viewing.

In his most interesting book, *Remote Viewers: The Secret History of America's Psychic Spies* (1997), Jim Schnabel cites a number of highly credible sources, including an American president, about the reality of remote viewing applied for military objectives. Here are some stunning statements that by now have found their place in the history of psychic phenomena:

> I never liked to get into debates with the skeptics, because if you didn't believe that remote viewing was real, you hadn't done your homework.
> Major General Edmund R. Thompson, US Army Assistant Chief of Staff for Intelligence, 1977–81, Deputy Director for Management and Operations, DIA, 1982–84 (Schnabel, 1997: cover).

> You cannot be involved in this for any length of time and not be convinced there's something here.
> Norm J., former senior CIA official who tasked remote viewers (Schnabel, 1997: cover).

There were times when they wanted to push buttons and drop bombs on the basis of our information.

Dr. Hal Puthoff, a former manager of the Remote Viewing Program (Schnabel, 1997: cover).

Stanford Research Institute in the United States was the venue where many of the original experiments were conducted. Physicist Hal Puthoff was the chief of the Remote Viewing Program there. Some of the personnel involved in this military programme, according to Schnabel (1997), included:

- Admiral Stansfield Turner, Director of the CIA 1977–91
- Major General Ed Thompson, Assistant Chief of Staff for Army Intelligence. He had special knowledge that the Russians had advanced techniques in psychic phenomena which were used for military espionage in remote viewing and long distance telepathic hypnosis
- Sergeant Mel Riley (1978–90)
- Sergeant Lyn Buchanan, Major Ed Dames and Colonel John Alexander from US Army Intelligence & Security Command
- Gifted remote viewer Ingo Swann, who was Puthoff's first test OBE subject
- CIA scientist Richard Kennett who worked with Patrick Price and Hal Puthoff
- Keith Harary, gifted remote viewer
- John McMahon, chief of the CIA's Office of Technical Service during 1974–76 and later the CIA's Deputy Director; he was a major supporter of remote viewing and became a remote viewer himself. He was convinced when he himself experienced stunning psychic phenomena
- Patrick Price, gifted psychic, highly consistent with the remote viewing of Ingo Swann. Price, through remote viewing, accurately described "details of a secret Pentagon facility in the hills of the West Virginia village of Sugar Grove..." Among its secret functions were the interception of intercontinental telephone

communications, and the control of US spy satellites. Price was also deadly accurate in his remote viewing in penetrating Russian installation at Mount Narodnaya in the remote northern Ural Mountains. The CIA confirmed the accuracy of Price's remote viewing.

Some achievements of the Program

Some of the targets 'remote viewed' with sensational accuracy in the early days included:

- a suspected low-yield nuclear test facility in Soviet Kazakhstan, with features confirmed only later by a spy satellite
- the location of a Soviet bomber that had crashed in the jungles of Zaire
- the construction of a new kind of huge Soviet ballistic missile submarine
- the activities of a Soviet intelligence officer in Washington, D.C.
- the code room of a foreign embassy.

From 1981 to 1995, five different US government-sponsored scientific review committees were given the task of reviewing the evidence for psychic phenomena. Reports were prepared by the Congressional Research Service, the Army Research Institute, the National Research Council, the Office of Technology Assessment, and the American Institutes for Research (the latter commissioned by the Central Intelligence Agency). While disagreeing over fine points of interpretation, all five of the reviews concluded that the experimental evidence for certain forms of psychic phenomena merited serious scientific study.

The book *Mind at Large* (ed. Tart, Puthoff and Targ, 2002), contains an excellent summary of the evidence for remote viewing. In the preface, physicist Russell Targ writes:

This program to study the applications of psychic abilities survived a formal Congressional investigation in 1978, after which it went on to provide valuable, otherwise unavailable information to almost every branch of the US intelligence community [Defense Intelligence Agency, Central Intelligence Agency, Army Intelligence, etc.] during the Cold War...As one of the scientists who conducted this research, I do not have to believe in extrasensory perception (ESP). I have seen it occur in the laboratory on a day-to-day basis for decades. As a physicist I don't have to believe in this phenomenon any more than I have to believe in lasers – with which I have also worked extensively (2002: xv).

The Legion of Merit is a US armed forces military award that is given for outstanding services and achievements. The United States government was so impressed by the results attained by remote viewer Joe McMoneagle that the US Congress and Senate awarded it to him. This award for brilliant psychic skills was passed by the US Congress and the Senate. The attestation reads:

While with his command, he used his talents and expertise in the execution of more than 200 missions, addressing over 150 essential elements of information. These EEI contained critical intelligence reported at the highest echelons of our military and government, including such national-level agencies as the Joint Chiefs of Staff, DIA, NSA, CIA, DEA, and the Secret Service, producing crucial and vital intelligence unavailable from any other source.

The official end of the Program

The CIA, at the request of Congress, took over the Remote Viewing Program and stopped its funding in 1995. Jim Schnabel claims that a large part of the problem was the closed-minded skepticism of scientists and engineers in the intelligence community. He says that the CIA wanted to have access to the remote viewers but " like many other agencies, it didn't want to take responsibility for it. That fear of embarrassment ...would follow the Remote Viewing Program wherever it went" (Schnabel, 2011).

The official reason given for closing down the Program was an unfavourable review by two scientists. However, according to Joseph McMoneagle's book *Mind Trek* (1997), these scientists were not shown 99 per cent of the documented results of remote viewing which were and are still classified, were forbidden to speak with any of the remote viewers or project managers, and were not given any means to evaluate the operational effectiveness of the information they were shown (McMoneagle, 1997: 218–29).

Even with these restrictions, both reviewers concluded that remote viewing is real. Statistician Jessica Utts, one of the two principal reviewers, wrote:

> Using the standards applied to any other area of science, it is concluded that psychic functioning has been well-established. The statistical results of the studies examined are far beyond what is expected by chance. Arguments that these results could be due to methodological flaws in the experiments are soundly refuted. Effects of similar magnitude to those found in government-sponsored research ... have been replicated at a number of laboratories across the world. Such consistency cannot be readily explained by claims of flaws or fraud.... (Utts, 1996: 3).

Surprisingly, the other principal reviewer, skeptic Professor Ray Hyman, agreed. He wrote:

> The statistical departures from chance appear to be too large and consistent to attribute to statistical flukes of any sort.... I tend to agree with Professor Utts that real effects are occurring in these experiments. Something other than chance departures from the null hypothesis has occurred in these experiments (Hyman, 1996: 57).

Remote viewing goes commercial

Since remote viewing has come out into the open, it appears to be proving its effectiveness in the marketplace. At the time of writing (2013), an Internet search on Google returned over 57 million entries for remote viewing.

Remote viewing (clairvoyance) has proved itself in many practical situations including detection of minerals (Ireland, 2009), stock futures (Targ, 2012: 133) and location of sunken ships (Schwartz, 2007).

Parapsychologist Stephan A. Schwartz, Visiting Professor at John F. Kennedy University (1981–83), is part of the small group that founded modern remote viewing research, and has successfully used remote viewing in archaeology. He has produced and written a number of television documentaries, and has written four books: *The Alexandria Project* (1983), *Mind Rover* (2001), *The Secret Vaults of Time* (2005), and his latest, *Opening to the Infinite* (2007). His website www.stephanaschwartz.com contains an extensive bibliography on remote viewing as well as details of his experiments with applied remote viewing.

Remote viewing in China?

According to Tim Rifat (1999), the Russian and Chinese military and intelligence agencies are also known to be heavily involved in remote viewing.

The Chinese are claiming that they have super psychics like Zhang Baosheng who reportedly can accelerate the molecular structure of their body to penetrate at will solid objects such as brick walls. They also claim they have highly gifted remote viewers. This means that the Chinese are certain to have highly gifted psychics who can read documents locked away in a solid safe (Dong and Raffill, 1997).

Paul Dong and Thomas E. Raffill in their book, *China's Super Psychics*, state:

54

China's vast population, encouraged by a government that assiduously promotes psychic research, has developed an unusually high percentage of practitioners with psychic abilities. It is estimated that China now has five thousand psychic children, three to five-hundred psychic adults, and more than thirty super psychics (Dong and Raffill, 1997).

Chapter 8

DEATHBED VISIONS

A new idea is first condemned as ridiculous and then dismissed
as trivial, until finally, it becomes what everybody knows.

PROFESSOR WILLIAM JAMES
AMERICAN PHILOSOPHER AND PSYCHOLOGIST

A ll over the world, people who are dying start talking to
loved ones who have already died. Sometimes they say
that they can see beautiful places in the spirit world and
hear beautiful music. Even a thousand years ago in France, the dying would tell of visions of God and of seeing those who had died
before them (Aries, 1982).

These 'deathbed visions' were rarely mentioned in the scientific literature until the late 1920s. Sir William Barrett, a professor of physics in Dublin, became interested when his wife told
him about one of her patients. As she lay dying, the woman said
that she could see her sister. No one had told the woman that her
sister had died three weeks before. This story was so interesting
to Professor Barrett that he began a systematic study. His book,
published in 1926, was called *Deathbed Visions*. In it he noted that
many times, at the moment of death people would see a friend or
relative at their bedside who they thought was still living. In all
cases, the person they saw had already died. Dying children often expressed surprise that the angels they saw waiting for them
did not have wings.

In the 1960s, Dr. Karlis Osis of the American Society for Psychical Research did a pilot study of deathbed visions that confirmed the findings of Professor Barrett. His findings showed:

- the most common type of vision was of people who had died before them
- the visions usually lasted a short time, five minutes or less
- the dying patients stated that the visitor had come to take them away
- it made no difference if the dying person did or did not believe in the afterlife
- most of the patients in the study had not received drugs which could confuse their minds (Osis, 1961).

Dr. Osis and Dr. Haraldsson

In 1977, Dr. Osis and his colleague, Dr. Erlendur Haraldsson, published *At the Hour of Death*. This book extended the original study and included reports from over a thousand doctors and nurses in India as well as the United States. It reported on the deaths of more than 100,000 people. These studies all recorded the same findings as the earlier studies.

According to the information provided to them by nurses and doctors, only ten per cent of people are conscious shortly before their death. Of this group, one-half to two-thirds have near-death visions. These people see their loved ones, see scenes of the next world and suddenly are very happy and excited for no medical reason. They concluded that these experiences are so extraordinary and so convincing that they cannot be explained by the physical condition of the patient or by the medication they have been taking.

Dr. Melvin Morse says that deathbed visions are "a forgotten aspect of life's mysterious process", and that they can comfort and help the dying patient and the family. In his book *Closer to the Light: Learning from the Near-Death Experiences of Children* (1993), he talks about several cases where dying children began to see visions

57

of the afterlife during the last few days of their lives. They described amazing colours and beautiful places and relatives they sometimes had not known existed.

Society for Psychical Research cases

There are many cases on record with the Society for Psychical Research where the spirit visitors were seen by others at the bedside of the dying person, sometimes by several persons at the same time:

- a deathbed apparition was seen by the dying woman, Harriet Pearson, and three relatives who were caring for her (*Journal of the Society for Psychical Research,* Feb 1904: 185–87)
- a young boy was dying and two witnesses independently saw his recently deceased mother at the child's bedside (*Proceedings of the Society for Psychical Research,* Volume 6, p. 20).

Recent research

Dr. Elisabeth Kübler-Ross claimed that patients, including children, slowly prepare themselves for death by having out-of-body experiences. They become aware of the presence of beings surrounding them who guide and help them. She claimed that everyone is met by a loved one at the moment of death. She said she saw many people suddenly becoming conscious and stretching their arms up to an unseen visitor (Kübler-Ross, 1971).

Maggie Callanan and Patricia Kelley (1997) talk of 'Nearing Death Awareness' which develops slowly as the dying person drifts for a time between two worlds. They claim that the dying communicate in symbolic language. They often talk about going on a trip, about places that they can see, about people no longer alive who are waiting for them. Many know exactly when their death will occur. They also make requests for reconciliation or the removal of some barrier to their departure. Callanan and Kelley also say that many times the dying will choose their preferred time of leaving, often waiting until a loved one has left the room for a minute.

Psychologist Dr. Carla Wills-Brandon, in her book *One Last Hug Before I Go: The Mystery and Meaning of Deathbed Visions* (2000), re-examined the research of Barrett and Osis. She also looked at many recent experiences. Her latest book, *Heavenly Hugs* (2012), is based on nearly 2,000 cases of departing visions and visits from deceased relatives and friends. She shows that at the moment of physical death, departed loved ones come back to the dying to help them cross over. These meetings are reported by people from a wide variety of cultural, ethnic and religious backgrounds.

Dr. Peter Fenwick and Dr. Elizabeth Fenwick published *The Art of Dying* in 2008. Subtitled *A Journey to Elsewhere,* the book is primarily about deathbed visions and visitations. They found that often, at the moment of death, the dying patient is seen to look at a particular corner of the room. They are concentrating and saying that a deceased loved one is there and waiting for them.

Shared death experiences

In his book *Glimpses of Eternity* (2010), Dr. Raymond Moody explores the area of shared-death experiences. There are many reports that people who are sitting at the bedside of a dying person experience travelling into the spirit world with them. They meet relatives who have already died and see that the dying person is welcomed. Moody also discusses a strange mist that is sometimes reported over a deathbed:

> They describe it in various ways. Some say that it looks like smoke, while others say it is as subtle as steam. Sometimes it seems to have a human shape. Whatever the case, it usually drifts upward and always disappears fairly quickly (Moody, 2010).

How to share the benefits of these experiences

In his book *Parting Visions* (1994), paediatrician Dr. Melvin Morse says:

- family members who know about the visions of the dying are known to spend more time at the dying person's bedside
- spiritual visions empower dying patients, making them realize that they have something to share with others
- spiritual visions remove all fear of dying in the patient and are enormously healing to the relatives
- they can prevent burnout on the part of nurses and doctors
- if attended to, they can dramatically reduce wasteful medical procedures that are often painful to the patient. He claims that 30–60 per cent of the American health care dollar is spent in the last few days of a person's life and "most of it is spent in useless procedures that do nothing to prolong life".

Chapter 9

AFTER-DEATH CONTACTS

It was clear that given proper preparation, people could see apparitions of departed loved ones... instead of telling a therapist how they feel about losing a spouse or child they could talk to the loved one directly.

DR. RAYMOND MOODY NDE PIONEER

After-death contacts have been studied scientifically since 1882 when a survey was conducted in England. Altogether 32,000 cases were recorded, 17,000 in English. It was published in Volume X of the Society for Psychical Research *Proceedings* for 1894 (Sidgwick, Johnson, Myers, Podmore and Sidgwick, 1894). Further studies were carried out by the American Society for Psychical Research and by the French researcher Camille Flammarion who compiled thousands of cases in his books *The Unknown* (1900) and *Death and Its Mystery* (1925).

Contacts occur in every country

In 1973 a University of Chicago sociologist asked a sample of 1,467 Americans if they had ever felt they had had contact with someone who had died. Twenty-seven per cent answered that they had (Greeley, 1975). A similar survey in Iceland (Haraldsson *et al.*, 1977) found that 31 per cent claimed to have had some visual contact.

Dr. W. D. Rees, a British physician, found that of a sample of widows in Wales, 47 per cent had had experiences – often repeatedly over a number of years – that convinced them that their dead husbands had been in contact with them (Rees, 1971: 37–41). An earlier British experiment by Dr. P. Marris (1958) had found a figure of 50 per cent.

When her husband died in 1983, Professor Sylvia Hart Wright and her son jointly had an experience that suggested he was trying to contact them. Two of her husband's male friends reported similar events. Wright started researching and interviewed almost a hundred healthy, everyday people who had sensed contact with the dead. The result was her book *When Spirits Come Calling: The Open-Minded Skeptics' Guide to After-Death Contacts* (2002).

All the evidence shows that when our loved ones die they go to a world which at first is just as solid and real as this one. In fact, they tell us that to them our life seems unreal. They are met by family members or friends and taken to live in houses with furniture and gardens and begin a rich and rewarding life. Time is different in the afterlife and for them it seems as though we are not separated. They tell us that when we sleep we visit them in their world. Although we miss them it is important to them that we go on with life and not get lost in grief.

Most still like to visit their families and loved ones and stay involved in their celebrations. Those who are too young to come on their own are regularly brought to visit. Our relationship with our loved ones is different but it still continues. (What happens when we die is dealt with more fully in Chapter 32).

Recent research shows that people who die make their presence known in a number of ways. These include helping others to:

(1) sense their presence
(2) hear their voice
(3) feel their touch

(4) smell something associated with them
(5) see them as if they were real
(6) see a flat vision of them like a photo
(7) experience one of these while half-asleep
(8) have a visit in a dream – an unusually vivid dream that one does not forget like a normal dream
(9) have an out-of-body experience and meet them
(10) receive a telephone call from the person who died (two-way conversations have been reported)
(11) experience electrical appliances such as lights, TVs, and radios going on and off
(12) receive a symbolic message, sign, meaningful coincidence, or synchronicity.

Dr. Melvin Morse, a paediatrician who has done many studies of death and dying, claims that it is rare for someone to lose a child and not see them again in a death-related vision (Morse and Perry, 1994: 135).

Contact dreams

Dream communication is the most frequently reported method of after-death communication. Researchers in cross-cultural studies found that about half of all reported spontaneous psychic experiences occurred in dreams.

Unlike normal dreams, contact dreams don't fade with time. They are incredibly vivid and you will be able to remember details even years later. The person who has died usually looks much younger and in perfect health. They are smiling and telling you that they are fine and happy. They tell you that they did not suffer during their passing and that they are with family members. You may wake up with a feeling that they have hugged and kissed you. Some contain evidence that suggest it was more than just a dream.

Mediums and out-of-body explorers tell us that our astral body lifts out of our physical body when we sleep and we actually visit with our loved ones in the afterlife. It is a world just as solid as ours but on a different frequency. Some contact dreams are fragments of memory of those visits. Those living in the afterlife are surprised that we don't remember anything about these visits, but we are told that when we finally cross over we will remember each one.

In some cases dream communications contain information that can be verified. One case, the Chaffin Will Case, was intensively investigated and accepted by the American courts. A father who had died appeared in the dreams of one of his sons and gave him details of how to find his last will (Fontana, 2005: 52–3).

Dianne Arcangel relates the case of Charles Vance in her book *Afterlife Encounters*. He began having recurring dreams about his deceased friend Murphy, who wanted to get a message to his widow, Lorraine, to look inside a wall in their house. Charles Vance eventually called Lorraine who broke into the wall. She reportedly found thousands of dollars hidden there. When Lorraine called her own daughter (who did not know Charles Vance), she found that the daughter had been having the same dreams but had disregarded them (Arcangel, 2005: 74–85).

Claire Sylvia, a dancer who had a heart-lung transplant, began having vivid dreams about her donor. She discovered: "He [was] tall, [had] sandy coloured hair and his name [was] Tim L." The story of how she finally traced the donor's family through a series of dreams is told in full in her book *A Change of Heart: A Memoir* (Sylvia and Novak, 1998).

Electrical disturbances

An increasing number of people report lights and appliances going on and off in a meaningful way and mobile phones turning on and playing voice messages from a loved one. This may or may not be deliberate on the part of the loved one. It could simply be a result of their electromagnetic energy coming into the system as they come close. Others report music boxes starting to play even though they have not been rewound. Sometimes telephones that are not connected will ring.

A good friend of ours, Richard C., tells us that for many months after the passing of his friend's son, both he and his friend would both hear the doorbell ring whenever they were discussing something to do with the afterlife. On one spectacular occasion they were talking to each other on the telephone when they heard 3–4 seconds of loud static followed by the son's voice saying "Hi Mum", followed by more loud static.

Another very frequent method that people are reporting is asking for a sign from a loved one and then seeing a significantly greater-than-chance number of rainbows, butterflies, coins, feathers or any other object associated with the loved one. While some instances can be argued away as the human tendency to seek patterns in random information, some people have so many unusual sightings that absolutely defy chance or coincidence.

The most frequent messages expressed

According to Bill and Judy Guggenheim's research published in *Hello from Heaven: A New Field of Research-After-Death Communication Confirms That Life and Love Are Eternal* (1997), the purpose of such contact is to offer comfort and hope to surviving family and friends. They want us to know they're still alive and that we'll be reunited with them when our time comes. Their most frequent messages, expressed verbally or non-verbally, are:

I'm okay... I'm fine... everything is okay... I love you... everything will be all right... I'm watching over you... I'll always be there for you... don't worry about me... don't grieve for me... please let me go... I'm happy... I'll see you again... go on with your life... please forgive... thank you... (Guggenheim, 1997).

Extreme grief can make it difficult for a loved one to contact you while you are awake. In these cases, the loved one will often try to impress thoughts onto you through dreams. And sometimes the person who has died will try to make contact through a friend or relative who is not so emotional. Judy Collier received a phone call from a casual acquaintance two months after her son's death. The friend said she had been contacted by Judy's son, Kyle. He had asked her to pass on a message to Judy – to quit kissing his ashes, which she had in an urn at home. In her book *Quit Kissing My Ashes*, Judy Collier relates to her readers all the signs she and her family have received that convinced them that Kyle is still very much part of their family and that they still have a relationship with him.

Apparitions at the time of death

A very large number of apparition cases involve a person who has recently died appearing to one or more loved ones to announce the fact of their death. In many such cases the death was unexpected and was later confirmed to have occurred immediately before the apparition. There are many cases of people hearing raps on the wall or hearing an object fall at the exact time of someone's passing.

Several documented and confirmed examples from various studies include:

- Second Lieutenant Leslie Poynter appeared to his sister in England, bent over and kissed her and then, smiling happily, faded from view. Two weeks later the family received a telegram informing them of his death earlier in the day on the same date (McKenzie, 1971: 116–117)
- Mrs. Pacquet's brother Edmund appeared to her six hours after he had drowned at sea and acted out how he had been caught around the legs by a rope and dragged overboard (cited in Rogo, 1974: 16–17)
- Mrs. Gladys Watson was awakened from a deep sleep by someone calling her name. Upon waking she saw her paternal grandfather who told her, "Don't be frightened. It's only me. I've just died." The grandfather had died unexpectedly a few minutes before (Spraggett, 1975: 45–6).

Contact agreements

According to Bennett (1939: 282), about one in 20 of the cases in the files of the Society for Psychical Research involves agreements where two people promise that whoever dies first will endeavour to appear to the other.

- Lord Brougham suddenly saw an apparition of a university friend he had not seen or thought about for years. Later he received a letter confirming that the friend had died in India at the exact time of the apparition (Cited in Johnson, 1971: 198–99)
- Mrs. Arthur Bellamy of Bristol made such an agreement with a school friend. She did not see her for many years. One night after the friend's death, Mr. Bellamy saw a lady sitting on the bed beside his sleeping wife. He later identified her from a photograph as the same friend (Bennett, 1939: 131–32).

There are many reasons why these apparitions cannot be regarded as hallucinations, wish fulfillment or the product of the unconscious mind.

1. The witnesses were normal

In many cases the witnesses were scientifically trained people of high credibility. In most of these cases the person was in a perfectly ordinary state of mind, free from shock or stress. The experiences were totally unexpected and took place in familiar surroundings. The witnesses were not mediumistic or telepathic. It was rare for witnesses to say that they had had more than one or two such experiences in a lifetime (Tyrrell, 1963: 23).

2. Objective phenomena

The appearance of an apparition often involves physical phenomena. Sometimes things move or break. Sounds like footsteps have been recorded on tape. Apparitions have been observed to cast a shadow, be reflected in a mirror, overturn furniture, leave a scent, ask for a lift, and even sign their name (Sidgwick *et al.*, 1894). In her book, *On Life After Death,* Dr. Kübler-Ross reports an encounter with Mrs. Schwartz, a former patient who had died. She writes: "I even touched her skin to see if it was cold or warm, or if the skin would disappear when I touched it".

3. Seen by more than one person

Many of the recorded cases have been seen by more than one person. In a case investigated by the Society for Psychical Research, nine people living in a house in Ramsbury, England, saw the apparition of a man who had died ten months before. They saw him many times both separately and as a group, from February until April. He was always seen sitting at his dying widow's bedside. His hand was placed on her forehead and he was visible for up to half an hour at a time (Holzer, 1965: 52–56).

Professor Hornell Hart, in his book *The Enigma of Survival* (1959), claims that between one-third and two-thirds of all apparitions are seen by more than one person. They are seen differently by each viewer according to the correct angle.

4. Giving information not known to the observer

In some cases people appear in order to save loved ones from danger. This happened to Elaine Worrell who lived with her husband Hal on the top floor of an apartment building in Oskaloosa, Iowa. One day she saw a young man in her hallway who led her downstairs into an apartment. There she found a young widow whom she barely knew. The young woman had slashed her wrists and was collapsed on a bed. After she recovered, the young woman showed Mrs. Worrell a photograph of her late husband. Elaine recognized it immediately as the young man who had led her downstairs and into the apartment (Holzer, 1963).

Dianne Arcangel's book *Afterlife Encounters* tells of a mother, Beverley, whose son Tommy was killed in an unknown way. After the funeral, Tommy came to his mother in an apparition. He told her to go quickly to a certain corner in Brooklyn where she would find his blood in the snow. She called the police who did a DNA test and found three eye witnesses and were able to solve his murder (Arcangel, 2005).

Psychomanteums – mirror-gazing

Dr. Raymond Moody became famous for his pioneering studies of Near-Death Experiences. He wanted to be able to help people have after-death contacts in a controlled setting. He knew that in Ancient Greece when people wished to contact a deceased loved one, they consulted an 'oracle' at a psychomanteum. This was a specially built setting which involved sensory deprivation and gazing into a mirror. Dr. Moody reconstructed the process with astonishing results. 85 per cent of his clients who go through a full day of preparation do make contact with a deceased loved one – but not necessarily the one that they are seeking to meet. In most cases this occurs in his specially built psychomanteum, but in 25 per cent of the cases it happens later in their own homes. Sometimes the client wakes up and sees the apparition at the foot of the bed (Moody, 1993: 97). Dr. Moody gives full instructions on how to create your own psychomanteum in his book *Visionary Encounters with Departed Loved Ones*.

Professor Arthur Hastings from the Institute of Transpersonal Psychology in Palo Alto, California, independently confirmed Dr. Moody's findings. He and his research team took 27 people through a three-hour process to contact a friend or loved one who had died. First, they spent some time remembering the loved one. Second, they sat in a darkened room lit only by a candle gazing into a mirror. Third, they discussed and reflected on the experience. Half of the participants said they had felt the presence of the person they wanted to contact. Participants reported that a variety of images appeared in the mirror. Some talked with their loved one. Others reported sounds, light, body sensations, and smells. Several specific messages were reported.

There were statistically significant reductions in bereavement responses over the entire group. These included unresolved feelings, of loss, grief, guilt, sadness, and a need to communicate. Participants also reported significant impact on their lives following the session (Hastings *et al.*, 2002).

After-death contacts can reduce intense grief

Dr. Craig Hogan is co-author with Allan Botkin, a clinical psychologist, of *Induced After-Death Communication*. The book describes a new kind of therapy which uses Eye Movement Desensitization and Reprocessing (EMDR). Dr. Botkin discovered the method while working with grieving Vietnam veterans. In 98 per cent of cases Dr. Botkin found he could induce an experience which allowed clients to feel they were having a vivid meeting with someone who had died. Initially Dr. Botkin thought that these experiences were hallucinations, but then he discovered that the observing psychologist could "tune into" and observe the encounter (Botkin and Hogan, 2005: 91–99).

In 2010 Rochelle Wright learned Dr. Botkin's method and redesigned it. She called her method 'Guided Afterlife Connections'. She uses the eye movements, but also plays music or sounds through a headset that alternate in volume between the left and right ears. Her method allows those in the afterlife to guide the experience and places no time limits on it. The Guided Afterlife Connections method has resulted in afterlife connections in one hundred per cent of the sessions in which it has been used to date. It is explained in the book co-authored by Rochelle Wright and Dr. Craig Hogan, *Guided After-Death Connections* (2011). The method can be used with grieving parents or anyone who wants to have an afterlife connection.

The connections may last for an hour or more and usually consist of active encounters with the deceased. The person having the connection receives messages, has conversations and experiences walking together, hugging, and even kissing. The people who have these experiences say that what they experienced was like no other experience they had ever had. They say it is quite different

70

to imagination, to drug-induced altered states of consciousness or dreams. In a number of cases, someone in the room with the experiencer has the same mental experience. Afterwards their reports match exactly. People learn information during the experiences they couldn't know that is afterward verified as being true.

The messages are more than simple reassurances that the person living in the afterlife is alive and happy. They provide guidance to the experiencer about how to live a full, happy life. They suggest specific actions they should take. The result in many cases is a huge change and the person having the experience decides to go forward in their lives with confidence and happiness.

Recently Dr. Hogan has finished the pilot and development phase of Self-guided Afterlife Connections. This is a method which uses a relaxation exercise instead of music through headphones. This is a method that people can use in their own homes without a medium or a therapist. So far it has been very successful. Details are available on his website http://selfguided.spiritualunderstanding.org.

Benefits of after-death contacts

OMEGA: Journal of Death and Dying published a study of the positive effects of after-death contacts:

> The encounters profoundly affected the participants' beliefs in an afterlife and attitudes toward life and death, and had a significant effect on their grief. Finally, post-death encounters had a healing effect on the participants by contributing to a sense of connectedness with the deceased. We conclude that health care professionals and counselors should be educated about post-death encounters so that the bereaved can share their experiences in a supportive and understanding atmosphere (N. Nowatzki & R. Kalischuk, 2009).

The Forever Family Foundation

In 2002 Bob and Phran Ginsberg lost their youngest daughter, Bailey, in a car crash. When they went to a grief support organization for parents, they found that the organizers tried to shut down any discussion about the afterlife. The parents ended up talking to each other in the parking lot. They decided that talking about and investigating the afterlife was the best method of healing their grief. This led to them creating the Forever Family Foundation which supports continued research into survival of consciousness. In addition to an active internet page, www.foreverfamilyfoundation.org, the Foundation co-ordinates afterlife discussion groups, runs a weekly internet radio programme, runs a mediumship certification programme and recommends reliable mediums. It also conducts lectures, workshops and conferences about the afterlife.

How to have an after-death contact

It is helpful to read about after-death contacts so that you can recognize when you have one. Many times people sense a contact but dismiss it as their own imagination. Contacts often come most strongly in the days following the death of a loved one, when you are most in need of comfort. This is the time when your loved ones are trying very hard to let you know that they are ok. Intense grief makes it harder for them to get their messages through. Dream contacts are often chosen as the easiest method. Some people report that receiving or learning Reiki or spiritual healing helps them to be more open to contacts.

George Meek in his book *After We Die What Then?* has this suggestion:

Sit quietly every few days and send loving thoughts to the loved one. Visualize where the loved one is. Speak out loud as though the loved one is present. Often, in fact, he is! Wish him well in his new surroundings. Of course, tell him that you miss him but that you are no longer grieving because you know that he has returned home, that he is among loved ones who are looking after his every want. State that you are very thankful for his love and companionship, and that you will meet again and continue your relationship.

Australian Medium Phil G. (Graham) recorded an excellent You-Tube video early in 2009 in which he describes a technique he calls "afterlife coffee time". His webpage www.philg.net.au has a number of resources to help you contact the person you miss.

Dr. Julia Assante is both an academic and a medium. She has been a professional medium and past-life therapist for over 40 years. Her accuracy in telepathy has been clinically tested at Columbia University. As a scholar, she has taught at Columbia and given talks at universities worldwide. Her latest book is *The Last Frontier: Exploring the Afterlife and Transforming Our Fear of Death* (2012). Chapter 16, "How to Make Contact," contains nearly 40 pages of detailed suggestions on how to interpret subtle signals and to initiate an after-death contact. It is highly recommended.

Chapter 10

MENTAL MEDIUMS TESTED

I tell you we do persist. Communication is possible. I have proved that the people who communicate are who and what they say they are. The conclusion is that survival is scientifically proved by scientific investigation.

Sir Oliver Lodge FRS

There is an impressive body of evidence which shows that there are many genuine, gifted mediums who have given an amazing amount of proven, objective evidence of survival.

Many types of mediums

The most common type of mediumship nowadays is mental mediumship. The medium works in good light and retains normal consciousness. He or she claims to be able to see, hear, smell or sense the presence of individual spirits.

In Western countries some mental mediums give demonstrations in Spiritualist churches, in halls and theatres. Sometimes there are thousands of people in the audience. As well, many conduct private consultations in person, by phone or by Skype. This is the kind of mediumship featured in popular television shows like *Medium* (based on the life of Alison Dubois), *Ghost Whisperer*, *Psychic Detectives*,

Sensing Murder, John Edward and *Lisa Williams*. There are many bestselling books by mental mediums like James Van Praagh, and exceptionally good movies like *Ghost* and *The Sixth Sense*.

Trance mediumship occurs when the medium enters an altered state of consciousness to bring forward information not normally known. Sometimes this is a light state similar to hypnosis. Sometimes the medium feels that he/she is an observer of another consciousness that is speaking/writing through her/him. In the USA this kind of mediumship is called channelling.

Sometimes the medium goes into a deep trance and becomes completely unconscious. They are completely unaware of what is happening. While the medium is in trance a 'spirit' takes over the medium's body and may talk in a different voice using totally different mannerisms and even speak in a foreign language. This kind of mediumship is usually practised in private groups called 'Circles'. The group members are called 'sitters'. A group gathering together with a medium is called a 'séance' which simply means a sitting.

There is also 'physical mediumship' which takes place in a completely dark room. Usually a group of about 6–8 people sit together for about an hour a week for several months to help the medium 'develop'. Then gradually they start to experience knocks, rappings, movement of objects. The medium usually goes into trance and begins to get instruction from a spirit who introduces him/herself as the 'control', the person speaking through the medium.

Some rare physical mediums are able to produce 'Independent Voice'. In this rare form of mediumship the voice of a person who has died comes from somewhere in the room, not from the mouth of the medium. And rarest of all physical mediums are 'materialization mediums' in whose presence spirits become solid and walk around the room.

The Church of England finds mediumship genuine

The systematic scientific investigation of mediums of various kinds goes back more than a 150 years. John G. Fuller, a respected journalist who investigated the evidence on mediumship, points out the problem created by its sheer volume:

> On examination, it is so persuasive that it points to a rational con-
> clusion that life is continuous, and that articulate communication
> is possible. One problem is that the evidence is piled so high that
> it is boring and tedious to go through it. Like the study of math-
> ematics and chemistry it requires painstaking labour to assess it
> (Fuller, 1987: 67–68).

He points out that it took a committee of the Church of England two years to assess the available evidence on mediumship. The committee was specially appointed in 1937 by Archbishop Lang and Archbishop Temple to investigate Spiritualism. They had frequent sittings with the top mediums in England. Seven of its members including a bishop, two canons, a Professor of Christian Religion, a prominent psychologist and a barrister issued a majority report based on their investigations. They concluded that:

> ... the hypothesis that [the spirit communications] proceed in some
> cases from discarnate spirits is the true one...The possibility that
> spirits of a low order may seek to influence us in this way cannot
> be excluded as inherently illogical or absurd, but it would be ex-
> tremely unlikely if there were not also the possibility of contact
> with good spirits (Church of England Report, 1937).

This report was considered so dangerous by Church conserva-tives that it was stamped 'Private and Confidential' and locked away for nine years before it was leaked to the media.

However, a number of Christian minsters and committed Chris-tians founded the Churches' Fellowship for Psychical and Spiritual Studies in 1953. Its aim has always been to help Christians under-stand "spontaneous gifts of the Spirit" and cope with bereavement by spreading knowledge of the afterlife. It takes a positive view of psychic abilities and mediumship as long as they are dedicated to living a fuller Christian life. A number of Christian minsters investigated mediums and wrote books about the evidence for the afterlife that they had received.

American Anglican minister Bishop James Pike wrote *The Other Side* (1968) about his experiences with mediums that convinced him beyond any doubt that he had communicated with his son Jim, who had committed suicide. Initially this was through English medium Ena Twigg. Then in September 1967 he appeared on a Canadian religious TV programme run by Allen Spraggett. The Rev. Arthur Ford went into a trance and brought through the Bishop's son who gave many evidential facts (Twigg and Brod, 1972: 137).

New Zealand Anglican minister Rev. Michael Cocks has written a book called *Afterlife Teaching From Stephen the Martyr* (Cocks, 2011) about his experiences sitting with a trance medium at the home of Thomas and Olive Ashman in the 1970s. During more than 200 sessions the spirit delivered advanced spiritual teachings as well as evidence of his identity.

Famous 'sitters'

The word 'sitters' also means people who consult a medium. It comes from the history of Spiritualism where people would sit in a darkened room to witness physical or trance mediumship. The word is still used when people consult a mental medium for a 'reading'.

Many famous and highly intelligent people have 'sat' regularly with mediums for years and have published personal testimonies to what they have experienced. One important one was *Many Mansions*. It was first published in November 1943 by Air Chief Marshal Lord Dowding who successfully led the British Airforce in the Battle of Britain.

Another was one of the finest minds of his age, Sir Oliver Lodge, who was made a professor of physics at 30. He was knighted and made a Fellow of the Royal Society in 1902. Lodge's original work in physics includes investigations of lightning, the voltaic cell and electrolysis, and electromagnetic waves. He became convinced of the afterlife after investigating mediums for more than 40 years (Lodge, 1916 and 1928).

It was well known that Abraham Lincoln attended séances in the White House during the American Civil War and was lectured by a spirit speaking through a trance medium on the necessity of freeing the slaves (Maynard, 1917).

Queen Victoria, the head of the Church of England, for years communicated with her deceased husband, Prince Albert, through a trance medium, John Brown. She brought all her children up as Spiritualists. The recent Queen Mother often used the services of the medium Lillian Bailey to communicate with her late husband, King George VI (Neech, 1957).

Sir Winston Churchill was a close friend of the trance medium Bertha Harris during World War II. She had many Sunday evening visits to Number 10 Downing Street during the war and predicted Pearl Harbor six months in advance of the attack. General Charles De Gaulle also consulted her regularly while he was in England during WWII after being introduced to her by Churchill (Meek, 1973: 140).

Many mental mediums pass scientific tests

Professor Gary Schwartz and colleagues at the University of Arizona conducted a number of research studies with some of the best known mediums in the United States including (in order of working with them) Laurie Campbell, John Edward, Suzanne Northrop, George Anderson. Anne Gehmen, George Dalzell, Allison Dubois, Catherine Yunt, Mary Ann Morgan, Janet Mayer, Christopher Robinson, Traci Bray, Sally Own, Mary Occhino, Debbie Martin, Doreen Molloy, Sally Morgan, Robert Hansen and Angelina Diana. Professor Schwartz writes:

These mediums have been tested under experimental conditions that rule out the use of fraud and cold reading techniques commonly used by psychic entertainers and mental magicians (Schwartz, 2001).

78

Details of his experiments in the Veritas Program and the published research reports based on them are available (Schwartz, 2001; Schwartz *et al.*, 2002). As well, Professor Schwartz worked with HBO to produce a 90-minute documentary called *Life After-life* made in 1999. It shows him conducting experiments with five of the mediums (and is available on YouTube).

It is important to understand how mental mediums work. They hear words, small segments of songs, see quick images and symbols and respond to feelings, emotions and sometimes tastes and smells. They have to interpret what they are seeing, feeling and hearing and sometimes make mistakes in doing so. Dr. Schwartz found that the best of the mediums he tested were about 80 per cent accurate.

Professor Archie Roy and Tricia Robertson

The PRISM studies (Psychic Research Involving Selected Mediums) were carried out by Professor Archie Roy and statistician Tricia Robertson on behalf of the Scottish Society for Psychical Research. Their five-year study of mediums resulted in three peer-reviewed papers published in the *Society for Psychical Research Journal*. Their three papers published in the *Journal of the Society for Psychical Research* (Robertson and Roy, 2001 and 2004) have never been seriously faulted. The third paper showed that even in triple-blind conditions, a good medium can deliver relevant information to a sitter with an odds-against chance of a million to one. One of the mediums that they tested extensively was Gordon Smith, one of Scotland's finest mediums, who demonstrates extensively in the UK.

Windbridge Institute

Mark Boccuzzi and Dr. Beischel founded The Windbridge Institute in the USA which has conducted many scientific tests on mental mediums. They published a number of peer-reviewed academic papers showing that mediums are getting very accurate results by means which are currently unknown to mainstream science.

The experiments proved that the mediums were not cheating or guessing. They concluded that the information reported by these mediums cannot be explained as a result of fraud or 'cold reading' (a set of techniques used by psychic entertainers in which visual and auditory cues from the sitter are used to fabricate 'accurate' readings) on the part of the mediums or rater bias on the part of the sitters.

You can read about the triple- and quintuple-blind experiments they have been carrying out in many of Dr. Julie Beischel's presentations on the internet and published articles (Beischel, 2007/2008; 2009). The Windbridge Institute website also has a list of mediums who have been certified as part of their research.

Dr. Julie Beischel has recently published an e-book *Among Mediums: A Scientist's Quest for Answers* (2013), an easy-to-read review of her ten-year research. Her writing is concise, non-technical, conversational, and entertaining. Dr. Beischel discusses her research investigating the accuracy of mediums. She also talks about her plans for furthering her research into potentially useful social applications of mediumship in fields including bereavement, end-of-life care and forensics.

On the Windbridge website is a very useful article "How to Get the Most Out of Your Mediumship Reading" (http://www.windbridge.org/reading.htm).

University of Virginia research

More than 40 years ago the Division of Perceptual Studies was set up at the University of Virginia's psychiatry department to research survival of bodily death. Recently Dr. Bruce Greyson announced that research conducted by Emily Kelly Ph.D, at the University, had replicated the work of the Windbridge Institute and found equally impressive results using elaborate control procedures (Greyson, 2008).

Dr. Ian Stevenson, who founded the Division of Perceptual Studies, did a lot of research on 'drop-in communicators'. These are spirit communicators who come through mediums without being known to anyone present. They can be highly evidential when they give information that can be verified because it shows that the information could not be coming from the mind of the medium or the sitters.

Dr. Ian Stevenson found 60 of these cases in the published research literature (see Haraldsson, 2008, for a summary). On one occasion he was contacted by some people in Tuscany, Italy, who told him that a spirit who claimed to be a Catholic priest had communicated through a non-professional medium there. The spirit had given his name as Father Giuseppe Riccardi. He said that he had been the parish priest in Canton, Ohio, and had been murdered by a parishioner. They asked if he could follow up to see if this could be confirmed. Dr. Stevenson contacted the Catholic authorities in Youngstown, Ohio, and found that a Father Riccardi, a priest in Canton, Ohio, had been shot and killed by a woman after mass (Greyson, 2008).

These contemporary studies generally repeat and extend the observations of early research into mediumship. They find that certain mediums can report accurate and specific information about the deceased loved ones of living people (called sitters). This is so even when the mediums know nothing about the sitters or their loved ones and cannot see or hear the sitters. Similar findings have been reported by many investigators (Braude, 2003; Fontana, 2005; Gauld, 1983).

Psychic artists

Some mental mediums who are also artists are able to draw the spirits that they see near to their sitters. Several books have been written where these drawings were compared with photos of the person while they were alive. Coral Polge who died in 2001 did thousands of portraits during the 54 years she worked as a psychic artist. Some of them, together with the photos of the subjects, have been captured in the book she wrote with Kay Hunter, *Living Images* (1997).

The work of Frank Leah who died in 1972 has been featured in a book by Paul Miller called *Faces of the Living Dead: The Amazing Psychic Art of Frank Leah* (Miller, 1943; republished 2010).

Rev. Rita Berkowitz is an American psychic-medium based in the Boston area who does mediumship readings, spirit drawings, or a combination of the two for her clients. She can do these over the telephone to anyone in the world, as well as in person, the drawings being sent by mail.

Bereaved parent 'tests' mediums

There are many excellent books by people who set out to find out whether they could contact their loved ones through a medium. Businessman Mark Ireland's son, Brandon, died from an asthma attack in 2004. Knowing that his father, Richard Ireland, was a deeply spiritual minister and renowned psychic and medium, Mark decided to conduct his own test sittings with mediums to see whether he could find convincing evidence of the afterlife. His book, *Soul Shift: Finding Where the Dead Go,* sets out the stunning readings he had with mediums Alison Dubois, Jamie Clark and finally with Laurie Campbell. The last reading was videotaped for the Discovery Channel.

Various organizations certify mediums

Many mediums in English-speaking countries belong to the religion of Spiritualism which began in 1848 in America. Spiritualist churches are found around the world, but are more common in English-speaking countries. In North America, many churches are affiliated with the National Spiritualist Association of Churches, and in the UK with the Spiritualists' National Union. These organizations test and certify their own mediums. The Arthur Findlay College in England conducts many courses for mediums and arranges certification. The Forever Family Foundation in the USA also tests and certifies mental mediums as does the Windbridge Institute.

Bob Olson is a former skeptic and private investigator who began investigating the afterlife (and psychic-mediums) after the passing of his father in 1997. He claims to have tested hundreds of psychics and mediums around the globe and has a website where he lists mediums who have passed his tests of authenticity. Today, Bob trains psychic-mediums on how to improve the structure and delivery of their readings based on principles of ability, ethics, integrity, responsibility, delivery and professionalism. He also publishes his own online list of 'genuine and legitimate mediums'.

How to have a good reading with a medium

Whilst there are many brilliant psychics and mediums, there are also some psychics and mediums who have a long way to go before reaching full development. And there are also frauds who pretend to be psychics and mediums. Their goal is to exploit your emotional state and take your money. Never give money to anyone who talks about removing a curse or who guarantees that if you pay money you will get a job, or meet the love of your life. And do not go to anyone who guarantees he/she will make contact with a particular person.

If you do want to have a sitting with a medium, try to get a recommendation from someone you know or from an organization that tests or certifies mediums. Good mediums can do readings by phone or Skype anywhere in the world. Do some research on 'cold reading techniques' so that you will not be tricked. Be pleasant and open but limit your answers to 'yes' or 'no'. Don't give away information like names that could come through in the reading as evidence. Keep a record of the reading and check things out afterwards.

Try to be open-minded and aware but not skeptical. You need to relax for at least 15–20 minutes before the reading starts and send out your thoughts to your loved one. Daily meditation in the days beforehand can help.

Chapter 11

PSYCHIC DETECTIVES

We had a serial murderer on our hands. But not enough evidence to identify the suspect. We had no witnesses. We contacted psychic Jeanne Borgen and she described the killer and led us to his capture and incarceration. I was a skeptic. Not any more!

LARRY HARDMEN
DETECTIVE, BATON ROUGE POLICE DEPARTMENT

For millions of people around the world today, watching the very popular and very successful television series *Psychic Detectives* (Superfine Films) and *Psychic Investigators* (Cineflix Productions) is their first experience of seeing evidential psychic-mediumship. In this chapter we are talking about 'forensic psychics.' These are the top one percent of psychics and mediums who can repeatedly produce accurate evidential details about the crime.

Police as witnesses

Police officers are very highly credible expert witnesses. So when you have a skeptical police chief or other police officer stating in his/her own words that psychics and psychic-mediums do have paranormal gifts, it is highly evidential. Cases on which *Psychic Detectives* (Superfine Films) and *Psychic Investigators* (Ciniflix Productions) are based are included in this book because the tough police officers were willing to give video testimony to millions of viewers around the world that the forensic psychics they worked with have genuine gifts.

On our webpage we have transcriptions of more than 80 police statements from some 60 police cases. These were given by serving and retired police officers who said that a particular psychic or medium was able to give them vital information that led to physical evidence to close a case. The gifted forensic psychics often named suspects, located a missing person or a body, or confirmed evidence about how the victim was killed that had not been released to the public.

This is about legitimate admissible evidence. It is the testimony of identified, reliable, expert witnesses that would be accepted in a court of law reported verbatim – in exactly the same words as were used originally. What can an uninformed, closed-minded skeptic say? That these police are all lying, are being fraudulent? That the police are all mistaken? That they are too gullible? Or that they are cold reading? If the psychics are all wrong, why do the police keep using them and say on the record that they will keep on using them? Below are just ten statements that police officers have made about the gifted psychics who helped them close cases.

Joyce Morgan names killers

When police had run out of leads in the murder of Angela Davies in Polo, Missouri, psychic Joyce Morgan was called in to assist. Among much valuable information, she stated that the motive was money. She gave the names of the two killers (Jimmy and Delmar), and identified one of the two from a photo album.

Police Chief John Rodriguez said:

> You'd be a fool not to use psychic Joyce Morgan. You have nothing to lose and everything to gain. Joyce Morgan does have a gift and she helps other people ... A homicide investigation is just like any other investigation. You pick up one piece at a time and what [the psychic] allowed us to do was to take several pieces from one

area – pieces from another area and we put it together to give us a pretty good idea what that puzzle looks like ... and from all that we go ahead and solve the case.

Police Deputy Roger Porter (Caldwell County Sheriff's Office) said:

Joyce Morgan is a good investigating tool to have around when you run out of all options. She does have a gift ... she helps other people ... and she is good at what she does. Anything Joyce Morgan told us about the case was used by the detectives ... and because of her help we took two people off the street who needed to be taken off the streets ...

(Court TV *Psychic Detectives*, "Family Ties", aired 22 February 2006).

Phil Jordan helps solve murder of four people

When police responded to a possible homicide at a local flower nursery in Oneida, New York, they were shocked to find four individuals killed execution-style. With conventional police methods not being successful, psychic Phil Jordan was brought onto the case. He sensed the motive was robbery, but that only valuable coins were taken. Police were shocked – it wasn't common knowledge that there was a coin shop housed in a corner of the business. Phil produced ten most relevant facts which led to the arrest and conviction of three murderers now serving 100 years in prison each.

Sheriff Bill Hasenaurer of Oneida Country Sheriff's Office said:

I accept the psychics' role in helping with murder cases – and I will call them again – because they get results. I am now a great believer in psychics helping the police.

Sergeant Lynton Clark of Oneida Sheriff's Office completely agreed about the use of psychics in solving murders. Kurt Hameline, Assistant D.A. of Oneida County stated words to the effect that using a psychic was critical to catching the murderers. (Court TV *Psychic Detectives*, "Blood Money", aired 6 September 2006).

Jeanne Borgen identifies serial murderer

When psychic Jeanne Borgen assisted police in Zachary, Louisiana, in a case involving the rape and murder of five women, she was able to tell the police that they had the wrong suspect. Among other things she told them that a key witness would lead them to the murderer. She described the suspect and told them details about his past. The witness was found and the murderer convicted.

Lieutenant David McDavid stated:

I've never dealt with psychics on a day-to-day basis ... My feelings are that if the good Lord gives you that [psychic] power, use it to assist law-enforcement in every way.

Police Forensic expert and consultant Ann Williams said:

Without psychic Jeanne Borgen, we would have been chasing our tails.... I wouldn't have found our witnesses.

Larry Hardmen, Detective Baton Rouge Police Department said:

We had a serial murderer on our hands. But not enough evidence to ID the suspect. We had no witnesses. We contacted Jeanne and she described the killer and led us to his capture and incarceration. I was a skeptic. Not any more!

(Court TV *Psychic Detectives*, "Eyes of a Stranger", aired 26 September 2007)

Georgia Rudolph names the killer and locates the body

When Jenifer McCrady went missing in Ohio, police had no leads. Detective Sergeant Dave Garvey called gifted forensic medium Georgia Rudolph. The medium told them: the missing person was dead; who had killed the victim and where they could find the body. Jenifer was found buried in Belpre, Ohio, brutally murdered by a gunshot to the head. Kevin Rings, Assistant District Attorney said:

> Without Jenifer's body being found we wouldn't have been able to file a charge against Mr. McCrady.... It would simply be an unsolved missing person case.

Detective Dave Garvey said:

> Georgia's guidelines and thoughts whatever you want to say ... led us to first find Jenifer ... we were able to get the bad guy who is now in jail ... and the family feels better.

Monica Tanner, a former employee of the Belpre Police Department said:

> Georgia made a world of difference. She solved the case (*Psychic Investigators*, "Till Death Do Us Part", aired 18 July 2009).

Etta Smith jailed for her psychic accuracy

When Etta Smith received psychic messages about the location of the body of murdered nurse Melanie Eurebe in December 1980, she passed the information on to detectives at Pacoima Police in Los Angeles. When the skeptical detective on duty would not act on the information, she drove to the location and found the body herself. A highly incompetent, negligent and unprofessional Los Angeles detective mistakenly charged her with murder and kept her in jail for several days. When the murderer was caught, she successfully sued the police department. She was paid thousands of dollars in compensation.

Police Detective Patrick Conmay on psychic Etta Smith:

Had it not been for Etta Smith this case would not have been solved as rapidly, or possibly not at all (*Psychic Investigators*, "Suddenly Psychic", aired 12 September 2009).

Debbie Malone, Australian psychic/medium

Debbie Malone, someone we know personally, is an acclaimed spirit medium who has assisted police departments across Australia in missing-persons and murder investigations for the last 16 years. Police officer Det. Sen. Const. Geoffrey Little is quoted in *Who Magazine* after working with Debbie Malone on a case:

I'm a skeptic but I just can't explain some of the things psychic Debbie Malone came up with that were just incredible. I was astounded ... as was the police woman who was with me. We were just amazed. I even sent some paperwork off to our Missing Persons Unit later to introduce Debbie to them. I think she is doing something with them now.... It can give you avenues of investigation that you didn't have. But then you have to get solid evidence to confirm what they've found. You can't use what they say. They can maybe help you find a body. They can maybe give you something that you didn't have before – something out of the blue. I said to other officers, I can't explain how she picked up what she did.

Psychics and mediums

Psychic abilities include telepathy (receiving information from the mind of another person), clairvoyance (direct knowing without the use of normal senses), and precognition (knowing things in advance). They have been proven in more than a hundred years of laboratory studies.

Some people focus their psychic gifts on gathering information from energies in the physical world. These people are called psychics, clairvoyants or remote viewers. Others focus their psychic abilities on communicating with the afterlife and are called mediums or psychic-mediums. All mediums have psychic gifts but in addition are able to contact people living in the spirit world. Many of the psychics who work with the police are in fact psychic-mediums but in the programmes are only shown to be working from clairvoyance rather than from spirit contact. Perhaps the directors of the programmes thought this would be less controversial.

Forensic psychics

Very few psychic-mediums are developed and reliable enough to be able to get information to solve crimes. The Australian version of the television programme *Sensing Murder* tested hundred psychic-mediums who applied to be on the programme. They were given a photo of a crime victim in a solved murder case and had to be able to give details of the crime – who the victim was, what happened and who the killer was. Only five out of a hundred in Australia were able to do this. In New Zealand, the figure was three out of 75. These are the ones we can call 'forensic psychics'.

Police become very frustrated with amateur psychics. Whenever there is a high-profile case they get hundreds of calls from people who have had a dream or a psychic flash. Some telephone the police or contact grieving relatives with what they think is information. They then tell the newspapers they have been called in 'to consult' on the case. This is especially annoying if the psychic is trying to promote a book or workshop. It wastes time and destroys the trust of police. It also makes it harder for police to work with gifted psychics in the future. And when the supposed involvement of the psychic does not bring results it adds to skepticism about psychics.

Police usually deny that they use psychics (even when they do) for very good reasons. Police are drilled in scientific procedures and forensic science. The culture is very skeptical and the police want to appear able to do their job properly without help. Government officials don't want to risk being criticized by the skeptical media. And the big reason is that a lot of time could be wasted by having hundreds of amateur psychics contacting them.

Read the full article where some 80 police officers confirm the gifts of forensic mediums (http:/snipurl.com/psychicdetectives).

Some police officers are themselves psychic

We all have some psychic abilities and it seems that many police officers themselves develop their 'intuition' and use their psychic skills very successfully in their work. Keith Charles in the UK, and Chuck Bergman and Riley G. Mathews Jr. in the USA, are all former police officers who have become full-time psychic-mediums and written books about their experiences. Phil Jordan, one of the psychic-mediums mentioned above, was also a former policeman.

And perhaps the best documented example of a psychic policeman was Pat Price who was the star remote viewer in the experiments conducted at the Stanford Research Institute. According to Dr. Russell Targ who worked closely with him, Pat Price told him that when he was the police commissioner in Burbank, California, he used to sit with the dispatcher in the police station and when he heard a crime reported, he would scan the city psychically and then immediately send a car to the spot where he saw a frightened man hiding (Targ, 2012: 50).

Dr. Russell Targ was with Pat Price and Dr. Hal Puthoff when Pat Price went to the police station in Berkeley in response to a call for help in the high-profile case of the kidnapping of heiress Patty Hearst. He says that they both saw Price identify and name the kidnapper, Donald DeFreeze, and point to his picture in a mug-book filled with hundreds of photos. He then described the location of the kidnappers' car. The police sent a car and found it within ten minutes (Targ, 2012: 58).

We cannot end this chapter without quoting the incredible case of Debra Martin, a level five Windbridge Certified Medium. According to Scott David on the CBS5 Arizona website, a woman approached the station seeking a medium. She was concerned about the death of her aunt in Peru. The family had been told that the woman had died of cancer and had been buried three months before. Debra Martin did a reading and received the information that the woman had been strangled. The murderer was a tall man with a lot of hair named Marcos. The issue was about a property matter. The family had the body exhumed. There was no trace of cancer but signs of strangulation. The police investigated and found that Marcos had forged papers to take over the aunt's property. Marcos was found guilty of murder and sentenced to 20 years in jail (video available on YouTube: *The Medium Who Solved a Murder*).

Sometimes a number of good psychic-mediums can work together and come up with the same information. Find Me is an Arizona, USA, organization of 110 talented psychics, retired law enforcement officers and professional search and rescue volunteers. The psychics volunteer to work collaboratively with law enforcement officials and families to find missing loved ones and solve homicides. They do not charge for their services. So far, in eight years they have solved or resolved 27 cases. The idea could be adapted for other countries.

Chapter 12

SENSING MURDER (NZ)
MENTAL MEDIUMSHIP

The mediums identify the exact date and time of the crime, the
gender, age, race, name and personality traits of the victim, the
circumstances of the death, where, when, how and why the victim
was killed and even the name of the killer in some murder cases!

VICTOR ZAMMIT

The television programme format for *Sensing Murder* was
developed by Danish Nordisk Film TV and has been sold to
many countries. In this chapter we will be dealing with the
New Zealand version of the programme (Ninox Television). Many
of the episodes are available on YouTube.

Seventy-five psychics and psychic-mediums applied to be involved
in the programme. They were given a photograph of the victim of
a little known solved murder case. They were asked to come up
with the details of the crime, the location and the killer. Only three
out of the 75 were able to do this. In the Australian version of the
programme, it was five out of a hundred. On the face of it, this is a
fairly quick and efficient way of screening psychic-mediums who
want to help solve crimes.

In each programme in the series, a little known unsolved murder in New Zealand is reconstructed. Two psychic-mediums with
no knowledge of the case are flown to the location of the crime on

separate days. They are kept under observation at all times and have no access to a computer. Usually they begin the process in a hotel where they are given a photograph of the victim which they usually keep face down. They are then filmed as they come up with details of the case. Later they are challenged to take a film crew to the exact location of the crime. The information given by the mediums is collated and compared with known facts. It is then given to a team of private detectives who investigate it and report back. The mediums who participate appear to be highly gifted and come up with incredible details about the cases, given that they only have a photograph to start with.

The only response by the skeptics is to claim fraud. This would mean that the whole programme would have to be a gigantic conspiracy involving all of the mediums, the producers, the production staff, the researchers, the crew, the detectives. The conspiracy would have to be maintained over years and survive staff changes and disagreements. The average person would not accept this explanation. Especially when it is well known that committing a fraud like that, if proved, would mean a prison sentence for everyone involved in the production of *Sensing Murder*.

I (Victor), as an expert in the admissibility of evidence, personally investigated two of the *Sensing Murder* mediums about their experiences with the programme. I was convinced there was no fraud involved – they had proved their legitimate psychic-mediumship gifts over the years in other situations. However, in the more than 20 episodes I watched, each of the mediums was able to get between 40 and 80 accurate pieces of information – accurately describing aspects of the case. This includes the victim's gender, age, race, name, personality traits, the circumstances of death, where, when and how the victim was killed and where he/she was found – and in many instances why the victim was killed. In all cases, they give a description of the killers and in some cases, the name/s.

The obvious question to ask is: where is the critical information about the victim coming from? These forensic psychic-mediums tell us that when they are producing the critical information, they are actually conversing with the victim who transmits information from the afterlife dimension. They say that they form a 'relationship' with the victim in spirit who sometimes comes through to them after the filming has stopped.

In the episode "Last Orders", Deb Webber from Australia and Kelvin Cruickshank from New Zealand were the mediums chosen to investigate. The facts of the case are very straightforward: Kevin O'Loughlin from South of New Zealand in 1993 was killed early one morning. The killers have never been caught.

Deb Webber was given a photo of the victim but decided not to look at the picture at first. All the following information she produced was correct.

I get a male energy ... 30 years old ... he's muscley ... had a mo [moustache] at one time ... he's flirtatious ... he tells me that he did all right in that department – [referring to womanizing] ... ...he tells me there was tension in his family life ... with his wife ... Leanne ...went through hard times fighting, arguing ... his name is Kevin but he says call me Kev ... he shows me he's doing manual work ... he's an outdoor manual worker ... he's a builder he says ...he's showing me water ...he's from the South he says ... his very close friend in his home-town died ... they were very close in the younger years ... played together ... the night of the murder he was enjoying himself ...in a nightclub ... I see people drinking ... he's having a good time ... but being a bit naughty but not bad naughty ... just naughty naughty ...he left the nightclub just to actually go home ... see him as a ... drunk ... staggering ...had drinks ...he was near a doorway ... near Dick Smith's. .. I keep getting the name Dick Smith ... I see him falling on the ground ... he was hit from behind ...getting stabbed ... but he got hit on the head first ...he's saying to me that for a moment he was trying to get help, trying to move ... he's collapsing ... he can't move now ... he had enemies ... he provoked people and pushed people ... he's had fights with a number of people ... the killer just killed him ... did not take anything ... Kev was confident when drinking ... his killer is in mid-20s age group ... known to have stolen a car or two ... known to the police ... [Deb Webber then asks the spirit victim about the name of the killer – Deb articulates the name of the killer but it was blocked by the television station for legal reasons] ... but there was another killer ... first name starts with B ... [Deb provides the first and second name of the killer – blocked again by the television station] ... there was a car involved ... looks like a utility-van ... there is a symbol on the car ... looks like a 'C' ...looks like a work-car or something ... there were some anger issues with the murderer and the brother of one of the girls he went out with ... they [referring to the brother and the victim] saw each other at the nightclub before the stabbing incident ... they're looking for the weapon still ... I'm told it's in a dirt-place out of town ... in Carlson Street something like that in the industrial area ... he was cutting through the car park when the incident happened ...

Deb Webber was able to identify the exact location of the crime and directed a driver where to go. She said: "... it's across the road ... no, not here but up further ... here ..." She then pointed to the exact spot where the victim was found and went on to describe the killer. "He is youngish 20s ..., has tattoos on one arm having short hair ... even shaven."

Here is some of what gifted forensic psychic-medium Kelvin Cruickshank stated in his hotel room about the same case. He too was given a photo of the victim, but Kelvin also decided not to look at the picture at first. All the information brilliantly produced by Kelvin was also correct.

... male ... handsome, good looking boy ... talks about his tan ... was a bit of a 'smoocher' [flirt] with the ladies ... definitely a ladies' man ... that's for certain ... his kids were taken away from him ... he screwed up ... 'L' [wife Leanne] significant ... name Kevin ... tells me to call him Kev ...woodchip to do with his job ... from the South ... he wants me to go to a place called

– sounds like 'Tianar' – there's a club now... he's there ... drinking ... he reckoned he was pretty pissed (excuse my language he said) ... he wasn't happy that day ...he was trying to forget all sorts of things ... he's in the car park walking ... two people involved [in the attack] ... attacker in car park ... he was hit on the head first ... he knew a lot of the people there ... they knew each other ... the person who killed him knew exactly where to hit ... multiple stab wounds ... I can see it ... they [the attackers] came from the back ... the killer has army connections ... he [victim] had betrayed somebody ... no didn't do drugs he said ... I see tennis picture ... sports connection ... it looks like a young person has taken him out ... not older person, not more than 23 or 24 years ...the police know who this person is ...

Kelvin then was able to give directions to the vicinity of the crime. He identified the exact place where the victim was killed. He then asked the spirit to name the killer and repeated the full name which was blocked for legal reasons...

... showing a person who is coming from behind ... is related to a person he had a fling with ... he's showing the female he had a fling with ... says he was promiscuous ... that he's been caught ... sports bar near Dick Smith's shop where he was eventually stabbed ...the tennis vision before now makes sense as there is a large picture of a tennis game going on ... yes this is the place where his head was pushed against this picture ... [in 1993 police found blood smears there] ... he's staggering towards the front door ... of Dick Smith's ... I feel like staggering then boom down on the ground ... [pointing to the ground] this is the place ...

Something significant with this particular episode of *Sensing Murder* is that both mediums independently came up with the identical unusual name of one of the killers. Deb Webber came up with the full names of both the killers.

Clearly, the objective analyst would be impressed by the sheer volume of accurate information given. Every episode is virtually like the one mentioned above with different victims – and sometimes with different psychic-mediums. One would think that scientists would want to investigate where all this sensational evidence is coming from and whether it can be duplicated by other exceptional mediums in other countries.

Chapter 13

TRANCE MEDIUMS INVESTIGATED

I shall not commit the fashionable stupidity of Regarding everything I cannot explain as a fraud

C. G. Jung

PIONEER PSYCHOTHERAPIST AND PSYCHIATRIST

Some mediums can go into a deep trance. They are unconscious and unaware of what is happening while a spirit person speaks through them. In psychic research this spirit is
then called the 'control'.

Three spectacular deep-trance mediums were investigated for many
years by gifted scientists and academics. They were never accused of
fraud. They co-operated willingly with every investigation and passed
every test. Their enormous contribution to proving the existence of the
afterlife will always be remembered.

Leonora Piper (1857–1950)

One of the most spectacular and outstanding trance mediums
who ever lived was the American Mrs. Leonora Piper from Boston. No one, not even the most hardcore closed-minded skeptic, after investigating her mediumship for almost 30 years, ever found
fraud or guessing or cold reading.

William James, professor of psychology at Harvard University, personally organized séances for Mrs. Piper for a year and a half. Then an Australian, Dr. Richard Hodgson, then the most closed-minded skeptic known, took over. And finally, Professor James Hyslop, professor of logic and ethics from Columbia University, took control of the investigations.

Michael Tymn, who recently published a study of Mrs. Piper's mediumship, points out that most people are not aware that Dr. Richard Hodgson conducted sittings with Mrs. Piper on the average of three times a week for some 18 years. As well, he organized numerous sittings for Professor William James, Sir Oliver Lodge, Professor James Hyslop, Professor William Newbold and others representing the Society for Psychical Research (Tymn, 2012b).

The George Pellew communications

In 1892 George Pellew, a young lawyer aged 32, died in an accidental fall. He was an acquaintance of Dr. Richard Hodgson. Like Hodgson, he had been skeptical about the afterlife, but promised that if he died he would try to contact Hodgson. Five weeks after Pellew died Mrs. Piper's control announced that a George Pellew was there and wanted to speak. [Hodgson used the name 'Pelham' in his report instead of his friend's real name, Pellew].

Over the next five years, from March 1892 to September 1897, Mrs. Piper continued to bring through detailed evidential messages from George Pellew. Hodgson was now in a unique position to ask his friend hundreds of questions about their relationship. Over several months, Dr. Hodgson introduced over 150 sitters, at séances, to Mrs. Piper while she was in trance. Thirty of these had known George Pellew while he was alive. The others had never met him. George Pellew was able to correctly identify all of the sitters whom he had known. Most of them reminisced with George Pellew as if he himself were there. His only mistake was to fail to identify a person whom he had not met since the person had been a very small girl!

Hodgson admits Mrs. Piper's mediumship genuine

Before investigating Mrs. Piper, Richard Hodgson had been an extreme skeptic. But that came to an end with Mrs. Piper. He wrote a 300-page report in which he confirmed the existence of the afterlife saying:

> ... at the present time I cannot profess to have any doubt but that the chief 'communicators' to whom I have referred in the foregoing pages, are veritably the personalities that they claim to be, that they have survived the change we call death, and that they have directly communicated with us whom we call living, through Mrs. Piper's entranced organism (SPR *Proceedings* Vol. 13, 1898, H 10).

Giants of science humbled

Some of the most eminent scientists and scholars, after scientifically investigating Mrs. Piper's mediumship, unanimously agreed in absolute, unqualified terms that she had proved the existence of the afterlife. Frederic Myers, one of the most distinguished members of the Society for Psychical Research, stated:

> Messages were given to me and certain circumstances indicated with which it was impossible that Mrs. Piper should be acquainted (Richet, 1927: 128).

Sir Oliver Lodge stated:

> I have assured myself that much of the information supplied by Mrs. Piper during trance has not been acquired by ordinary everyday methods and precludes the use of the normal sense channels (Richet 1927: 128).

Professor William James, initially an extreme skeptic, later admitted:

> I am absolutely certain that Mrs. Piper, in a state of trance, knows things of which it is impossible that she should have had any knowledge in the waking state (Richet, 1927: 128).

Professor Hyslop, in his book *Life After Death,* wrote:

> I regard the existence of discarnate spirits as scientifically proved and I no longer refer to the sceptic as having any right to speak on the subject. Any man who does not accept the existence of discarnate spirits and the proof of it, is either ignorant or a moral coward. I give him short shrift, and do not propose any longer to argue with him on the supposition that he knows anything about the subject (Hyslop, 1918).

Anyone wanting absolute convincing evidence of the afterlife is urged to read the full story of the investigations in Michael Tymn's new book *Resurrecting Leonora Piper: How Science Discovered the Afterlife* (2012).

Mrs. Gladys Osborne Leonard (1882–1968)

Known as the British Mrs. Piper, Gladys Osborne Leonard is considered one of the greatest deep-trance mediums ever. She became well known in London after physicist and psychic researcher Sir Oliver Lodge and his wife visited her anonymously on 25 September 1915. He and his wife became convinced that she had given them absolute proof of genuine messages from their son Raymond. All of the details were published in Lodge's 1916 book *Raymond.*

Investigations into Mrs. Leonard's mediumship were then conducted by the most noted psychic researchers of the time: Rev. C. Drayton Thomas, Rev. Vale Owen, James Hewat McKenzie, Mrs. W. H. Salter and Whately Carington.

The material which came through Mrs. Leonard did so in a variety of ways, many of which were used by the researchers to determine its origin. They include:

- 'Book Tests', in which a spirit would direct a sitter to a certain book in a certain place in his or her home where, on a given page, the sitter would find a meaningful message. The Reverend Charles Drayton Thomas, a member of the Society for Psychical Research, conducted 348 tests over a two-year period. The messages were given by his father in the spirit world through Mrs. Leonard; 242 tests had positive results, 46 indefinite, and 60 failures. A control experiment was carried out by the Society for Psychical Research. A number of people were asked to open a book at random to see if a passage on the page contained a message which might apply to them personally. Out of 1,800 separate book items, the percentage of complete and partial successes was only 4.7 per cent. This was much less than the 70 per cent positive results in the tests with Mrs. Leonard.

- 'Proxy Sittings', in which a person seeking information from a loved one would ask someone else to go and see the medium on his/her behalf. The person seeking the contact did not know the medium or the person going to sit on their behalf. This showed that the medium was not reading the body language or the mind of the sitter

- 'Cross-Correspondences', in which part of a message would come through her mediumship, part through another medium.

Susy Smith's book *The Mediumship of Mrs. Leonard* (1964) has a detailed account of her magnificent contribution.

Mrs. Eileen Garrett (1893–1970)

Another well known and very much investigated trance medium was Mrs. Garrett. Her early adult life was marked by illness and many personal tragedies. She had experienced the death of three sons, a husband

and a fiancé, as well as many difficulties. She travelled to the USA in 1940. There she allowed herself to be tested by many noted scientists and parapsychologists and, in 1951, founded the Parapsychology Foundation. Over the years, it published several fine journals, newsletters, and reports, many under her presidency. Mrs. Garrett herself hosted 28 annual international conferences on parapsychology and related sciences. The Foundation also supported many projects in afterlife research including the Karlis Osis work with deathbed visions.

One of Eileen Garrett's more memorable communications as a medium was the case of the airship, the R101, which crashed in France on 5 October 1930. It was on its first overseas voyage and 48 people were killed. Two days after the crash, Mrs. Garret was being tested as a medium at the National Laboratory of Psychical Research when she suddenly fell into a deep trance. The captain of the airship, Flight Lieutenant H. C. Irwin, began to speak through her, giving listeners a highly technical account of how the airship had crashed. What he said was taken down in shorthand and a copy was submitted to the Air Ministry. According to the experts, the information that came through Mrs. Garrett was unknown at the time and was a hundred per cent accurate in every detail. The case is considered one of the most evidential in proving survival after death.

George Chapman (1921–2006)

One of the most stunningly evidential recent examples of trance mediumship was the partnership of George Chapman who died in 2006 with deceased doctor William Lang who died in 1936. Dr. Lang had been an eye specialist at London's Middlesex Hospital up until 1914.

For 60 years the late Dr. Lang conducted 'spirit operations' on patients referred to him by other doctors while George Chapman was in trance. He performed these operations with either no physical contact or a very light touch. The success rate of these operations was very high. Over the years Laurence Harvey, Stanley Holloway, Patricia Neal, Barbara Cartland and Roald Dahl were among those said to have sought the spirit doctor's help. A dental surgeon, S. G.

Miron, wrote a book about the remarkable healings, *The Return of William Lang* (1973), after his own wife was cured.

Although physical healing was an important aspect of Chapman's work, he stated that the main purpose of Dr. Lang's manifestation was to convince people of the reality of life after death. He also stressed the importance of testing the spirit to ensure its authenticity, and cross-checking any claims made with information available from physical sources.

Dr. Lang's daughter, Marie Lyndon Lang, was initially skeptical that her father was manifesting through George Chapman. But after hearing his voice, observing his mannerisms, and asking personal questions concerning events which only she and her father knew about, she made this declaration: "The person who speaks through George Chapman and claims to be William Lang is, without a doubt, my father."

For 31 years until her death at the age of 94 in May 1977, Marie Lyndon spoke regularly with her deceased father through George Chapman. At her request, however, both her intimate connection to the increasingly popular Dr. Lang and her consultations with him were kept secret until her passing.

Dr. Lang's granddaughter, Mrs. Susan Fairtlough, reacted with anger when she heard that a healer was 'pretending' to be her grandfather. But after meeting George Chapman and Dr. Lang, Mrs. Fairtlough had this to say:

> To my great horror, or rather, stupefaction, the man who was in this room was indisputably my grandfather. It was not him physically, but it was his voice, his behaviour. It was unquestionable. He spoke to me and evoked precise events of my childhood. And I was so impressed that all I could say was, 'Yes, grandpapa. No, grandpapa' (Fisher, 2001).

After meeting Dr. Lang for the first time in December 1969, Dr. Robert Laidlaw of New York told how he discussed in a professional manner certain ophthalmological conditions and techniques, and added: "I fully believed then, and I believe now, that I was conversing with the surviving spirit of a doctor who had died some 30 years ago" (cited Fisher, 2001).

George Chapman's mediumship met his own criteria of evidence:

- the spirit communicator should speak as near as possible to the way he spoke on earth
- he should use the same phrases and mannerisms
- he should manifest other personal characteristics
- he should be able to give dates, names and details of his earthly experiences that can be verified
- he should be able to discuss intimate matters with relatives and colleagues still on earth.

Chapter 14

WRITING

MEDIUMS

Brazilian Spiritists like to make a clear distinction between what they call *escrita automatica* or 'automatic writing', and what they call *psicografica*. The former is held to be no more than the manifestation of one's subconscious, while the latter is that of a separate entity, presumably a spirit.

GUY LYON PLAYFAIR
PARANORMAL INVESTIGATOR

A writing medium is able to go into a light trance and allow their hand to be taken over by a spirit person. Sometimes they write at an incredibly fast speed, in languages unknown to the medium, about subjects totally outside their knowledge. This is also called 'psychography'. Sometimes the writing is exceptionally small and sometimes it can only be read in a mirror, but usually it comes through complete without the need for editing.

Rev. Stainton Moses, one of the greatest and most evidential mediums of the 19th century, wrote a book in which he discussed his own experiences and those of other individuals. He claimed that during an out-of-body experience from 'the other side' he saw how it was done:

It was not done, as I had imagined, by guiding my hand or by impressing my mind, but was by directing onto the pen a ray which looked like a blue light. The force so directed caused the pen to move in obedience to the will of the directing spirit. In order to show me that the hand was a mere instrument not essential to the experiment, the pen was removed from the hand, and kept in position by the ray of light which was directed upon it. To my great astonishment it moved over the paper and wrote as before (Moses, *Direct Spirit Writing*, 1878).

Carlos Mirabelli

In 1919 the *Academia de Estudos Psychicos* "Cesar Lombroso" was founded. Mirabelli submitted himself for experiments in trance speaking, automatic writing and psychical phenomena. A report was published in 1926. It speaks of 392 sittings in broad daylight or in a room illuminated by powerful electric light (in 349 cases, in the rooms of the Academy), attended by 555 people. Many of the people who were writing through Mirabelli were well known international figures and wrote in different languages (cited in Fodor, 1934).

Chico Xavier – 100,000 pages of published spirit writing

Chico Xavier from Brazil had very poor eye-sight and only a very basic primary education. However he was a gifted medium and from the earliest age was able to see and hear the spirit of his mother who had died when he was only five. This brought him into conflict with his family and the Catholic Church. He learned about mediumship when he met some Spiritist mediums (those following the teachings of Allan Kardec) who helped to heal his sister of mental illness.

Once he understood his gift, he began to sit with a pencil in his hand and his eyes closed. He would then write pages of hand written books, always without a mistake, on highly spiritual subjects. It is reported that using this method he produced more than 100,000 pages of spirit writing which was published in 412 books, including some in foreign languages in which he was not fluent. His books sold an estimated 50 million copies, the profits of which were all channelled into charity work.

Chico also produced thousands of psychographed letters for grieving parents containing messages from their sons and daughters who had crossed over into Spirit. The Spiritist Medical Association of São Paulo conducted a survey of some of those letters in 1990. They found that 93 per cent of the letters contained correct names of relatives. As well, 35 per cent of them were signed with the signature of the person who had died (da Rosa Borges, 2010).

Chico Xavier refused to take any money himself for his books which were very popular. Instead, he donated the copyright of all these works to be used by Spiritist charities to help the needy. Each day poor people queued outside his home in Uberaba to receive free food and to speak a few words with him. Many people thought he was a saint. Celebrities were among regular visitors to his home seeking advice from him, or the spirits who communicated through him. Xavier's work produced religious teachings, novels, and works of philosophy.

On 2 April 2010, a date on which Chico Xavier would have turned 100, a movie biography about his life *Chico Xavier o Filme* was launched. Another film *Nosso Lar* (*Our Home*) was made in the same year. It shows a representation of the afterlife based on one of Chico's books transmitted by a doctor. English translations of Chico Xavier's books and versions of both films with English subtitles are available on the Internet.

Chapter 15

THE CROSS-CORRESPONDENCES

Taken as a whole, the Cross-Correspondences and the Willett scripts are among the most convincing evidence that at present exists for life after death.

COLIN WILSON, AFTERLIFE RESEARCHER

Some of the best evidence for the afterlife came through writing mediums under the direction of the no-longer-living Frederic W. H. Myers, a Cambridge classics scholar and writer of the late 19th century.

He was also one of the pioneers involved in the investigation of the afterlife. When he was alive, he wanted to find a way of proving that information transmitted through mediums could not have come from their own unconscious minds.

The method he thought up was cross-correspondences – a series of messages to different mediums in different parts of the world that on their own would mean nothing, but which when put together would make sense. He and his fellow leaders of the Society for Psychical Research felt that if this could be done it would be a high level of proof of the afterlife.

After he died in 1901, more than a dozen different writing mediums in different countries began receiving a series of incomplete scripts signed by Frederic Myers. Later, there were scripts signed by his fellow leaders of the Society for Psychical Research, Professor Henry Sidgwick and Edmund Gurney, as they too had died. The scripts were all about unusual classical subjects and did not make sense on their own. But the mediums were told to contact a central address and send the scripts there. When the scripts were put together they fitted like pieces of a jigsaw puzzle.

In all, more than 3,000 scripts were transmitted over 30 years. Some of them were more than 40 typed pages long. Together they fill 24 volumes and 12,000 pages. The investigation went on so long that some of the investigators, such as Professor Verrall, died during the course of it and began communicating themselves.

The writing mediums used by Myers and the others from the afterlife were not highly educated and all the messages transmitted were outside their learnt knowledge and experience. On one occasion, one of the mediums, Mrs. Coombe-Tennant, was conducting a discussion using 'automatic writing' between the spirit entity of Professor Sidgwick and his living colleague, G. W. Balfour, on the 'mind–body relationship', 'epiphenomenalism' and 'interactionism'. She complained bitterly that she had no idea what they were talking about and lost her temper that she was asked to transmit such difficult things.

Myers did say it was extremely difficult to send his messages from the spirit world across to the mediums. In a communication through the medium Mrs. Holland he described it as being like:

> ...standing behind a sheet of frosted glass which blurs sight and deadens sound dictating feebly to a reluctant and somewhat obtuse secretary (Cummins, 1932).

The information transmitted in the Myers experiments was so accurate that it stunned the members of the Society for Psychical Research. The evidence is absolute. All the original documents are on file. There are at least eight complete sets of copies in existence for any investigator to study. For those who have the initiative to investigate, sufficient information is available. And whilst for the investigator of the Myers Cross-Correspondences the information available is challenging, the rewards are evidentiary proof of the afterlife.

One person who took the time to study the Cross-Correspondences in depth was the former atheist, Colin Brookes-Smith. After researching them, he stated in the *Journal of the Society for Psychical Research* that survival should now be regarded as a sufficiently well-established fact to be beyond denial by any reasonable person. Further, he argued that this conclusion should not be kept in the obscurity of research records but should be presented to the public as "a momentous scientific conclusion of prime importance to mankind."

Swan on a Black Sea

Another very convincing piece of evidence for the afterlife was provided by one of the writing mediums who had received some of the Myers communications.

Mrs. Coombe-Tennant died in 1956 at the age of 81. Using her pen-name Mrs. Willett, she transmitted from the afterlife a long and detailed book of personal memories. She used the medium Geraldine Cummins who had never met her or her children. Published as *Swan on a Black Sea: The Cummins–Willett Scripts*, as they are sometimes also known, are considered by many, including Colin Wilson, to be "The most convincing proof of the reality of life after death ever set down on paper" (Wilson, 1987: 183).

The Myers Cross-Correspondences have successfully showed, using the experiential scientific method, that what was transmitted from the medium was not from the medium's own unconscious.

Chapter 16

PHYSICAL MEDIUMSHIP – LABORATORY EXPERIMENTS

Instead of listening to the medium relaying spirit messages, the sitter can actually be physically touched by what are claimed to be spirit hands.

DAVID FONTANA

A physical medium produces phenomena that can be seen, heard or felt by everyone present. It is a very rare form of mediumship that usually takes years to develop. A dedicated group of around six people, known as a Circle, meet weekly and sit patiently for an hour or two in a darkened room. Usually one person (the medium) sits in a curtained-off enclosure called a 'cabinet'. This is to allow the psychic force to be concentrated in one place. Eventually, the medium starts to go into a trance and the group starts to make contact with a 'control' – a spirit who gives the Circle direction on how the mediumship will be developed.

Some of the phenomena that develop in physical mediumship include bangs and raps which will answer questions in a code (one rap for Yes, two for No). Objects start to move with no apparent cause. When we visited a physical Circle in England, as soon as the lights were turned out, a large table which had luminous tape on its side moved around the room with no apparent cause. When everyone present put their hands lightly on its top, the table was levitated high in the air. At other times, it rocked on its legs to answer Yes or No to questions and to spell out messages.

As the mediumship develops there may be apports. Small objects like flowers or jewellery, coins or small statues are dematerialized from somewhere else and brought into the room and re-materialized. There can be spirit lights – small lights of different colours that move around the room – sometimes hovering in front of people. Whispered voices are heard and people are touched by materialized hands. Some of the most highly developed kinds of physical mediumship are Independent Voice and materialization which are dealt with in coming chapters.

Physical mediumship has been known throughout history; every indigenous culture seems to have had physical mediums – sometimes called shamans, or 'Wu' in China (Jones-Hunt, 2011). The Bible is full of reports of physical mediumship. In 1901, US ethnologist Waldemar Bogoras travelled to Siberia to visit a shaman of the Tchouktchi tribe. Bogoras heard strange voices filling the room. The voices seemed to come from all corners and spoke English and Russian. It was the first known case in which direct spirit voices were caught in a recording (Macy, undated).

Investigated by scientists in controlled conditions

From the middle of the 19th century, physical mediumship became very popular in the United States and all over Europe. Some of the best physical mediums of the day were investigated at length by the top scientists who concluded that the effects were real and there was no fraud going on (see Tymn 2011 for a full discussion).

Sir William Crookes, British chemist and physicist, carried out several investigations with American medium Kate Fox, one of the Fox sisters whose mediumship had started the Spiritualist movement in the US in 1848 (*see* Chapter 2). Crookes recorded that, simply by placing her hands on any substance, Kate Fox had the ability to engender raps loud enough to be audible at a considerable distance

– even rooms away. On one occasion, as Crookes held both of Fox's hands in his left hand, a luminous hand materialize before him, took a pencil from his right hand, wrote a message on a sheet of paper and cast the pencil down, fading into darkness (Inglis, 1977: 264).

William Crookes also conducted many experiments with physical medium Daniel Dunglas Home. Home was unusual in that he could produce all the effects in lighted conditions. Dozens of highly credible witnesses independently gave testimony that when Home went into trance, heavy pieces of furniture would be levitated. Sir William claimed to know of more than 50 occasions on which Home was levitated "in good light" (gas light) at least five to seven feet above the floor. In another carefully set up experiment, an accordion (brought by Crookes) played by itself when placed near Home. In these experiments, Home's hands and feet were restrained and the accordion was placed inside a wire cage. Crookes and two of the other witnesses present stated that they distinctly saw the accordion "floating about on the inside of the cage with no visible support" (Crookes, 1874: 14).

Professor Alexander von Boutlerow, professor of chemistry at the University of St. Petersberg, tested both Daniel Dunglas Home and Kate Fox and obtained similar results.

Home always claimed that his powers came from people who had died and continued to live in the afterlife. But Crookes was careful not to talk about 'spirits' for fear of further upsetting the scientific establishment. Instead, he talked about a new force which he called 'psychic'. Sir William's wife, Lady Ellen Crookes, was more willing to speak plainly about her observations. She said that she saw the accordion in the experiment taken from Home's hand by "a semi-transparent distinctly human form" which sank into the floor after playing the accordion.

Experiments repeated

Crookes' experiments with physical mediums were repeated by scientists in England and Europe, the United States, Canada and Brazil.

Dr. Eugene Osty, head of the Metaphysic Institute in Paris, proved under laboratory conditions that a young medium, Rudi Schneider, was able to produce genuine physical phenomena without fraud. He set up a table with an infrared beam across it. The beam would set off several cameras if anything crossed it. Even under these conditions, the spirit control of Rudi Schneider was able to move objects on the table. As it did so, a galvanometer began to register the 'pulsation' of an invisible intelligence. As Carrington states: "It was somewhat like taking the pulse of an invisible being standing before them in space!" (Carrington, 1973: 54).

In France and Germany, between 1909 and 1913, Baron von Schrenck-Notzing carried out a series of carefully conducted experiments and independently confirmed William Crookes' psychic findings.

Ectoplasm

Nobel Laureate Charles Richet, a professor of physiology at the Sorbonne, discovered that one of the causes of the psychic force which causes physical mediumship is a substance he called ectoplasm – a word he made up meaning 'substance brought out of the body'. It is a mysterious substance made up of white or colourless blood cells which physical mediums are said to have a lot of. Professor W. J. Crawford, from the University of Belfast, conducted long and meticulous studies of ectoplasm with the Goligher Circle and published three books about it – all supporting the claims of Crookes and Richet.

Dr. Jan Vandersande

Jan W. Vandersande has published more than 80 scientific articles. He holds a doctorate in physics and has served professorships at the University of Witwatersand, South Africa, as well as at Cornell University. Dr. Vandersande has worked at the Jet Propulsion Laboratory and is currently the communications director for Viaspace Inc. In his recent book *Life After Death: Some of the Best Evidence* (2008), he talks about his own experiences sitting in a physical mediumship Circle in South Africa with Mickey and Sarah Wolf. Over an eight-year period, he witnessed physical phenomena such as trumpets flying around the séance room, direct voice and ectoplasm.

Kai Müegge and the Felix Experimental Group

In Germany, The Felix Experimental Group is one of the few groups in the world currently working with ectoplasmic physical mediumship that welcomes scientific investigation. The medium, Kai Müegge, bases his mediumship on the techniques of Austrian physical medium Rudi Schneider. The leader of the spirit team claims to be Hans Bender, who while alive was a famous German parapsychologist. Rudi Schneider is another member of the spirit team.

In June 2012 we attended one of Kai's séances in Frankfurt, Germany, and in December 2012, another in Sydney, Australia. In both séances we witnessed unexplained movement of objects, spirit lights and massive amounts of moving ectoplasm which we could see in red light. In the Sydney séance, we were able to see a moving hand-like form emerging from the ectoplasm. In the German séance, we saw a small statue take form before our eyes.

The Felix Experimental Group has a very detailed website which is regularly updated with photos.

Why are there so few physical mediums?

Physical mediumship used to be very common in the last part of the 19th century and up until the 1920s. It was a time when there was little organized entertainment, no opportunities to work and study at night, and no electricity in most homes. People who lived close to each other would gather in their own homes. Many formed 'Family Circles' sitting in dimly lit gatherings of family and friends who lived close by.

Physical mediumship is not something that anyone can develop. You need to have certain elements in your body to be able to produce an abundance of ectoplasm. As well, you need a supportive environment and a harmonious group of people with enormous patience to sit without any results for year after year. And physical mediumship is extremely draining physically and emotionally. Many physical mediums are also superb mental mediums and find that they can reach many more people using mental mediumship.

Estelle Roberts, for example, was a superb physical materialization and direct-voice medium. She also filled the Royal Albert Hall in London (with a capacity in excess of 5,000 people) on over 20 occasions giving demonstrations of mental mediumship. In the 1950s, she visited both Houses of the British Parliament and gave stunning demonstrations of mental mediumship.

However, there has been an increase in interest in physical mediumship over the last few years. We know of a few Circles which are sitting privately and getting good results. Over the last few years, some Circles report that they are working with new forms of energy that are faster to develop and safer for the mediums. The Scole Group, described in the next chapter, was one of those groups.

Chapter 17

THE SCOLE EXPERIMENT

I invited the Scole Group to my old country house on the Island of Ibiza... I can therefore guarantee that the results of the Scole Group are in every respect hundred per cent genuine.

DR. HANS SCHAER
ATTORNEY AND BUSINESSMAN

The Scole Experiment is a recent example of physical mediumship. It is a well-documented experiment, witnessed by a number of people of the highest credibility. Scole is a village in Norfolk, England. These experiments were conducted in the home of Robin and Sandra Foy (in Norfolk), and also in the United States, Ireland and in Spain over a period of six years. There were 500 sittings from December 1992 to November 1998.

The Group began with two mediums, Alan and Diana Bennett, delivering messages from a non-physical group. Many of these messages contained personal information that nobody else could have known about. Soon the messages came in the form of voices which everyone in the room could hear. Many of the experimenters experienced physical touch. A large table was levitated. Then came the materialization of the people and objects.

Senior scientists and investigators who participated in the Scole Experiment included Professor David Fontana, Professor Arthur

Ellison and Montague Keen. Over the six years there were many others who attended as senior scientists and guests in the actual experiments: Dr. Hans Schaer, a lawyer; Dr. Ernst Senkowski; Piers Eggett; Keith McQuin Roberts; biologist Dr. Rupert Sheldrake; Professor Ivor Grattan-Guiness – all with scientific or other relevant background. There was a host of other highly credible witnesses who have had years of experience in dealing with the paranormal.

The participants and some of the investigators have been interviewed on the documentary film *The Afterlife Investigations.*

In the United States, a considerable number of scientists, including a number of senior scientists from the National Aeronautics and Space Administration (NASA), attended sessions. There were also scientists from the Institute of Noetic Sciences, based near San Francisco. Grant and Jane Solomon, who wrote a book on the experiments, report that, after the Scole Group experiments, some 15 scientists from the NASA group formed their own psychic group to continue to communicate with afterlife entities (Solomon, 1999: 73, 189).

During these experiments, the 'spirit team' working from the afterlife made it clear that it was they who were causing psychic phenomena. This was accepted by everyone who participated. There was no suggestion that the effects were being caused by the unconscious minds of the sitters or by 'super ESP'. The members of the 'spirit team' identified themselves. The 'spirit scientists' identified themselves. And at regular intervals, there were guest observers from the spirit world like Helen Duncan, who when alive had been a very gifted physical medium.

Apports

More than 50 small objects (apports) were materialized. These included a silver necklace, a Churchill coin, a small rose quartz crystal ball, a 1940 British penny, a 1928 one-franc piece token, a silver charm of the "Grim Reaper". Most astonishing were original copies of *The Daily Mail* dated 1 April 1944, and an original copy of *The Daily Express* dated 28 May 1945. The paper was tested and found to be genuine.

Photograpy

The spirit team did some interesting experiments with photography. They imprinted images and writing on rolls of film. The films were bought new by the three outside experimenters, Professor David Fontana, Professor Arthur Ellison and Montague Keen. They remained in a locked box which was held by them, and were developed by them. The images included photos of people and places, sometimes from the past. Some had verses or poetry and drawings that took some effort to identify. There were also pictures of other dimensions and the beings that inhabit them. Eventually, video cameras were able to record images of non-human living beings.

Spirit lights

Some of the most spectacular phenomena of the Scole Experiment were the materialized spirit lights. They whirled around the room performing various manoeuvres. Occasionally, these lights would throw out beams, as well as pass through solid objects. When they touched people, there was a definite sensation. Sometimes, people could feel the lights go right through their bodies and come out the other side. The speed, the different movements and the other phenomena performed behind the lights were just overwhelming. All the witnesses stated it was impossible that the lights could have been produced by a trick. All of the phenomena were accompanied by sudden and dramatic drops in temperature.

This is how scientist Piers Eggett, one of the eyewitnesses, described the light:

> This was a small ball of white light which moved around the room in all directions, sometimes at great speed, leaving a trail like a firework by persistence of vision... At times the light hovered in

mid-air, and then touched some of the sitters, giving them a small electric shock (Eggett, undated).

According to other eye witnesses, the normally single light-point would:

- dart around at great speed and perform elaborately patterned dances
- settle on outstretched hands and jump from one to the other
- enter a crystal and remain as a small point of light moving around inside the crystal
- strike the top of the table with a sharp rap or the glass of the dome or dish with a 'ping' and do this repeatedly while remaining visible as a sharp pinpoint of light
- respond to requests, such as coming to sit on parts of the witnesses' bodies and lighting them up
- move in time to tape-recorded music
- produce 'lightning flashes' in an area of a large room some three to three and a half meters distant from the group sitting round a table (in Spain)
- undertake several aerial 'bombing raids' on the table-top. The raids would hit it very audibly and visibly. Then they would come out again from an area immediately below the table (Los Angeles)
- change shape from a pinpoint of light to a generalized irradiation
- move at very high speed making perfect geometric shapes within a foot or two of visitors' faces. But they made no sound and did not create any air movement.

A master magician's testimony

Skeptics may argue that these effects could be produced by stage magicians using long hollow strands of fiberglass with laser lights projected through them. This was certainly considered by James

Webster, a professional stage-magician. He is a former member of the Magic Circle, and has more than 50 years experience in psychic research. On three occasions, he attended sittings with the Scole Group and published reports. His conclusion was clearly set out in a letter to the English newspaper, *Psychic World* (June 2001):

I discovered no signs of trickery, and in my opinion, such conjuring tricks were not possible, for the type of phenomena witnessed, under the conditions applied....

The end of the Scole Experiment

The Scole Experiment came to an abrupt end in December 1998 at the request of the spirits overseeing the experiment. Robin Foy explains the circumstances in his highly recommended book *Witnessing the Impossible* which contains notes about every one of the 500 sittings. It is the only authoritative guide to the Experiment. The Scole Group members were told:

We must tell you that the work at Scole was very important. The links that were made have already enabled inter-dimensional energies and wisdom to assist the changes to future earth consciousness. Therefore, this final mission is to seal the doorway that has been created, and to end ALL communications – I repeat ALL communications (Foy, 2008: 546).

The Scole Report says all phenomena genuine

The three members of the Society for Psychical Research who were the principal investigators of the Scole phenomena were Montague Keen, Professor David Fontana and Professor Arthur Ellison. Between them, they had more than 50 years of experience investigating physical mediumship. They wrote a Report that was presented to the usually highly skeptical Society for Psychical Research (available from Saturday Night Press Publications).

The Report stated that all the phenomena they had witnessed were genuine. This view was accepted by other members of the SPR who attended a study day on the Scole Experiment several months later. According to Montague Keen, speaking on behalf of the three experienced investigators who wrote The Scole Report, "None of our critics has been able to point to a single example of fraud or deception" (Keen and Ellison, 1999).

The authors of The Scole Report challenged any critics of the phenomena to produce the same phenomena fraudulently under identical conditions. Nobody then or since has ever attempted to meet this challenge.

For the open-minded skeptic, the evidence collected over a period of six years with more than 500 sittings by the Scole Experimenters is absolute. Many regard the Scole Experiment as the greatest recent afterlife experiment conducted in the Western world.

Sadly, it is no longer possible for people to experience personally the wonders that visitors to the Scole Group experienced in the early 1990s. The next best thing is to watch the video *The Afterlife Investigations*, produced by Tim Colman (www.theafterlifeinvestigations.com). There are also long interviews with the Scole investigators Professor David Fontana, Montague Keen and Dr. Rupert Sheldrake on YouTube.

Chapter 18

'INDEPENDENT VOICE' MEDIUMS

This American woman has a mysterious gift which enables those who sit in the same room with her to learn of the continued existence of those whose physical bodies have perished. The possession of this strange power is acquired by no virtue of her own; she was born with it...To exhibit it, all she has to do is to sit passively in a chair, preferably in pitch darkness.

VICE ADMIRAL W. USBORNE MOORE
AUTHOR OF THE VOICES

'Independent Voice' mediumship, sometimes called 'direct voice' mediumship, is a form of physical mediumship. People who have 'died' can be heard talking in their own voices which do not come from the vocal cords of the medium. Usually the development of this ability takes many years of sitting with a group of people in a darkened room.

We have been privileged to experience Independent Voice mediumship on many occasions with physical medium David Thompson. William, David's 'control', will sometimes use Independent Voice rather than full materialization to save energy. What is amazing is the rapidity with which the voices move around the room – from being right up near the top of a ceiling to being six inches (fifteen centimetres) away from your ear an instant later. Some voices are as soft as a whisper and others boom out so loudly that you are sure all the neighbours can hear them.

When the Independent Voice medium is first developing, the voices sound like whispers and you have to listen very carefully to hear them.

The spirit communicators often ask for a 'trumpet' – a cone which can amplify the sound. This can be made out of heavy paper or thin cardboard or even metal. When the spirit force gets stronger it will pick up the trumpet and carry it around the people sitting in a Circle around the medium. Spirit communicators use the trumpet to whisper private messages into the ears of particular people. The trumpet generally remains connected to the medium with ectoplasm and it is very important for sitters not to reach out and touch it. The medium is usually unconscious in deep trance. In some cases, with development, the medium can be conscious and join in the discussions.

The voices can come through in many languages not known by the medium. Dr. Neville Whymant, a professor of linguistics at Oxford and London Universities, claims he has heard 14 different languages used during 12 sittings with medium George Valiantine. They included Chinese, Hindi, Persian, Basque, Sanskrit, Arabic, Portuguese, Italian, Yiddish, German, and modern Greek.

In his book *Psychic Adventures in New York* (1931), Dr. Whymant explains that he was invited to attend a séance with direct-voice medium, George Valiantine, because he was an expert in Oriental Languages. When a spirit came through and began speaking in an ancient Chinese dialect, Whymant identified him as Confucius. He took the opportunity to ask the spirit about an ancient Chinese poem; the meaning of one line of the poem did not make any sense. The spirit then recited it with corrections so that the meaning was clear. Whymant submitted the amended text to the Chinese professors in several universities.

John Sloan (1871–1951) and Arthur Findlay (1883–1964)

One of the greatest Independent Voice mediums in the UK was John Sloan. For many years, he gave sittings without charge to small groups of friends. One of his long-term sitters was Arthur Findlay who, until he met Sloan, was an agnostic stockbroker. Findlay was finally convinced that the voices were coming from the afterlife when he heard the voice of his own deceased father and a family friend. They told him something not known by any living person. Findlay began a lifetime's study of psychic science and produced the series of wonderful books listed in the Bibliography.

Leslie Flint (1911–1994)

Another Independent Voice medium who was thoroughly tested in recent times was Leslie Flint. In his presence, while his mouth was taped shut or full of water:

> … literally thousands of different voices of discarnate persons have been tape-recorded for posterity, speaking in different dialects, in foreign languages unknown to me and even in languages no longer spoken on this earth (Flint, 1971: 170).

Because direct voice mediumship is a form of physical mediumship which depends on ectoplasm, it usually has to take place in total darkness. This severely restricts which venues can be used. Leslie Flint used to give sittings in the front room of his own home.

However, in 1946, Noah Zerdin, one of the supporters of Leslie Flint, organized for a lightproof cabinet to be built so that Leslie Flint could demonstrate to large audiences. Leslie Flint would sit inside the cabinet in total darkness on the stage in a well-lit theatre. Microphones were placed outside the cabinet to pick up the voices and the spirit communicators could speak directly with members of audiences of up to 2,000 people.

Leslie Flint's autobiography, *Voices in the Dark*, gives many examples of evidential sittings which were carried out both in private and in large demonstrations.

Not cold reading

The information coming through a Flint sitting was not, as some critics of mediums claim, vague suggestions which could apply to anyone. Take, for example, the following conversation between a young airman killed in World War II speaking in his own voice and his parents. He had initially appeared at a séance attended by Lord Dowding, giving his name as Peter William Handford Kite, and asking that his parents be contacted at an address he gave.

The parents accepted an invitation to attend a second séance and for close on 40 minutes, Peter came through and told them the following which his parents confirmed to be true:

- of a joke he had made before he died, about buying an Alsatian
- that his mother had put a photograph of himself and photographs of his grave in Norway in her bag that morning
- that he liked the cherry tree they had planted for him in the memorial garden
- that his bedroom had not been changed in the six years since he died
- that he had not liked the wallpaper in his bedroom
- that his father was still driving his car although it was too small for him.

SPR Tests

In 1948, Flint submitted to a series of experiments conducted by scientists from the Society for Psychical Research. The *Psychic News* of 14 February 1948 reported in detail one experiment where he conducted a séance with adhesive tape pressed over his lips. Bandages were tied over the tape, and his hands and legs were tied to a chair. The observers concluded that, in spite of the above restrictions, the voices were soon speaking with their usual clarity, even shouting. Some 12 persons in the room all heard more than enough to convince the most stubborn skeptic.

Another expert who investigated Leslie Flint and thoroughly vouched for his authenticity was Professor William R. Bennett, from the department of electrical engineering at Columbia University. He wrote:

My experience with Mr Flint is first-hand; I have heard the Independent Voices. Furthermore, modern investigation techniques not available in earlier tests corroborate previous conclusions by indicating that the voices are not his. But to be thorough, one should consider the possibility of live accomplices... This suggestion became untenable for me during his visit to New York in September 1970, when, in an impromptu séance in my apartment, the same voices not only appeared but took part in conversations with the guests (Flint, 1971: 220).

Lawyer identifies judge's voice

Aubrey Rose (eminent lawyer, OBE and CBE) attended many sittings with Leslie Flint and claims that through Flint he received "the most detailed evidence of survival of the individual beyond this life".

In his autobiography, *The Rainbow Never Ends* (2005), he states that his investigation into the afterlife began when he heard a tape recording of a voice he recognized as that of deceased Judge, Lord Birkett, speaking through Leslie Flint. Rose became a close friend of Leslie Flint and went on to become a spiritual healer himself.

The Woods-Greene recordings

The many hundreds of communications received through Leslie Flint would have been lost and forgotten were it not for the fact that they were recorded, first on wire or paper tapes and later on better quality tapes. Initially, it was by Sidney George Woods who sat with Leslie from 1946 onwards. In 1953, he was joined by Mrs. Betty Greene who gave him important assistance.

In 1956 the voice of Ellen Terry, a famous actress of the British stage, who had died in 1928, came through to Leslie Flint's Home Circle and said:

> The tapes you record give us an opportunity to reach many people in all parts of your world. We shall bring various souls from various spheres to give talks and lectures. You are very important to us because we know that you are sincere. We know that we can achieve a great deal through you, and that is why we want you to come at regular intervals. Much depends on this regular contact. We want you to keep it and not break it (Flint, 1971).

For the next 15 years, George Woods and Betty Greene sat regularly with Leslie Flint and 'interviewed' 500 spirits from all walks of life. The spirits answered questions about what had happened when they died. Most were surprised to find that they were still 'alive' and that their surroundings were as natural and lifelike as on earth. These tapes are now available on the internet through the Leslie Flint Educational Trust. Author Neville Randall worked with George Woods to prepare a summary of what the tapes tell us about the afterlife in his book, *Life After Death* (1975).

The Anni Nanji recordings

There are 66 recordings of casual conversations between one of Leslie Flint's regular sitters and his wife, Anni, who was in the afterlife. She was speaking to her husband in Independent Voice through Leslie Flint over a 12-year period (between 1971 and 1983). You can listen to them online. They talk in casual conversation like any married couple. The wife tells her husband that he comes to visit her when he is asleep and asks if he remembers visiting her (http://wwwleslieflint.com/recordingsnanji.html).

Emily French (1831–1912) and
Edward C. Randall (1860–1935)

Another American Independent Voice medium who was thoroughly investigated over many years was Mrs. Emily French of Buffalo, New York. For 14 years, this frail elderly woman sat in a séance every week at the home of Edward C. Randall and his wife, with their close associates. Randall was a leading lawyer from Buffalo. For five of those years, they were joined by a prominent judge, Dean Shuart of Rochester, "a learned jurist and man of such impeccable character that he had been repeatedly elected to the responsible office of Surrogate Judge". Every person who attended the Circle was initially skeptical, and sure that the voices were fraudulent. And each person was allowed to conduct however many exacting experiments they needed to be convinced that they were genuine.

In 1905, Edward C. Randall wrote to Dr. Isaac K. Funk, a prominent psychic researcher and co-owner of the publishing house, Funk and Wagnalls. He asked him to arrange for Mrs. French to be scientifically investigated. Dr. Funk agreed on condition that Mrs. French would come to New York City. She was to conduct sittings every day for two weeks in the homes of people she did not know surrounded by highly experienced and skeptical observers.

Mrs. Emily French was then 72 years old, extremely feeble and frail with a dangerous heart condition, and almost totally deaf. After a long journey, she sat with Dr. Funk with barely any time. She was surrounded by people who were skeptical of her. And night after night she produced magnificent direct voice evidence of the afterlife. The full favourable results of these detailed tests were

131

published by Dr. Funk in his book, *The Psychic Riddle* (1905), and are reprinted in Chapter 11 of N. Riley Heagerty's excellent collation of the work of Edwin C. Randall, *The French Revelation* (1995, and on the internet as a pdf file).

Etta Wriedt (1859–1942)

We cannot end this chapter without mention of Mrs. Henrietta (Etta) Wriedt whom Michael Tymn, author of several books about past mediums (including *The Voices*) nominates as the best medium ever. He writes:

> Wriedt was studied and validated by such esteemed researchers as Sir William Barrett, a physics professor who co-founded the SPR, Sir Oliver Lodge, a physicist remembered for his pioneering work in electricity and radio, Sir Arthur Conan Doyle, the physician who created Sherlock Holmes, Dr. John S. King, a physician who founded the Canadian branch of the SPR, and Vice Admiral William Usborne Moore, a retired British naval commander-turned-researcher. Lady (Dr.) Florence Barrett, Sir William's wife, who was dean of the London School of Medicine for Women, is said to have been skeptical of all mediums until she sat with Mrs. Wriedt and heard from deceased relatives in their own voices (Tymn, 2011).

Mrs. Wriedt spoke only English with a strong American accent. But the voices that came through her spoke with many different English accents as well as Arabic, Croatian, Serbian, Dutch, French, German, Hebrew, Hindustani, Spanish, Italian, Norwegian, Welsh, Scotch and Gaelic (W. U. Moore, 1913).

Independent Voice mediumship has given many thousands of people, fortunate enough to communicate directly and at length with their loved ones, proof beyond reasonable doubt that their loved ones continue to exist in the afterlife.

Why is direct voice mediumship so rare today?

Leslie Flint answered this question in his autobiography. He wrote:

Except possibly in the privacy of Home Circles, physical mediumship like my own gift of independent direct voice ... is practically non-existent. For this I blame the times we live in and the tempo at which we live our lives. Physical mediumship is an inborn gift but it takes a long time and much patience to bring it to its full development. In my case it took seven years of sitting in a dedicated Circle regularly and without fail to bring my gift to its fruition. The rush and bustle of today with its demand for instant success, instant results, instant mediumship cannot produce the great mediums both mental and physical who were available to researchers in more leisurely times (Flint, 1975: 213).

Chapter 19

MATERIALIZATION MEDIUMSHIP

I know it happened. I was there. I met these real people, materialized from the world beyond death, hundreds and hundreds of times. And I have the written records, the tape recordings, the photographs, the solid objects – 'gifts' teleported through the dimensions, as evidence.

TOM HARRISON
SON OF MATERIALIZATION MEDIUM MINNIE HARRISON

Of all the evidence for the afterlife, there is nothing as convincing as materialization. You sit in a locked room where there is a small number of people present. Security is tight and it is impossible for anyone to enter or leave the room. You all hold hands and know each other's voices. Suddenly there is another living breathing person among you, walking around, touching you, making jokes and sharing insights about the spirit world.

Wendy and I have been fortunate enough to have experienced materialization mediumship with David Thompson on more than 200 occasions. We have been present at many reunions, in an atmosphere charged with emotion. People who died days, months, or years before walk across the room, talk in their own voices and share memories and embrace their loved ones. They come with messages of love and concern: thanks for looking after me in my final days; you were right about the afterlife; I'm sorry I never told you I loved you; look after yourself and be happy; give my love to the family and tell them I'm fine.

Over the last 20 years, hundreds of people have seen David Thompson's demonstrations of materialization mediumship in Australia, England, the United States, Germany, Switzerland, Spain and elsewhere. Video testimonials from people who were reunited with their loved ones are contained on his Circle of the Silver Cord website.

Could it be fraudulent?

While there have been fraudulent mediums who tried to make money by fooling people, there is also a large amount of evidence from top scientists that physical mediumship is real, that Independent Voice mediumship is real, that ectoplasm is real and that materialization is real. Professor Richet, winner of the Noble Prize for Physiology studied materialization, and writes in his book, *Thirty Years of Psychical Research*:

> I shall not waste time in stating the absurdities, almost the impossibilities, from a psycho-physiological point of view, of this phenomenon. A living being, or living matter, formed under our eyes, which has its proper warmth, apparently a circulation of blood, and a physiological respiration which has also a kind of psychic personality having a will distinct from the will of the medium, in a word, a new human being! This is surely the climax of marvels. Nevertheless, it is a fact (Richet, 1923).

The archives of the (British) Society for Psychical Research and the American Society for Psychical Research contain numerous accounts of materialization mediums who were investigated for years by some of the leading scientists and professors of the day – people like the 19th-century chemist and physicist Sir William Crookes, Professor W. J. Crawford and Dr. Gustave Geley. But many of the best materialization mediums like Minnie Harrison and Rita Goold sat for years for family and friends, without charging a cent, not bringing any attention to themselves.

What is ectoplasm?

We are told that groups of scientists in the afterlife work with physical mediums to create communication between the dimensions. They extract elements from the body of the medium and from the sitters and the furniture and use it to make a mysterious substance called 'ectoplasm'. Ectoplasm can be manipulated into hardened rods and spirit can direct these rods to move large object like tables and chairs, and to levitate a person. It can also be moulded into an artificial voice box or stretched out flat like a sheet of material with which spirits cover themselves in order to lower their vibrations and become solid.

The word ectoplasm from the Greek meaning literally "exteriorized substance" was coined by Charles Richet, professor of physiology at the Sorbonne in Paris, winner of the Nobel Prize and member of the prestigious Institut de France who investigated it for 30 years. Richet's conclusion was:

> There is ample proof that experimental materialization (ectoplasmic) should take definite rank as a scientific fact (Richet, 1927: 112).

In its primary stage, he found that it is invisible and intangible, but even then it can be photographed by infrared rays and weighed. In its secondary stage, it becomes either vaporous or liquid or solid with a smell somewhat akin to ozone. In its final stages, when it can be seen and felt, it has the appearance of muslin and feels like a mass of cobwebs. At other times, it is moist and cold and, on rare occasions, dry and hard. Its temperature is usually about 40 degrees fahrenheit (Butler, 1947: 75), which accounts for the observation of a drop in temperature around physical phenomena.

Baron von Schrenck-Notzing, a Munich physician, showed that ectoplasm is composed of leucocytes – white or colourless blood cells – and epithelial cells which are from the various protective tissues of the body. During materialization it is taken from the bodies of the medium and the sitters.

Scientist Gambier Bolton (author of *Ghosts in Solid Form*) conducted more than a hundred test materializations, with Florence Cook and five other mediums during a period of seven years, which were all documented in detail consistently confirming the experiments of Sir William Crookes who took photographs of a materialized spirit standing beside the medium. Dr. Geley and Professor Richet conducted experiments in physical mediumship in France. During one meeting, some 150 people, including scientists, witnessed materialization (Fodor, 1960: 131). Baron Schrenck-Notzing in *Phenomena of Materialization* sums up hundreds of experiments conducted for a period of five years with Eva C.:

> We have very often been able to establish that, by an unknown process, there comes from the body of the medium a material, at first semi-fluid, which possesses some of the properties of a living substance, notably that of the power of change, of movement and of the assumption of definite forms (Schrenck-Notzing, 1920).

We personally have seen ectoplasm in red-light conditions with mediums David Thompson and with Kai Müegge of the Felix Circle in Germany. In both cases, it seemed to be a sparkling, living, moving substance – not at all like rolled-up cheesecloth as some skeptics claim. Recently, Kai Müegge has produced some excellent photos of ectoplasm forming in his mouth. You can clearly see that the texture is like spun cotton candy. Other photos show that it emerges from the pores of his tongue (see Felix Experimental Group website).

Weight loss

Professor W. J. Crawford was a lecturer in mechanical engineering at Queen's University, Belfast, who conducted long and meticulous studies of ectoplasm. He wrote three classic books: *The Reality of Psychic Phenomena* (1916), *Experiments in Psychic Science* (1919), and *The Psychic Structures in the Goligher Circle* (1921). He found that during materialization, the weight of his medium dropped from 120 pounds to 66 pounds. Professor Crawford found that all of the physical manifestations of his mediums – lifting of tables, moving of objects etc. were achieved by the construction of ectoplasmic rods, struts and cantilevers. In his *Psychic Structures,* he provides photographs of ectoplasm being used to lift tables.

George Meek (1987) found that during materialization séance, there is a temporary weight loss from both the medium and the sitters as a substance is withdrawn from their bodies. In his own experiments, he found a weight loss of 27 pounds – about 10 kilos – shared among the medium and 15 physicians, psychologists and others who made up the research team (Meek, 1987: 69).

Alexander Aksakov, the Russian psychic investigator, recorded testimonies of ten witnesses who saw the partial dematerialization of medium Mme. d'Esperance's body from the waist downwards and, with the testimonies of those present, published the full story in his *A Case of Partial Dematerialization* (1896).

But why can't they turn on the lights?

Every medium's ectoplasm is different but one of its key properties is that some of its forms are extremely sensitive to light and other radiation. In some circumstances, even flashing a torch drives the substance back into the medium's body with the force of snapped elastic. Bruises, open wounds and haemorrhage may result.

Fodor (1932) lists the following examples of mediums being hurt by the sudden retreat of ectoplasm:

Kluski received an open wound from a violent retreat of ecto-plasm. Conan Doyle quotes the case of a medium who exhibited a bruise from the breast to the shoulder caused by the recoil of the band. Evan Powell, at the British College of Psychic Science, suffered a bad injury on the chest owing to an unintended violent movement of a sitter, touched by an ectoplasmic arm. Haemorrhage may also result from sudden exposure to light. Dennis Bradley speaks of an instance in which George Valiantine got a ... bruise, ... about two inches by three, on the stomach by the shock of returning ectoplasm when a powerful electric light was suddenly switched on in his garage which faced one of the windows of the séance room (Fodor, 1932).

Leslie Flint was hurt by ectoplasm when his impromptu demonstration of his mediumship to a group of fellow soldiers in his barracks during World War II was interrupted by one of the sergeants barging in and switching on the overhead light. Flint writes:

This caused the ectoplasm which the other side had taken from me to make the etheric larynx through which they speak to rush back into my body and I felt as though I had been kicked in the solar plexus (Flint, 1975: 128).

In November 1956, police raided a séance in Nottingham hoping to prove that the medium was fraudulent. They grabbed materialization medium Helen Duncan (*see* next chapter), strip-searched her, and took endless flashlight photographs. They shouted at her that they were looking for beards, masks and shrouds. They found nothing, but Helen was badly injured by the ectoplasm which rushed back into her body when the lights were turned on. A doctor was summoned and discovered two second-degree burns across her stomach. She was so ill that she was immediately taken back to her Scottish home and later rushed to hospital. Five weeks later she was dead.

Alec Harris was a leading Welsh materialization medium who died in 1974. According to a report in *Psychic News* by Maurice

Barbanell, at a séance Barbanell attended there were 30 different materialized figures clearly seen in good red light. The figures walked about ten feet from the cabinet where the medium could clearly be seen sitting in trance. They had long conversations with their loved ones in many different languages not known by the medium. Sir Alexander Cannon claimed that he had conversed with two Tibetans in their ancient language (*Psychic News*, August 1946).

However, not long after this report, Alec Harris moved to South Africa. There he was severely injured in a séance when two skeptical reporters grabbed a materialized spirit which dissolved in their grip. They also set off flash cameras they had previously hidden in the séance room, hoping to capture evidence of fraud. They found nothing, but the ectoplasm had recoiled back into Alec Harris' body. His wife Louie wrote:

> When Alec came out of trance, he was patently very ill. He had a severe pain which persisted for some weeks in his solar plexus. A doctor was called. He treated Alec weekly for many months. Rohan (the materialized spirit guide) too, suffered adverse effects and needed, we were told by the scientist, a period of recuperation...I noticed a great change in Alec after the exposure attempt. His health was not as robust as before. Something seemed to have gone out of him. He slowed down considerably. Alec had always been such an energetic person, constantly looking for things to do about the home. Now everything seemed to be an effort (Harris, 2009).

Because of this sensitivity to light, most physical mediums have to work in total darkness or, occasionally, in very low red light. Those responsible for their safety have to use extreme care in selecting sitters who can be trusted to stay seated and hold hands during materialization.

Tom Harrison returns

Between 1946 and 1954, Tom Harrison witnessed 1,500 solid ectoplasmic materializations in good red light through his Home Circle with his mother, Minnie Harrison, as the medium. All the spirit people were accepted by relatives or close friends who came as guest sitters. More details and special photos are available in Tom's book *Life After Death: Living Proof.* Tom impressed all who met him as an extremely credible witness. (Readers interested can also see his video, *Visitors From the Other Side:* Saturday Night Press).

Tom Harrison's wife, Ann, confirmed to us that after Tom had crossed over on 23 October 2010, he communicated through a medium the following day. Since that time, she has had many contacts with him through mental mediumship, trance and, from August 2011, materialization with three different mediums, and also later direct voice.

In a séance with physical/materialization medium David Thompson at the Acacia Centre in Spain, Ann says that although the materializations were in the dark, "there was no doubt that it was him by his distinct voice and phraseology". Tom spoke to Ann and kissed her forehead before moving audibly across the room to speak to friends who could vouch that the voice was his.

Rita Goold

In the early 1980s, the English medium Rita Goold based in Leicester, UK, began to produce physical phenomena in her Home Circle. She was told that she had an abundance of an energy "as old as time itself" and that this energy could be used to materialize spirits without the dangers of ectoplasm.

We interviewed several people who attended Rita Goold's séances and they all confirmed the contacts they had experienced. Gwen and Alf Byrne confirmed that in August 1982, they received a phone call that Russell, their son who had died in 1963 at the age of nine, had materialized at Rita Goold's mediumship Circle. He had given the name and address of his parents and asked that they be contacted. They travelled to Leicester for séances and were reunited with Russell on more than 100 occasions. He was able to shine a torch on different parts of his body to show he was fully materialized. After these experiences, Gwen started a support group for bereaved parents. Gwen and Alf are interviewed on the video *Science of Eternity* (Parts 4, 5 and 6) which is on YouTube. She also wrote a book called *Russell* (Byrne, 1994).

Pat Jeffrey was a member of Rita Goold's Circle and she confirmed that her own son had materialized on numerous occasions. Michael Roll, whom we have known for many years, confirms that his own father materialized at a Rita Goold séance in 1983 and gave him solid unmistakable proof of his identity.

Eddy Grenyer, an English medium, confirmed that he had been invited to séances with Rita Goold on eight or nine occasions along with his close friend, Alan Crossly. He claims that sometimes the silhouettes and solid forms of the spirits could be seen. He was present on one occasion when Raymond Lodge, the son of Sir Oliver Lodge, 'visited' the Circle and conversed with the sitters. There were 'spirit lights' produced and sitters could see the clear outline of Raymond's boots and army uniform. He did not look completely solid but he was clearly materialized.

Other famous European and North American materialization mediums

Some of the most famous materialization mediums of the last two centuries include Daniel Dunglas Home and Florence Cook who were investigated in a laboratory by Sir William Crookes. 'Franek Kluski' was a Warsaw medium who materialized animals. His mediumship was verified by Dr. Gustav Geley and Professor F. W. Pawlowski. Others include: Elizabeth S. and May E. Bangs (known as the Bang Sisters, of Chicago), Arnold Clare, Margery Crandon, Stella Cranshaw (better known as 'Stella C.'), Frank Decker, the Eddy Brothers, William Eglinton, Gordon Higginson, Cecil Husk,

Rev. Stainton Moses (an Anglican clergyman), Estelle Roberts, Rudi and Willy Schneider, Hunter Selkirk, and Jack Webber.

The best photos of materialization

Photos of materialization in progress can look very strange. Professor Richet, who was the world's leading expert on ectoplasm, observed that materializations are usually gradual, beginning with a rudimentary shape and then complete forms and human faces only appearing later on. He wrote:

> At first, these formations are often very imperfect. Sometimes they show no relief, looking more like flat images than bodies, so that in spite of oneself, one is inclined to imagine some fraud, since what appears seems to be the materialization of a semblance, and not of a being. (Richet, 1923: 486).

Sitting with Kai Müegge, we ourselves saw a hand forming out of a pile of ectoplasm. At first, it was quite distorted and then gradually it became clear what it was. However, some of the most interesting photos we have seen were taken of medium Ethel Post Parish and her guide, Silver Belle, in 1953 on infrared film. The pictures are taken at ten-second intervals and show the medium sitting in a cabinet. A white smoky substance is drawn from her and in front of the audience gradually assumes the shape and features of a young Indian girl. They can be seen online at http://www.gotsc.org/MaterializationSilverBelle.htm

Some of the best photographs of materialization throughout history are contained on the Felix Circle website.

Brazilian evidence

There have also been many wonderful materialization mediums in Brazil, and one of the greatest was Carmine Mirabelli (1889–1950) who produced fantastic physical phenomena witnessed by scientists from many parts of the world.

In 1927, there appeared in Brazil a book entitled *O Medium Mirabelli*, containing a 74-page account of phenomena which occurred in broad daylight – at times in the presence of up to 60 witnesses at the same time representing the leading scientific and social circles of Brazil. Among those who gave their names as witnesses were the President of Brazil, the Secretary of State, two professors of medicine, 72 doctors, 12 engineers, 36 lawyers, 89 men of public office, 25 military men, 52 bankers, 128 merchants and 22 dentists as well as members of religious orders (*Zeitschrift fuer Parapsychologie*, 1927: 450–462).

The testimony of so many prominent credible witnesses cannot easily be overlooked. In Brazil a committee of 20 leading men, headed by the President of Brazil, was set up to interview witnesses and to decide what should be done to scientifically investigate Mirabelli's powers. It was decided in 1927 to mount a series of controlled investigations by the newly established Academia de Estudos Psychicos using the same controls as European mediums had submitted to.

The investigators of Mirabelli divided into three groups. One group dealt with spoken mediumship and had 189 positive sittings (sittings which produced positive results). A second group investigated automatic writing and had 85 positive sittings and 8 negative sittings (sittings which produced no results). A third group investigated physical phenomena and had 63 positive and 47 negative sittings. Of the positive sittings, 40 were held in daylight and 23 in bright artificial light with the medium tied up in a chair in rooms which were searched before and after (Inglis, 1984: 223).

Physical mediumship and materialization

At a well-attended séance in São Vicente, the chair on which the entranced Mirabelli was sitting rose and floated in the air two meters above the floor. Witnesses timed its levitation for 120 seconds. On another occasion, Mirabelli was at the da Luz railroad station with several companions when he suddenly vanished. About

15 minutes later, a telephone call came from São Vicente, a town 90 kilometres away, stating that he had appeared there exactly two minutes after he had disappeared from da Luz.

At a séance conducted in the morning in full daylight, in the laboratory of the investigating committee in front of many people of note including ten men holding the degree of Doctor of Science:

- the form of a little girl materialized beside the medium
- Dr. Ganymede de Souza who was present confirmed that the child was his daughter who had died a few months before and that she was wearing the dress in which she had been buried
- another observer, Colonel Octavio Viana, also took the child in his arms, felt her pulse and asked her several questions which she answered with understanding
- the form of Bishop José de Camargo Barros who had recently lost his life in a shipwreck appeared in full insignia of office
- he conversed with those present and allowed them to examine his heart, gums, abdomen and fingers before disappearing.

At another séance conducted at Santos at half past three in the afternoon before 60 witnesses who attested their signatures to the report of what had happened:

- the deceased Dr. Bezerra de Meneses, an eminent hospital physician, materialized
- he spoke to all of the assembled witnesses to assure them that it was himself
- his voice carried all over the room by megaphone
- several photographs were taken of him
- for 15 minutes, two doctors who had known him examined him and announced that he was an anatomically normal human being
- he shook hands with the spectators

- finally, he rose into the air and began to dematerialize, with his feet vanishing first followed by his legs and abdomen, chest arms and last of all head
- after the apparition had dematerialized, Mirabelli was found to be still tied securely to his chair and seals were intact on all the doors and windows
- the photographs accompanying the report show Mirabelli and the apparition on the same photographic plate.

At another séance under controlled conditions, Mirabelli himself dematerialized to be found later in another room. Yet, the seals put upon his bonds were intact as were the seals on the doors and windows of the séance room (Inglis, 1984: 226).

Chapter 20

THE HELEN DUNCAN INJUSTICE

Facts often appear incredible only because we are ill informed and cease to appear marvelous when our knowledge is extended.

Sir Francis Bacon

Helen Duncan was a magnificent physical/materialization medium from Scotland, and one of the most important women in psychic history. Her story is given its own chapter in this book because:

- three hundred witnesses of the highest credibility volunteered to give evidence in Duncan's favour when she was accused of fraudulent mediumship in 1944. Some 42 witnesses, including a Royal Air Force Wing Commander, stated in court under oath that Helen Duncan was a genuine materialization medium, explaining in detail their psychic experiences with her. Many senior barristers and QCs, when canvassed, stated that this was indeed 'unique'
- this meant that under oath and for posterity, highly accredited witnesses stated in very clear terms, from their own experience, the reality of materialization, of meeting their loved ones
- the case of Helen Duncan is often brought up by closed-minded skeptics who claim that all physical mediums were/are fraudulent

147

"as proved by Helen Duncan's convictions". But when we look at the evidence rather than the media and the rhetoric, we find that there is no credible evidence that she was fraudulent.

Throughout the years of World War II, Helen Duncan reunited many grieving relatives with servicemen who had died. But she was also bringing through information that had not been released to the public. In a séance in Edinburgh on 24 May 1941, Albert, her control, announced that HMS *Hood* had been sunk earlier that day in the North Atlantic. The time of this séance was 3:30 pm. Brigadier Firebrace, a very enthusiastic believer in Spiritualism who was the Head of Military Intelligence in Scotland, attended that séance. He returned to his office and telephoned the Admiralty to see whether the 'rumour' of the sinking was true. At that time it was denied. By 9:30 p.m., as he was leaving the office, a telephone call was received from the Admiralty confirming the sinking at 1:30 p.m. that day.

In November 1941, at a Helen Duncan séance at Portsmouth, a sailor materialized and was reunited with his mother. He told the assembled sitters that his ship, HMS *Barham*, had recently been sunk and he had been severely burnt to death. The editor of the *Psychic News*, Maurice Barbanell, innocently telephoned the British Admiralty to enquire whether this was true and if it was true why the Admiralty had not advised the sailor's mother about the loss of her son. Military intelligence was furious. For security reasons and for public morale, news of the sinking had been withheld and had been classified 'top secret'.

After the Second World War, Brigadier Firebrace, the head of Military Security for Scotland, confirmed that Helen Duncan had been under surveillance from that time onwards. He also claimed that in early 1944, he received a call from Scotland Yard asking how Helen Duncan could be prevented from giving out information in the lead-up to the coming invasion of Europe (see interview in video *Britain's Last Witch Trial*).

National Security thought that a medium of Duncan's caliber could easily get hold of the most politically sensitive secret information:

where the Allies were going to land on D-Day. One can understand the concern of the Admiralty for secrecy of such an important event. But one cannot understand the way the Admiralty dealt with a frail woman, who had six children and a disabled husband to support, by sending her to jail for nine months. The way the Admiralty conspired to put her away was outrageous, immoral, unconscionable and violated every human and legal right of a human being who did nothing except help people communicate face to face with their loved ones who had 'died' and were living in the afterlife.

The informer who complained to the police about Helen Duncan in January 1944 was Stanley Worth, a naval officer employed by the Admiralty. He was the nephew of the most senior detective at Scotland Yard and a close personal friend of the chief constable at Portsmouth. He knew nothing about mediumship and he was discredited under cross-examination.

Claiming that Helen Duncan was a fraudulent medium, he led a police raid on the séance. The police hoped to find white sheets, fake beards and other crude equipment for impersonating spirits. Helen Duncan and the people present at the séance invited police to search them and the room. Nothing was found. There was absolutely NO evidence that fraud was taking place.

Fraudulent mediums were usually charged under the Vagrancy Act, dealt with in the local court, and given a fine of five shillings. However, the Home Secretary had instructed local police not to enforce the law during wartime for a variety of reasons, including the cost and time involved in prosecuting such a trivial matter. However, Helen Duncan was denied bail for four days and then her matter was transferred from Portsmouth to the Central Criminal Court of England and Wales (in London). She was then charged, under the Witchcraft Act of 1753, with pretending to call up spirits.

Helen's barrister did not raise the issue of government conspiracy and instead brought in expert witnesses to show that she was a genuine medium. He submitted a declaration by Will Goldston, the well known professional magician and illusionist, and three other leading magicians Henry Rigoletto, Dr. A. E. Neale, and Dr. O. H.

Bowen. They stated that in 1932 they had witnessed in a test séance things that could not have been done through trickery. The crown case consisted of the claim that Helen Duncan or an accomplice was pretending to be all of these 'materializations.' They claimed that she had been dressing up in a sheet and using false beards, wigs, etc. But when the police had 'raided' her séance, while she was in trance and producing materializations, they had found no sheet, no false beards, no wigs, no accomplice – indeed, no evidence of fraud whatsoever. For three days, witness after witness said it would be impossible for them to be tricked by dolls or masks because they had seen spirits building up from the floor directly in front of them and then sinking into the floor after speaking.

Typical testimony

- Nurse Jane Rust testified on oath at the Old Bailey, among other things, that she, through Helen Duncan, actually met a loved one again – her husband who materialized from the afterlife and kissed her. "I have never been more certain of anything in my life before", she said. She stated that she had been enquiring for 25 years as a skeptic but it was only when she met Helen Duncan that she was able to actually meet her loved ones including her mother who had passed on (Cassirer, 1996: 68)
- a high ranking Air Force officer, Wing Commander George Mackie, stated on oath that through Helen Duncan's materialization gifts he actually met his 'dead' mother and father and a brother (Cassirer, 1996: 72, 115)
- James Duncan (no relation), a jeweller, testified that both he and his daughter had seen his wife materialize on eight different occasions, in good light. Duncan had seen her close up at a range of 18 inches, and they had talked of domestic matters including a proposed emigration to Canada that they had previously kept secret. He had, he said, not a shadow of a doubt that the voice was that of his wife. He also claimed to have seen

materializations of his father, who was about his own height and bearded, and his mother (Cassirer, 1996: 103)

- Mary Blackwell, President of the Pathfinder Spiritualist Society of Baker Street, London, testified that she had attended more than 100 materialization séances with Helen Duncan, at each of which between 15 and 16 different entities from the afterlife had materialized. She testified that she had witnessed the spirit forms conversing with their relatives in French, German, Dutch, Welsh, Scottish and Arabic. She claimed that she had witnessed the manifestation of ten of her own close relatives including her husband, her mother and her father – all of whom she had seen up close and touched (Cassirer, 1996: 87)

- leading journalist and medium, Maurice Barbanell, testified that he had seen Helen Duncan and her materialized spirit 'control' at the same time from inside the medium's cabinet (Cassirer, 1996: 134)

- the best known journalist and drama critic in London, Hannan Swaffer, testified that he had sat with Helen Duncan in controlled tests on five or six occasions and found her ectoplasm to be genuine. He also stated that he had seen genuine ectoplasm in sittings all over the world more than 50 times (Brealey and Hunter, 1985: 210)

- Lilian Bailey, a leading London medium who gave sittings for the British royal family, testified that she was quite sure that her mother and her paternal grandmother had manifested (Cassirer, 1996: 89)

- Dr. John Winning, an assistant to the Medical Officer of Health of Glasgow, said that he had sat with Mrs. Duncan 40 times and had seen 400 materializations. He had heard many voices, several languages, and a number of dialects spoken by materializations. These included Scottish, Irish, American, Hebrew and German. Once he had heard Gaelic spoken (Cassirer, 1996: 208).

Denied the right to prove her innocence

Helen Duncan's attorney was certain that if the jury could attend a demonstration of her mediumship, they would be convinced that she was a genuine medium. He had attended such a demonstration after the trial had started and was overwhelmed. The Recorder (judge) at first refused saying that it would be a waste of time, yet allowed the jury to decide that Helen Duncan would not be allowed to prove her innocence. The prosecution objected and the jury followed its lead.

The verdict and sentence

As expected, Helen Duncan was found guilty and sentenced to nine months in prison. She was denied the right to appeal and was sent to the notorious Holloway Women's Prison where she served six months. According to the official Helen Duncan homepage, the warders refused to lock her cell for the duration of her sentence and she continued to apply her psychic gifts for the benefit of warders and inmates alike.

The English and Scottish Law Societies individually and together expressed disgust at the miscarriage and 'travesty of justice' in the Helen Duncan tragedy created by cowardly, armchair-violent men to do untold harm to a spiritual person.

Further materializations

After being released from jail, Helen Duncan eventually resumed her mediumship. Even though she was ill with diabetes, her mediumship was still spectacular. For example:

> At a séance in Stoke-on-Trent, in one case an airman materialized for his mother, complete with the birthmark that he had on his face before his passing. Another man materialized for his wife, lacking the two fingers that he had lost while working. Further proof was

given on the occasions when Albert, over six foot in height, brought Helen, only five foot and four inches, out of the cabinet, entranced, and stood beside her. To demonstrate their separateness even further, Albert would ensure that the sitters could see Helen while he was standing, and speaking up to four feet away (Nicholls, undated).

The death of Helen Duncan

In 1956, the Nottingham police again raided a séance Helen Duncan was giving. The police knocked on the door of a private home without a search warrant on the supposed complaint of two police officers who had earlier attended one of her séances. The police had technical knowledge that materialization usually has to be conducted in semi-darkness and that, if the lights are put on suddenly, very serious injury or death to the medium can occur. When they were admitted to the home, they made for the medium's cabinet and grabbed the medium. More men arrived and took flash photographs. The whole house was searched and even the medium's luggage gone through. But just as at Portsmouth, nothing incriminating was found. The medium was left unconscious and, according to a doctor who was called, in deep shock and likely to die if moved (Brealey and Hunter, 1985: 13).

Helen Duncan's daughter Gena writes that there was no doubt the police raid was the cause of Helen's death five weeks later. She says that Helen had burn marks the size of a saucer on her breast and abdomen (Brealey and Hunter, 1985: 155).

Helen Duncan returns

Since her death, Helen Duncan has returned on many occasions through other materialization mediums. We have been present on two occasions when she materialized through David Thompson in order to talk to one of her grandchildren who was present. She also returned during the Scole Experiment (Foy, 2008).

Helen Duncan was claimed to be one of the main members of the Spirit team working with English materialization medium Rita Goold in Leicester, England, in the early 1980s. Rita's séances were all held in the dark and no ectoplasm was used; Helen Duncan said her death was one of the reasons they were not using ectoplasm. On many occasions, she materialized and had long conversations through the mediumship of Rita Goold with Alan Crossley who had written a biography of her (Crossley, 1975).

Psychic News assistant editor Alan Cleaver reported that he had attended one of Rita Goold's séances when Helen Duncan's daughter, Gena Brealey of Luton,z Beds, visited the Circle to see whether it really was her mother communicating. He writes:

> Within minutes she knew. Helen apported to her daughter a single red rose. This had a special significance known only to the two of them. When she was given the rose, Gena broke down in tears of joy and cried, "What greater proof could I have?" For more than an hour, mother and daughter spoke to each other about intimate details only they knew, often using Scottish slang they then had to 'translate' to the other sitters. Afterwards, Gena declared: "Yes, it is my mother. There is no doubt about it" (*Psychic News*, No. 2,646, Saturday 26 February, 1983).

Gena (Brealey) worked with Kay Hunter to write a biography of her mother called *The Two Worlds of Helen Duncan,* first published in 1985 and reprinted since (Brealey and Hunter, 2008). On my website I have an article which argues that there is no evidence that Helen Duncan was not a genuine medium. (http://victorzammit.com/duncan.htm)

Chapter 21

SPIRIT VOICES ON TAPE – ELECTRONIC VOICE PHENOMENA

I didn't say that it was possible, I just said that it happened!

Sir William Crookes

For more than 50 years, experimenters all over the world have been tape-recording 'paranormal voices'. These are voices which can only be heard when the tape is played back. Many of the very short messages claim to be from loved ones who have passed on. These are not just random noises or words – they use the experimenter's name and answer questions.

There are thousands of researchers around the world who have been researching this most fascinating psychic phenomenon. It is particularly relevant to my argument since it follows strict scientific procedures. The experiments have been duplicated under laboratory conditions by researchers in many different countries. Persistent investigators get a powerful shock when they decide to investigate electronic voice phenomena. By using the proper method of tape recording, they are likely to hear voices of loved ones or friends who have died.

Colin Smythe and Peter Bander

That's exactly what happened to Dr. Peter Bander. He was a senior lecturer in religious and moral education at the Cambridge Institute of Education. Before he started his investigation, Dr. Bander stated that it was impossible for those who are 'dead' to communicate with us. He said that it was "not only far-fetched but outrageous" to even think about it (Bander, 1973: 3).

When publisher Colin Smythe asked Peter Bander to get involved with the voice phenomena in 1972, Bander's answer was an absolute 'No'. So Colin Smythe himself experimented on a tape recorder, following the procedures outlined in Constantine Raudive's book, *Breakthrough* (1971). He asked Bander to put the tape recorder onto Record for a few minutes. Then he rewound it and let it play. After ten minutes, he was about to give up when suddenly, Bander says:

> I noticed the peculiar rhythm mentioned by Raudive and his colleagues... I heard a voice... I believed this to have been the voice of my mother who had died three years earlier (Bander, 1973: 4).

Controlled experiments rule out stray radio signals

Later, Colin Smythe published *Voices from the Tape,* in which there are four pages of photos showing different participants in Bander's later experiments. These were carried out under the strictest control conditions. On one occasion, EVP experiments were conducted in soundproof studios to filter out stray broadcasts. In the space of 27 minutes, some 200 voices were received. Comments from observers quoted in Bander's book include the following (Bander, 1973: 132):

Ken Attwood, chief engineer of Pye: "I have done everything in my power to break the mystery of the voices without success; the same applies to other experts. I suppose we must learn to accept them."

Dr. Brendan McGann, director of the Institute of Psychology, Dublin: "I have apparently succeeded in reproducing the phenomena. Voices have appeared on a tape which did not come from any known source."

A. P. Hale, physicist and electronics engineer: "In view of the tests carried out in a screened laboratory at my firm, I cannot explain what happened in normal physical terms."

Sir Robert Mayer LL.D., D.Sc., Mus.D.: "If the experts are baffled, I consider this is a good enough reason for presenting the Voice Phenomena to the general public."

Ted Bonner of Decca and RTE said: "This is no trick. This is no gimmickry; this is something we have never dreamed of before" (Bander, 1973: 106).

Pioneers of EVP

Peter Bander's experiments were inspired by the research of Dr. Konstantin Raudive. Dr. Raudive worked in Germany to duplicate the research done by Friedrich Jürgenson who, by chance in 1959, rediscovered the Voice Phenomena.

Raudive's classic research under the English title *Breakthrough* (1971) was based on 72,000 voices he recorded. Work on the Voice Phenomena had actually started in the 1920s with Thomas Edison, who believed that there could be a radio frequency between the long and short waves which would make possible some form of contact with the other world.

It is worth noting here that the pioneers of radio and television – Guglielmo Marconi, Edison, Sir Oliver Lodge, Sir William Crookes, John Logie Baird – were all convinced of the reality of spirit communication and were using their professional skills to demonstrate it. Marconi, one of the developers of wireless radio, was reportedly working on a system to communicate electronically with the afterlife at the time of his death.

The first voices were captured on phonograph records in 1938 and on tape recorders in the early 1950s. Since the Bander book was published in 1973, the work has been taken up by thousands of researchers in many countries.

The Vatican supports EVP

Unknown to many Christians – including Catholics, Protestants and Fundamentalists – the Catholic Church has been actively positive and encouraging towards investigation of the Electronic Voice Phenomena:

- Two of the earliest investigators were Italian Catholic priests, Father Ernetti and Father Gemelli, who came upon the phenomena by chance while they were recording Gregorian Chants in 1952

- Father Gemelli heard his own father's voice on the tape, calling him by a childhood nickname, saying: "Zucchini, it is clear, don't you know it is I"

- Deeply troubled by Catholic teaching in regard to contact with the dead, the two priests visited Pope Pius XII in Rome

- The Pope reassured them:

   Dear Father Gemelli, you really need not worry about this. The existence of this voice is strictly a scientific fact and has nothing to do with spiritism. The recorder is totally objective. It receives and records only sound waves from wherever they come. This experiment may perhaps become the cornerstone for a building for scientific studies which will strengthen people's faith in a hereafter (Italian Journal *Astra*, June 1990, quoted in Kubis and Macy, 1995: 102)

- Pope Pius' cousin, the Rev. Professor Dr. Gebhard Frei, co-founder of the Jung Institute, was an internationally known parapsychologist who worked closely with Raudive, a pioneer in the research. He was also the President of the International Society for Catholic Parapsychologists. He himself is on record as stating:

All that I have read and heard forces me to believe that the voices come from transcendental, individual entities. Whether it suits me or not, I have no right to doubt the reality of the voices (Kubris and Macy, 1995)

- Dr. Frei died on 27 October, 1967. In November 1967, at numerous taping sessions, a voice giving its name as Gebhard Frei came through. The voice was identified by Professor Peter Hohenwarter of the University of Vienna as positively belonging to Dr. Frei (Ostrander and Schroeder, 1977)

- Pope Paul VI was well aware of the work being done from 1959 onwards on the Elecronic Voices by his good friend, Swedish film producer Friedrich Jürgenson, who had made a documentary film about him. The Pope made Jürgenson a Knight Commander of the Order of St. Gregory in 1969 for his work. Jürgenson wrote to Bander:

I have found a sympathetic ear for the Voice Phenomenon in the Vatican. I have won many wonderful friends among the leading figures in the Holy City. Today 'the bridge' stands firmly on its foundations (Ostrander and Schroeder, 1977)

- The Vatican also gave permission for its own priests to conduct research into the voices. Father Leo Schmid, a Swiss theologian, collected more than 10,000 of them which he discusses in his book *When the Dead Speak*, published in 1976, shortly after his death

- Another Vatican-approved researcher was Father Andreas Resch who, as well as conducting his own experiments, began courses in parapsychology at the Vatican's school for priests in Rome (Kubris and Macy, 1995)

- In 1970, the International Society for Catholic Parapsychologists held a conference in Austria, and a major part of that conference was concerned with papers on the Electronic Voice Phenomena

- In England, in 1972, four senior members of the Catholic hierarchy were involved in the famous Pye recording studio tests conducted by Peter Bander

- Father Pistone, Superior of the Society of St. Paul in England, said in an interview after the tests:

  I do not see anything against the teaching of the Catholic Church in the Voices, they are something extraordinary but there is no reason to fear them, nor can I see any danger.

  The Church realizes that she cannot control the evolution of science. Here we are dealing with a scientific phenomenon; this is progress and the Church is progressive. I am happy to see that representatives of most Churches have adopted the same attitude as we have: we recognize that the subject of the Voice Phenomena stirs the imagination even of those who have always maintained that there could never be any proof or basis for discussion on the question of life after death. This book and the subsequent experiments raise serious doubts, even in the minds of atheists. This alone is a good reason for the Church supporting the experiments. A second reason may be found in the greater flexibility of the Church since Vatican II, we are willing to keep an open mind

160

on all matters which do not contradict Christ's teaching
(Bander, 1973: 103)

- His excellence, Archbishop H. E. Cardinale, Apostolic Nuncio
  to Belgium, commented:

  Naturally it is all very mysterious, but we know the
  voices are there for all to hear them (Bander, 1973: 132)

- The Right Reverend Monsignor Professor C. Pfleger commented:

  Facts have made us realize that between death and resur-
  rection there is another realm of post-mortal existence.
  Christian theology has little to say about this realm
  (Bander, 1973: 133)

- Bander's book contains a photograph of the Right Reverend
  Monsignor Stephen O'Connor, Vicar General and Principal Roman Catholic Chaplain to the Royal Navy, listening to the play-
  back of a recording on which a voice had manifested claiming
  to be that of a young Russian naval officer known to himself
  who had committed suicide two years earlier. Dr. Raudive had
  recorded the message independently at an earlier session

- Since the 1970s, the Vatican has continued to sponsor extensive
  research into all areas of parapsychology including Electronic
  Voice Phenomena

- In 1997, Father Gino Concetti, one of the most competent theo-
  logians in the Vatican, said in an interview:

  According to the modern catechism, God allows our
  dear departed persons who live in an ultra-terrestrial
  dimension, to send messages to guide us in certain difficult moments of our lives. The Church has decided not

to forbid any more the dialogue with the deceased with the condition that these contacts are carried out with a serious religious and scientific purpose (in the Vatican newspaper *Osservatore Romano* – cited in Sarah Estep's *American Association Electronic Voice Phenomena Inc. Newsletter*, Vol. 16 No. 2, 1997).

Clearly, the Catholic Church realizes that science is making enormous, inevitable, irreversible and cumulative progress which nobody is in a position to stop.

ATransC (Association TransCommunication)

The American Association for Electronic Voice Phenomena (AAEVP) was founded by Sarah Estep in 1982. It has now evolved into the Association TransCommunication (ATransC) under the leadership of Tom and Lisa Butler. While EVP is still an important part of its focus, the new name reflects the international nature of its membership. Its focus is on 'objective evidence for survival', which includes those phenomena that can be documented with technology including physical mediumship.

ATransC is a teaching/learning organization, and offers support to those interested in working with EVP and learning to be more objective in understanding the paranormal voices. Tom and Lisa Butler's book, *There Is No Death and There Are No Dead* (2003), is a wonderful introduction to scientific investigation of the afterlife. It was written to teach people about these phenomena and to help them learn how to record paranormal voices (see the Association TransCommunication website).

The Association's website, atransc.org, also includes personal experiences, research reports, examples and techniques. For more direct help, the Idea Exchange is an online discussion board. It is reserved for members only as a safe place to ask for help, discuss concepts and share examples.

A number of ATransC members have written moving, detailed accounts of their evidential transcommunication with transitioned loved ones for the quarterly ATransC News Journal and website. Martha Copeland's *I'm Still Here* tells the story of how Martha continues to work with her daughter, Cathy, who is on the other side. Martha is one of the founders of a group within ATransC known as the Big Circle. Cathy has come through with children who are on the other side to connect with their loved ones who are participating in the Recording Circle.

Sandra Champlain's new book, *We Don't Die: A Skeptic's Discovery of Life After Death* (2013), traces how she learned how to record EVPs after attending a workshop with Tom and Lisa Butler. She was successful using the noise of rain on the roof and the noise of a running shower as background noise.

Tom and Lisa Butler warn new practitioners about the human tendency to try to find meaning in random sounds. It suggests that experimenters always get honest feedback from friends or the online community without telling them what they think is being said. The organization's Ideas Exchange can be of considerable help in this regard.

They also do not recommend radio-sweep technology. Units called a 'ghost box' or 'spirit box' are being sold for more than $1,200 US. Even though they are easy to work with and there is always an output, there are no reliable studies showing that radio-sweep actually produces EVP. An exception is when noise from very rapid radio-sweep, without recognizable live voices, is used as background noise for transform EVP.

You can support and participate in research in transcommunication by joining the Association TransCommunication. As a public service funded by members, the website at atransc.org provides over 400 pages of relevant information. Sarah Estep's book, *Voices of Eternity*, is also available as a free download.

Chapter 22

INSTRUMENTAL TRANS-COMMUNICATION (ITC)

For the first time in 8,000 years of recorded history, it can now be said with certainty that our mind, memory, personality and soul will survive physical death.

GEORGE MEEK

Since about 1980, psychic researchers have claimed that contact with people who have died has also been made via radio, over telephones, on television, on answering and fax machines, and computers.

This more extended and recent voice contact is called Instrumental Trans-communication or Extended ITC or even Trans-dimensional Communication. It is highly evidential in that the contact is repeatable, is occurring in laboratories throughout the world, and is being subjected to close scientific scrutiny. When it is perfected, ITC has the potential to be the most revolutionary and persuasive evidence for the afterlife.

According to Mark Macy, a leading researcher in this area, throughout the 1990s, the research laboratories in Europe received extended, two-way communication with spirit colleagues. This was almost daily through telephone answering machines, radios and computer printouts. His book *Miracles in the Storm* outlines how scientists working for the International Network for Instrumental Trans-communication (INIT), which he founded in 1995, received from the afterlife:

- pictures of people and places in the afterlife on television that either appeared clearly on the screen and remained for at least several frames, or which built up steadily into a reasonably clear picture over multiple frames

- text and picture files from people in the afterlife which appeared in computer memory or were planted on disk or similar recordable media

- text and images of people and places in the afterlife by way of fax messages.

In America, the pioneers of this work were George and Jeanette Meek and William O'Neil who worked to establish Spiricom. This was a piece of electromagnetic equipment which allowed two-way real-time audio communication between Bill O'Neil and Dr. George Jeffries Mueller, a deceased college physics teacher. By the autumn of 1980, Dr. Mueller's voice, although quite buzzy, was loud and understandable. Meek recorded more than 20 hours of dialogue between O'Neil and Mueller. Unfortunately, the device needed their particular combination of energies to work.

The reader is referred to a book written by John G. Fuller called *The Ghost of 29 Megacycles* (1981). This 351-page book describes in detail George Meek's highly credible research, and the evidence he produced to show that life goes on after we die. It is recommended to the serious seeker.

Radio Luxembourg experiments

In West Germany, Hans-Otto Koenig, an electronics and acoustics expert, tried a different method. He developed sophisticated

165

electronic equipment using "extremely low-beat frequency oscillators, ultraviolet and infra-red lights.'" On 15 January 1983, he was invited to appear on Europe's biggest radio station, Radio Luxembourg. At that time, it had a listening audience of millions across Europe. Koenig was asked to give a live radio demonstration of his newly developed ultrasound technique of conversing two-way with those who had died.

Koenig installed his equipment under the watchful eyes of the Radio's own engineers and the presenter of the programme, Herr Rainer Holbe. One of the Radio's staff asked if a voice could come through in direct response to his requests. Almost immediately a voice replied:

"We hear your voice" and "Otto Koenig makes wireless with the dead" (Fuller, 1981).

Other questions were asked. But then announcer Holbe, shaken by what he and everybody else had heard, stated:

I tell you, dear listeners of Radio Luxembourg, and I swear by the life of my children, that nothing has been manipulated. There are no tricks. It is a voice, and we do not know from where it comes (Fuller, 1981).

The station issued an official statement afterwards that every step of the programme had been carefully supervised. The staff and engineers were convinced that the voices were paranormal (Fuller, 1981).

Naturally enough, more intensive public work was done by Koenig. Other experiments were carried out with Radio Luxembourg with similar success (Fuller, 1981: 339). One particular voice came through, stating, "I am Raudive." When Dr. Raudive was alive, he had written the book *Breakthrough* referred to earlier. In it, he gave full details about his own experiments with the EVP – more than 72,000 voices from those who had 'died' were recorded.

166

Black and white television pictures

In 1985, Klaus Schreiber in West Germany devised a way to get pictures on television tubes of persons who had died. The tubes used "an opto-electronic feedback system". There was positive identification, in many cases through accompanying audio communication, including audio-video contact with deceased family members.

Schreiber's work was closely supervised by experienced investigators. Professor Ernst Senkowski and Rainer Holbe of Radio Luxembourg, both of whom knew Schreiber personally. They were satisfied that his results were genuine (Fontana, 2005).

At the same time in Luxembourg, Maggy and Jules Harsch-Fischbach received images on a television screen after previously being told to expect them in an ITC audio communication. Present were investigators Professor and Mrs. Senkowski, Professor Resch and George Meek. These images were of the same quality as those recorded by Schreiber (Fontana, 2005).

Computer contact

In 1987, Jules and Maggie Harsch-Fischbach claimed to have established computer contact with the afterlife. They were able to ask technical questions to beings in the afterlife and receive high-speed print-outs of the replies. Also, in 1987, they claimed to have received TV picture sequences of good quality in the presence of experienced investigators (Locher and Harsch-Fischbach, 1997).

According to Kubris and Macy, by 1993 the research team in the afterlife was able to access the hard drives of computers. They were able to leave detailed, computer-scanned images as well as several pages of text. The computer-scanned images were far more detailed and less subject to distortion than the video images. They showed scenes in the afterlife of earth-like mountains, lakes and gardens, and pictures of children who had died who had grown older in the afterlife. Researchers in our dimension were able to direct questions to their counterparts in the afterlife dimension and receive answers by telephone, radio, TV, computer, or fax (Kubis and Macy, 1995; Locher and Harsch-Fischbach, 1997).

The first colour television picture of a spirit entity was reported in October 1995. A German researcher, Aldof Homes, awoke with a strong feeling to try an experiment with his colour TV set. He had been receiving paranormal video images on his monochrome TV. But this time, he received a telephone call from a spirit colleague telling him to turn on his colour TV. He turned it on and trained his camcorder on the picture tube. At that instant, an image of the early Swedish EVP experimenter Friedrich Jürgenson, who had died seven years earlier, appeared on the screen and remained there for 24 seconds.

He then heard a loud, cracking noise coming from the next room. Upon entering the room, he found his computer had been switched on paranormally. On the screen he found a typed message to him: "This is Friedel from Sweden. I am sending you a self-portrait..." (Mark Macy, World ITC website).

Paranormal phone calls

There have been many reports of people answering the telephone and hearing the voice of someone they know has died. Others have received calls from individuals who – they have later found out – had died before the call was made. Parapsychologist Scott Rogo and Raymond Bayless spent two years investigating. Their book *Phone Calls From the Dead: The results of a two-year investigation into an incredible phenomenon* was published in 1979. English parapsychologist Cal Cooper has written an updated version, *Telephone Calls From the Dead* (2012).

During a period of several weeks in 1994, five American ITC researchers received phone calls from fellow researcher Konstantin Raudive who had died in 1974. These were George Meek, Mark Macy, Sarah Estep, Dr. Walter Uphoff and Hans Heckmann (a close friend and colleague of George Meek). In each case, the phone call mentioned the previous phone calls. The calls were tape recorded and analyzed by voice experts. In 1996, one two-way taped conversation between Dr. Konstantin Raudive and Mark Macy lasted for 13 minutes (Continuing Life Research video, *ITC Today*, 1997).

A number of researchers began to question the phone contacts, suggesting that they might be a hoax. Then, German ITC researcher Adolf Homes received a text file on his computer in Germany giving details of the phone calls. His computer had not been connected to the internet, and the message had simply appeared on the screen. The message said other successful contacts had been made with China and Japan by telephone and fax.

Professor Ernst Senkowski, who coined the term 'Instrumental Trans-communication', began investigating the field from 1974. A professional physicist, Dr. Senkowski was a scientific research fellow at the Institute of Physics at the Mayence University and a UNESCO expert on physics at the National Research Centre in Cairo, Egypt. His book *Instrumental Trans-communication* (see World ITC website) is a detailed scientific investigation of this exciting method of communicating with the afterlife. In a videotaped interview he talks about his experiences receiving a phone call from the 'dead' Friedrich Jürgenson, in the presence of French scientific witnesses.

INIT contact-field problems

Mark Macy writes that the wonderful contacts being received by the International Network for Instrumental Trans-communication came to an abrupt end in the late 1990s. He claims that this was because of "doubts, fears, envy, resentment, and other troubled feelings" which created dissonance and broke the 'contact field'. This issue is well known in physical mediumship where the presence of even one skeptical or resentful sitter in a group can affect the phenomena.

Sonia Rinaldi and the Brazilian team

One of the leading researchers in this field today is Sonia Rinaldi who leads the biggest ITC (Instrumental Trans-Communication) association in Brazil, Associação Nacional de Transcomunicadores (ANT), with nearly 700 members. She recently announced new contacts received via computer, answering machine, telephone and video camera.

Sonia has been helping people by making phone calls to the beyond since March 2001. Parents who have lost children make an appointment with Sonia in advance. They are instructed to prepare ten questions. When they call on the appointed day, Sonia has one phone in her hand and leaves an extension phone open for those in the spirit world to participate. The telephone is connected into the MIC jack of her computer and all conversations are recorded directly into the computer. The questions are asked leaving ten seconds between each question and the recorded conversation lasts about 12 to 15 minutes. After the session is over, Sonia prepares a final recording of the session resulting in seven to eight minutes of pure dialogue between parent and deceased child. The parents are then able to hear their loved one's voice and decide if it is their child who is speaking, identifying not only the voice itself, but also details and information which only the parents know. Sonia has made 169 well-documented calls, all of them witnessed and under scientifically controlled parameters.

Sonia has discussed these findings on a number of television programmes in Brazil. Her work is based on scientific control and her website contains scientific declarations issued by the most respected university in Brazil, Universidade de São Paulo. At public meetings in Brazil and in the United States, large numbers of members and visitors were able to receive direct answers from loved ones in the spirit world.

Marcello Bacci's voices

Another long-term experimenter in ITC is Marcello Bacci. For 40 years he has been receiving paranormal voices on a regular basis in his laboratory in Grosseto, Italy. Bacci uses an old valve radio tuned to white noise in the short-wave band. For many years, he has been holding sessions on Friday nights with parents who have lost deceased sons or daughters who claim to be able to hear the voices of their deceased children. Many books have already been written about his work, and Bacci today continues his research using his old valve radio.

Many researchers have visited Bacci's laboratory to test the phenomenon of the Bacci voices. Physicist Salvatore Mario Festa worked with Bacci analyzing the voices weekly for six years. Here is part of a report he wrote for World ITC:

The phenomenon of the voices of Bacci is authentic, there is no trick of any sort! After approximately 30 minutes of waiting, during which Marcello moves the tuning knob between 7 and 9 MHz looking for a zone of white noise, the silence is broken by Marcello's voice announcing that "he hears them". Immediately after, something sensational happens: in the zone of white noise above mentioned, all radio signals stop and one, predominant, noise takes over. This sound is similar to the noise of the wind. Marcello then talks to the radio and calls out "FRIENDS we are here, can you please make yourselves heard?" And them, who are waiting for nothing else, they do exactly that and with such determination! I am not going to run through what happened thereafter, because all the experts are well familiar with what happens: clear and convincing messages are heard, messages filled with esoteric content and answers more or less in line with the questions asked. What can be said about the voices of the 'youngsters', who always generate the most extraordinary emotions amongst those present? When the 'youngsters' talk, a heart-warming and all-embracing atmosphere is created in the room.

Technical studies have been carried out in order to verify the paranormal nature of the phenomenon over more than 30 years. Professional independent researchers, such as Daniele Gullà, Dr. Marabini and Paolo Presi, among others, have investigated the voices and analyzed them using the most sophisticated electronic equipment. The voices are received only when the experiment is personally performed by Bacci, which means that a certain level of mediumship by the experimenter is needed. A similar effect was noted in the experiments carried out in the 1980s by William O'Neill with the Spiricom device.

Dr. Anabela Cardoso

Another leading figure in ITC today is Dr. Anabela Cardoso. A professional Portuguese diplomat and animal rights campaigner, Dr. Cardoso has an impeccable career record. Her work has been studied in depth by Professor David Fontana. In his book *Is There an Afterlife?* (2005), he eloquently outlines Dr. Cardoso's work.

Her book *Electronic Voices: Contact with Another Dimension?* (2010) describes the astounding experiences that transformed her life since she started ITC research in 1997. Her book is an excellent starting point for anyone interested in experimenting with this method. She presents extracts of conversations with her deceased loved ones and other personalities who insist that they are alive in the afterlife. Many of these conversations were witnessed by researchers. She explains how she uses the Direct Radio Voice method. She uses a number of radios tuned to different white noise frequencies; the voices come through and can be heard by all present, and conversations take place. Several examples are included on a CD that accompanies the book.

One of the frustrations of working with ITC is that the communication can be interrupted for no apparent reason. At the end of her book, Dr. Cardoso describes how, after a break of more than two years, the direct radio voices resumed in August 2009 and are continuing.

As well as her wonderful work as an individual experimenter, Dr. Cardoso has taken on the role of coordinator of the work, running an international ITC journal which has been published quarterly since March 2000. Now in the second decade of its existence and with an International Editorial Board, the ITC Journal publishes articles by leading researchers and specialists who have achieved successful results with ITC, among them Adrian Klein (Israel), Anabela Cardoso (Portugal), Carlo Trajna (Italy), Carlos Fernández (Spain), Carlos Luz (Brazil), Cristina Rocha (Brazil), Daniele Gullà (Italy), David Fontana (UK), Enrico Marabini (Italy), Ernst Senkowski (Germany), François Brune (France), Jacques Blanc-Garin (France), Nils O. Jacobson (Sweden), Paola Giovetti (Italy), Paolo Presi (Italy), and Sinesio Darnell (Spain). Copies on all issues are available on her website.

International conferences on ITC

The 'First International Conference on Current Research into Survival of Physical Death, with Special Reference to Instrumental Trans-communication,' was held by the ITC Journal in Vigo, Spain, in April 2004. The *Proceedings* are available in the form of a soft-covered book of 192 pages and contain copies of all the 14 papers delivered at the conference. The papers are in either English or Spanish (with one paper in French).

The 'Second International Conference on Current Research into Survival of Physical Death with Special Reference to ITC' was held in Vigo from 28 to 30 April, 2006. It featured presentations by a number of leading European and US authorities on ITC, such as Daniele Gullà, Dr. Sinesio Darnell, Hans-Otto König, Dr. Anabela Cardoso, Professor Ernst Senkowski, Professor Salvatore Mario Festa, and Sylvia Hart Wright. Also included were contributions on other aspects of research into survival from Professor David Fontana, Dr. Enrico Marabini, Mario Varvoglis, Dr. Alexander Trofimov, Dr. Walter von Lucadou, Jean Pierre Girard and Dr. Peter Fenwick.

You can see from the ITC journals available on Dr. Cardoso's website that these conferences were huge gatherings of hundreds of highly qualified serious investigators. They came from a range of professional backgrounds and many countries.

There are many physicists, chemists, biologists, psychologists, engineers and highly qualified psychic researchers working in this area, sharing amazing video and audio materials received through ITC.

All of the experimenters working in ITC say that it is most important to have a group of people who are united, harmonious and lacking in ego. They need to have a passionate desire for contact with the aim of helping mankind. There also needs to be a strong favourable link with a deceased person who is willing to work with the group.

ITC is still in its infancy but we have already seen detailed evidence of the afterlife attested to by people of the highest integrity and credibility. We know that there are teams of scientists working in the afterlife who are equally keen to open this channel of communication between their world and ours.

Chapter 23

THE OUIJA BOARD

The borderland between the worlds of the living and the dead appears to be a kind of psychic jungle or 'outlaw territory', thronged with vicious, psychopathic personalities. If they can find and attune themselves to a victim, their destructive natures can operate with even less restraint than they did while embodied.

Ian Currie
AUTHOR AND PSYCHIC RESEARCHER

The ouija board is one of the most widely used methods of 'untrained' spirit communication. It is a primitive form of physical mediumship. The name is taken from the French and German words for yes – Oui and Ja. It consists of a flat board with the letters of the alphabet, some numbers, punctuation marks, and Yes and No printed on it.

Psychics and experienced mediums believe the responses to the ouija board are sometimes made by human and non-human entities. They say that contact is most usually with the lowest entities who operate close to our own 'wavelength'.

Psychic investigator Professor Archie Roy says using a ouija board is like picking up total strangers in a bar and inviting them home (Roy, 1996: 176). If contact is made with a refined spirit, the response will usually be polite and uplifting. If contact is made with very low spirits, the communication will be rude, unintelligent, and vulgar. Sometimes they will curse and swear to shock those around him or her.

The materialist view is that the messages come from the sub-conscious or unconscious minds of the 'players' – a form of 'automatism'. For years, the ouija board has been sold in toyshops and game departments in the USA. People used it for fun or for personal advantage such as trying to get winning numbers for gambling, etc. But no skeptic has been able to explain how groups of normal decent people suddenly get horrible messages. Some get curses and all manner of terrifying threats from the ouija board.

Stoker Hunt, who researched the effects of using the ouija board, summarizes a common pattern of communication that develops between users of the board and the 'force' with which they communicate:

> The invader focuses on the victim's character weaknesses... If one is vain, appeals to vanity are made. "I need your help", the seducer will say, "and only you can help me." ... The entity is malicious and does not hesitate to lie, misrepresent itself (usually as a deceased loved one) and flatter. It's better for the invader, of course, if the victim is alone, isolated, exhausted and ill.

> Thus, the entity will encourage its victims to drop real friends and rely only on ouija communication for counsel, advice and companionship. To this end, it will recommend dangerous stunts and wild adventures while discouraging healthy activities and proper medical care. The victim will feel an uncontrollable desire to use the board or write automatically at all hours of the day and night. If need be, the invader will terrify its victim, materializing in ghastly form, inducing grotesque visions, inciting poltergeist activity, causing objects to appear out of the blue, delivering false or tragic news, levitating objects, perhaps levitating the victim. All these things and more might be done – not as ends in themselves but as a means to an eventual complete possession (Hunt, 1985: 86–87).

Mediums from around the world consistently report that some people who die live in despair in the lower vibration regions closest to the earth. These areas are sometimes called the lower astral regions. Many spirits are caught in these areas by their addictions and attachments. They want to continue to experience the things that they used to enjoy while alive – excitement, alcohol, smoking, sex. If they could think loving thoughts or had some other positive spiritual attributes, they would not be in the condition they are in. If they even had the capacity to ask for help to relieve their misery, someone would come to help them.

Some EVP experimenters (*see* Chapter 21) have recorded voices coming from this level that swear, whisper threats and sometimes talk in a clearly hostile tone (Lazarus, 1993: 158).

It seems that a ouija board can be highly dangerous to anyone who is highly susceptible, anyone with any type of emotional or personality disorder, or anyone who has been using mind-altering drugs. The experts advise that under no circumstances should it be used by a child or by anyone who does not have a strong sense of their own identity (Covina, 1979). There have been cases of psychiatric illness which seem to have come about as a direct result of playing with the board. Dr. Carl Wickland, an American psychiatrist, wrote his classic work on mental illness *Thirty Years Among the Dead* in 1924. In it, he warns:

> The serious problem of alienation and mental derangement attending ignorant psychic experiments was first brought to my attention by cases of several persons whose seemingly harmless experiences with automatic writing and the ouija board resulted in such wild insanity that commitment to asylums was necessitated... Many other disastrous results which followed the use of the supposedly innocent ouija board came to my notice and my observations led me into research in psychic phenomena for a possible explanation of these strange occurrences (Wickland, 1924: 29).

Dr. Wickland found that he was able to cure many of these cases of diagnosed insanity. His wife was a trance medium and he allowed her to be taken over by the spirit which he claimed was obsessing the psychiatric patient. He found that many of these entities were unaware that they had died. Without any knowledge of the afterlife, they found themselves in a kind of twilight or dream condition. With help from higher intelligences on the other side, he was able to persuade them to leave the aura of the patient whose light had attracted them.

Hugh Lyn Cayce, the son of the famous American psychic Edgar Cayce, gives many case histories of negative ouija experiences. In his book *Venture Inward* (1964), in a chapter on Automatic Writing and Ouija boards, he states that stories of people getting into extreme difficulties following both these practices are:

> ... not uncommon, unfortunately. The frightening thing about them is that they can be duplicated by the thousands from the case histories of present-day inmates of mental institutions all over the world (Cayce, 1964).

Paul Beard, as President of the College of Psychic Studies in England, studied many cases of ouija-board obsession. He concluded that habitual use of the board or automatic writing can bring about prolonged contact with a malevolent dead person who can infiltrate the victim's protective aura and then make contact with the victim at any time by 'talking' in a 'voice' or through 'thoughts' in the victim's head. This can lead to "practically continuous evil suggestions which may involve visual hallucinations" (Beard, 1970).

Ian Currie claims to have encountered a number of ouija board possession cases which are all strikingly similar. The communicating entities try to get the victim 'hooked'. They urge them to use the board at all hours of day and night. Then they begin to offer false and destructive advice. Finally, the victims begin to hear a persistent voice either externally or inside their head saying things like "kill yourself so that you can join me" (Currie, 1998: 242–3).

Martin Ebon outlines his negative ouija experiences in *The Satan Trap* (1975). He claims that he began by being thoroughly skeptical about anything to do with the occult but became addicted to the board when it accurately predicted New York's 1973 flood. It also gave him accurate 'inside' information about the death of a famous gossip columnist.

Another woman who warned against the board was medium Susy Smith. In her 1971 book *Confessions of a Psychic*, she writes:

> Warn people away from ouija and automatic writing until you have learned how to be fully protected. They say that innocent efforts at communication are as dangerous as playing with matches or hand grenades. They have me as Exhibit A of what not to do, for I experienced many of the worst problems of such involvement. Had I been forewarned by my reading that such efforts might cause me to be mentally disturbed, I might have been more wary (Smith, 1971).

A few years ago, we came upon a serious case of a young man who had been using a ouija board. He had been asking for winning numbers for gambling purposes. For some time, he had indeed been winning and became very excited about the information given him by his new 'friends'. But when he tried to give up using the board, he began to be obsessed by voices. He found himself woken up at one or two in the morning in great terror, literally being squeezed and suffocated by a presence which claimed that it was owed a debt.

Physical medium Marion Dampier Jeans recently shared a story of how a dare to the communicating spirits to show themselves physically led to poltergeist-like effects. In a private communication to us, she wrote:

> In a place in the middle of England, I had to help a family who one evening thought for entertainment they would try the ouija board. It began well, but then 40 minutes into the communication, they asked the spirits to prove they were spirit. The light in the hallway suddenly was lifted out of the ceiling and hurled at the

family as they sat around the board. The tap in the kitchen was suddenly turned on, and the table where they sat began to shake. The family ran from their home which was why I was invited to walk with them into their house. I could see where the light bulb had been smashed. The water was still running and had damaged lots of things. This makes you wonder why people want to play with this. In many cases, it is people who have no respect for spirit communication and treat it as a parlour game.

Positive communications

There have, however, been instances where working with a ouija board led to the opening of psychic or mediumship abilities that led to positive long-term communications.

Dr. Horace Westwood was a Unitarian minister in Canada at the beginning of the 20th century. After becoming interested in spirit contact, he bought a ouija board. Nothing happened until 11-year-old Anna, the daughter of his cousin, began to touch the planchette. When she was blindfolded it spelled out long detailed messages even when the letters were randomly scattered. Within a week, Anna developed the power of automatic writing. Not long after the automatic writing began, Anna wrote messages from two apparently different sources. One signed her name 'Ruth' and the other 'Ralph.' They claimed to have been stenographers in Washington, D.C., in the employment of the US Government, and said they had died together about two years earlier while in their late twenties. Under their influence, Anna soon was able to type quickly while blindfolded (she had never learned to type); read a book that was placed in the next room; play chess and play the piano far better than she had previously been able to; talk about hunting and trapping with professionals although she had never learned about them. She did these things while fully conscious when 'the spirits' were present. When the spirit team left six years later, all these abilities disappeared (Westwood, 1949).

Pearl Curran and her friend, Emily Grant Hutchings, were married women in Illinois, USA, with time on their hands in 1912. Mrs. Hutchings bought a ouija board and took it to Mrs. Curran's house, and they began regular sessions with it. Nothing much came through for about a year. But from July 1913, a sudden rush of communications began with the message: "Many moons ago I lived. Again I come. Patience Worth my name. If thou shalt live, so shall I."

As Pearl became more and more interested in the numerous messages the women were receiving from Patience, she began spending more time on the ouija board. However, it soon became clear that the ouija-board method was far too slow to deal with the huge amount of material she was receiving. So Pearl tried automatic writing (*see* Chapter 14). Between 1912 and 1919, she dictated through the board five million words – epigrams, poems, allegories, short stories and full-length novels. Her collected works fill 29 bound volumes; 4,375 single-spaced pages. There were five full-length novels, the most successful being *The Sorry Tale,* a 300,000-word story of the earthly life of Jesus. It was reviewed as follows in *The New York Times* (8 July 1917):

This long and intricate tale of Jewish and Roman life during the time of Christ is constructed with the precision and accuracy of a master hand. It is a wonderful, a beautiful and noble book.

'Patience Worth' also wrote over 2,500 poems. She won a national poetry contest in which 40,000 contestants submitted multiple entries. She was regularly published in America's most prestigious annual poetry anthology. One of her greatest admirers was the publisher William Reedy, who was on the award-selecting committee for the first Pulitzer Prize for poetry. He was a regular visitor to Pearl's house, and he said of her poems:

They contain passages of bewitching beauty, of rare high spirits, of pathos. It does not equal Shakespeare or Spencer. It is not so great as Chaucer. But if there be any intelligences communicating

poems by ouija board or otherwise... it is good poetry, better poetry than we find in our magazines as a rule – poetry with a quality of its own (Hunt, 1985: 31).

The Seth books

Another famous literary relationship which began with ouija communication was that between a spirit named Seth, and Jane Roberts
and her husband. On the Roberts' fourth try of the ouija board in 1963,
an entity introduced himself as 'Frank Withers'. He said he had most
recently lived on earth as an English teacher and had died in 1942.
Later he explained that he preferred to be called 'Seth', and had a special mission to help people better understand themselves and reality.

He appeared to Jane and her husband and began talking through
Jane while she was in trance. Through Jane, Seth has dictated several
bestselling books which have dealt with the nature of reality, reincarnation, dreams, astral travel and the nature of God. He has given step-by-
step advice to his readers on the development of meditation techniques
and ESP. He has diagnosed illnesses, correctly described the contents
of buildings and rooms many miles away, and materialized as an apparition in well-lit settings (see Roberts, 1974, 1994, 1997a, 1997b).

What is most interesting about the ouija board literature is the
extent to which it is consistent with other areas of afterlife research.
This includes research with mediums, with electronic voice phenomena, with instrumental transcommunication, poltergeists and
physical mediumship. It is simply impossible to explain the different
kinds of communication that one receives when entities of different
levels are communicating – often in quick succession – purely on
the basis of the unconscious of an individual or a group.

Dr. Alan Gauld and 'drop-in' communicators

As well, there have been a number of startling cases of 'drop-
in communicators' coming through the board. These are entities

which give correct and verifiable details of names, addresses, occupations and sometimes a large number of other details. Dr. Alan Gauld investigated 37 of these. They had appeared among 240 alleged communicators in a ouija board Circle which met in a Cambridgeshire home between 1937 and 1954 (Gauld, 1966–72: 273–340).

In his paper for the Society for Psychical Research, Dr. Gauld explains how he followed up the details of some of these, in some cases more than 20 years after the original communications had been made. In four cases, he had been able to verify a significant number of details.

In the case of Gustav Adolf Biedermann, he was able to verify the personality of the communicator and the following specific information:

> I lived in London
> My house was Charnwood Lodge
> Nationality German
> Correct name Adolf Biedermann
> I was always known and called Gustav
> I was a Rationalist
> I was turned 70 when I passed away
> I had my own business
> I am associated with the London University
> I passed over a year ago

Dr. Gauld points out that in these cases the sitters did not seek publicity or money. He was convinced that there was no way they would have gone to the trouble of accessing the public documents he was able to obtain. And if they had gone to the trouble of researching many sources, why would they leave them for more than 20 years on the off-chance that somebody would happen to investigate?

Chapter 24

POLTERGEISTS

Minds are like parachutes. They only function when they are open.

LORD THOMAS DEWAR

The word 'poltergeist' is from German and means 'noisy spirit'. Research into this area from the United States, Brazil, England, Scotland, Ireland, Canada, Finland, Germany, France, Italy, Malta, India and Russia and other countries shows that poltergeists really exist and behave in the same way.

Thousands of cases

There have been thousands of poltergeist incidents recorded. Many people have seen solid objects flying in the air, huge kitchen cabinets levitating, plates, glasses and clothing set on fire. Often stones are thrown to break windows. Sometimes, human voices are heard shouting obscenities. In the most extreme cases, scratches, cuts and bite marks can appear on people and human forms can be seen. Usually, they stop after a few months.

Michael Gross, a British writer, has written a scholarly annotated bibliography of 1,111 sources about poltergeist cases from different countries (Gross, 1979). Colin Wilson has produced a very easy to read and comprehensive 382-page book packed with cases. It is called *Poltergeist: A Classic Study in Destructive Hauntings* (Wilson, 2009). Guy Playfair's book, *This House is Haunted,* is an excellent description of an English case – the Enfield poltergeist.

Sometimes, experienced police officers have witnessed and testified to this poltergeist phenomenon that cannot be explained other than by a disturbed intelligence from the afterlife. Many times, professional mediums were able to contact the poltergeist who was able to explain why it was disturbed.

In Britain

One of Britain's most amazing poltergeist activities was at the Harper home in Enfield and lasted for more than 15 months in 1977, starting in August 1977 and ending in October 1978. Mrs. Harper, a divorcee, lived there with her four children, two boys and two girls, aged 7 to 13.

The disturbances which did not come from physical-human origin were witnessed by a number of different people with different backgrounds and different religious beliefs, including skeptics. There were police, politicians, psychologists, psychiatrists, journalists and social workers who all reported the poltergeist activities.

Two long-term investigators of the case were a writer, Guy Lyon Playfair – an experienced observer of poltergeist activities in Brazil – and Maurice Grosse, a motivated member of the Society for Psychical Research (SPR). Playfair and Grosse estimated that over 2,000 inexplicable incidents were observed by at least 30 witnesses.

Some of the activities of this particular poltergeist included:

- throwing household items around. Chairs were smashed, children's toys were seen flying in the air, thrown from an invisible source
- lighting fires
- draining the power out of the journalist's camera and other electronic batteries, immediately after the batteries had been charged

185

- throwing an iron grille from the bottom of the fireplace across the room narrowly missing Jimmy, one of the Harper boys
- ripping a heavy gas fire out of the wall.

One of the poltergeists replied to an investigator that he was "Joe Watson". Asked the reason for the activity, the poltergeist answered: "I was sleeping here" – implying everybody else was a trespasser!

A hollow appeared on one of the pillows – as if an invisible head was resting there. This was witnessed by the investigator, Guy Playfair. Voices saying "F--- off you", "I was sleeping here", and, "I like annoying you" were heard directed towards Playfair.

In the United States

Thousands of poltergeist cases have been reported in the United States. In one well-attested case, police were called to the home of Mrs. Beulah Wilson of Pearisburg, Virginia, on 19 December 1976. The police had ignored her previous complaints about a poltergeist but when they went into the house they witnessed the destructive behaviour of some invisible intruder. Dishes, wooden chairs and other household items were smashed. In this particular incident, the police witnessed the amazing sight of a 200-pound kitchen cabinet floating in the air without any means of support (*The Geneva Times*, 6 January 1977).

In Germany

A most powerful poltergeist activity occurred in a lawyer's office in the Bavarian town of Rosenheim in 1967.

The poltergeist activity centered around a young 18-year-old secretary, Annemarie Schneider. One morning, when she first got the job at the office, she walked down the entrance hall. Witnesses stated that:

- the hanging lamp started to swing
- the lamp in the cloakroom started to swing, too

- a bulb directly above her exploded.
- the fluorescent lighting went out in the next room.

At other times:
- loud bangs were heard
- all the lights in the office went out at the same time
- electrical fuses would blow without any cause
- cartridge fuses ejected themselves from the sockets
- all four telephones would ring simultaneously with no one on the line
- calls were frequently cut or interrupted for short periods
- telephone bills suddenly soared to very high levels
- developing fluid in the photostatic copiers would often spill out without any disturbance
- investigating technicians captured swinging lamps and frames on cameras
- physicists F. Karger and G. Zicha could not find anything wrong with the electrical and other material things in the office
- drawers were witnessed opening by themselves
- twice, a 400-pound cabinet was seen to move by itself.

Professors, journalists, police and other witnesses testified to the poltergeist phenomenon. Professor Hans Bender, a parapsychologist who also investigated this special poltergeist, stated that the poltergeist phenomenon was centered around Annemarie. When Annemarie had to leave to work somewhere else, the poltergeist phenomenon stopped abruptly.

Elsewhere, in 1969 in Nicklheim Germany, it was reported that parascientists investigated apportations – the moving of solid objects 'by themselves' from one place to a different place. Parascientists communicated with this particular poltergeist and instructed it to remove perfume bottles from one room to be taken outside. Soon afterwards, in the presence of many witnesses, these bottles were seen falling from the sky.

The materialist explanation

Beginning with Frank Podmore's book *On Poltergeists* in 1887, materialists have consistently argued that they are caused either by fraud or by the 'unconscious energy' of the person at the centre of the disturbance. Professor William Roll, in his book *The Poltergeist* (1972), claimed that the cause was a psychologically disturbed individual, usually a child at the time of puberty. The person is called 'the focus'. He called this 'recurrent spontaneous psychokinesis' (RSPK) and claimed it had nothing to do with spirits.

While this 'exteriorization of energy' may be part of the cause, it is clearly not the whole story. It does not explain why no poltergeist activity occurs in the overwhelming majority of houses inhabited by adolescents reaching puberty, most of whom experience sexual frustration and anger. If the energy of young people at puberty is the cause of poltergeist activity, then more than half of the world where early teenagers reside would be pestered by poltergeist activity.

Nor does the materialist theory explain:

- poltergeist activity usually lasting only for a relatively short time (on average 2–6 weeks) whereas puberty and the supposed sexual frustration goes on for a number of years
- materializations of goods, and ability to start a fire
- apparitions
- the voices of mature-aged persons being heard
- very heavy furniture being lifted
- poltergeist stone-throwing which occurs in many countries
- poltergeist capacity to accelerate vibrations of solid objects and transport these objects into a different house
- verbal or code responses by the poltergeist to questions and commands
- some poltergeist activities being extremely vindictive and harmful
- some poltergeist utterings being disgustingly filthy and obscene

- some poltergeists exhibiting personalities of vicious older males
- some poltergeists being gentle and even playful
- poltergeist activity immediately ceasing once the entity is contacted through a gifted medium and persuaded to move on.

A kind of physical mediumship

Many of the actions seen in poltergeist phenomena are also seen in physical mediumship. The laboratory experiments conducted by Sir William Crookes with medium Daniel Dunglas Home remain to this day the only major laboratory study of macro psychokinesis ever undertaken. Professor Charles Tart in his chapter on Psychokinesis says that Crookes observed:

> ... major movements of physical objects occurred under good observation in hundreds of case.... Alas, we don't seem to have a D. D. Home around nowadays! (Tart, 2009: 151–157).

We do know that many physical mediums were at the centre of poltergeist activity when they were in the early stages of developing their mediumship:

- Daniel Dunglas Home was thrown out of his home by his aunt at age 17 when furniture started moving on its own near him (Lamont, 2005)
- Florence Cook at age 15 was sacked from her position as an assistant school teacher because in her presence books and pencils flew around, chairs kept following her, and tables were moving on their own (Fodor, 1934)
- Brazilian medium Mirabelli was sacked from his job as a shoe salesman at age 23 because the shoes kept jumping off the racks
- British medium/healer Matthew Manning from the age of 11 was at the centre of poltergeist activity – various items were moved

or disappeared, there were loud knocking and creaking sounds, objects flew violently around the house, and signatures of dead writers appeared on his bedroom wall. Matthew later learned to channel his energies into healing and the phenomena stopped (Owen, 1974).

We also know that some spirits have admitted to causing poltergeist-like phenomena when they wanted to get attention. Bishop James Pike writes in his book, *The Other Side* (1969), about his experiences after his son, Jim Jr., committed suicide. Shortly after his son's death, Pike says that books vanished and reappeared, safety pins opened indicating the approximate hour of his son's death. Half the clothes in a closet were disarranged and heaped up and the air conditioning was turned up high the way his son had liked it. When he had a session with trance medium Ena Twigg, his son came through and said: "I came to your room, I moved books, I knocked on the door – came to your bedside – you dreamt about me and spoke to me" (Twigg, 1972: 126). After this communication the disturbances stopped.

Dr. Ian Stevenson in his paper "Are Poltergeists Living or Are They Dead?' (1972) presents three cases to show that sometimes poltergeists are caused by spirits of the dead. Some of the points where he suggests a spirit is the cause include cases where:
- objects seem to be carried and deposited gently
- the subject is disadvantaged or injured by the phenomena
- meaningful responses are obtained from raps
- apparitional and visual phenomena often occur early and abundantly
- communications come through mediums from apparent spirit personalities
- the phenomena ceases upon intercession, placation or exorcism.

In the introduction to the most recent edition of his book *Poltergeist: A Classic Study in Destructive Hauntings* (2009), Colin Wilson explains that he finally accepts the spirit explanation. He says that he was influenced by respected psychic investigator Guy Lyon Playfair, and by British psychic investigator Montague Keen, who both gave him examples of poltergeist cases caused by spirits. Wilson also claims that following the sudden death of 300,000 people from the tsunami in Indonesia, Sri Lanka, Thailand and other neighbouring nations in 2004, poltergeist phenomena were in 'plague' proportions. This he says was a clear indication of spirits not able to move on.

Chapter 25

XENOGLOSSY

I came across this patient in hospital (a blue-eyed blonde), in the hospital bed, coming out of anaesthetics speaking in the Italian language. She said she never learnt the Italian language, she never had Italian friends and she never went to Italy.

PETER RAMSTER

PAST LIFE RESEARCHERS AND FILM MAKER

One of the most amazing psychic phenomena is xenoglossy; the ability to speak or write a foreign language a person has never learned. It comes up during trance mediumship, writing mediumship, Independent Voice mediumship and in past life regressions.

Fraud, genetic memory, telepathy and cryptomnesia (the remembering of a foreign language learned earlier in life) are sometimes suggested as causes. But when all these possibilities are eliminated, two other explanations are left. Either memories of a language learned in a past life or communication with a discarnate entity – a spirit person.

There are many cases on record of adults and children speaking and writing languages which they have never learned. Sometimes this happens spontaneously. More often, it occurs while the person is under hypnosis or in an altered state of consciousness. In some cases, it is only a few words remembered, but in other cases, the person becomes totally fluent. In some cases, they are able to talk with native speakers or speak in obscure dialects which have not been used for centuries.

- Dr. Morris Netherton reports one case of a blonde, blue-eyed 11-year-old boy who under hypnosis was taped for 11 minutes as he spoke in an ancient Chinese dialect. When the tape was taken to a professor at the Department of Oriental Studies at the University of California, it turned out to be a recitation from a forbidden religion of Ancient China (Fisher, 1986: 202)

- American medium George Valentine under trance conducted séances in Russian, German, Spanish and Welsh. The Brazilian medium Carlos Mirabelli spoke and wrote long technical documents in more than 30 languages including Syrian and Japanese in the presence of scientists and crowds of up to 5,000 (Lazarus, 1993: 121)

- In 1977, doctors at a state penitentiary in Ohio, USA, discovered that a convicted rapist named Billy Mulligan had become possessed by two new personalities, both of whom communicated in a different language. Mulligan was born and raised in the USA and spoke no foreign languages. But when taken over by Abdul, Mulligan could read and write in perfect Arabic; as Rugen he spoke perfect Serbo-Croat (Lazarus, 1993: 83).

The most obvious explanations of these kinds of cases are either deliberate fraud or that the person concerned learned the language in early childhood without being aware of it. Careful investigators always take care to thoroughly investigate these two possibilities.

Dr. Ian Stevenson

Dr. Ian Stevenson was a leading, much-respected scientist in the United States. He did specialized research in this area and his book *Xenoglossy* (Stevenson, 1974) is one of the leading scientific studies.

193

In it, he documents a study he made of a 37-year-old American woman. Under hypnosis, she experienced a complete change of voice and personality into that of a male. She spoke fluently in the Swedish language – a language she did not speak or understand when in the normal state of consciousness.

Dr. Stevenson's direct involvement with this case lasted more than eight years. The study involved linguists and other experts and scientists who meticulously investigated every alternative explanation.

Fraud was ruled out for a number of reasons which Stevenson outlines in his study. The subject and her physician husband were thoroughly investigated. Both the husband and wife were considered by their local community to be honest and decent, and their behaviour exemplary. Certainly, there was no motive for personal profit. On the contrary, they experienced a great deal of inconvenience to fully complete the study over many years. They did not want publicity and agreed to the publication of the study only if their names were changed to protect their privacy.

Cryptomnesia – the recollection of a foreign language learned in the earlier years of a person's life – was also ruled out. Years of investigation of the subject failed to raise any possible suggestion that either she or her parents had learnt the Swedish language in her younger years. Nor had she associated with anyone Swedish.

Another case Stevenson investigated with equal care was reported in the July 1980 edition of the *Journal of the American Society for Psychical Research*. It involved an Indian woman named Uttar Huddar. At the age of 32, she suddenly took on the personality of a housewife of West Bengal in the early 1800s. She began speaking Bengali instead of her own language, Marathi. For days or weeks at a time, speakers of Bengali had to be brought in to enable her to communicate with her own family.

Author Lyall Watson describes a case of a ten-year-old child, an Igorot Indian living in the remote Cagayon Valley in the Philippines. The child had never had any contact with any language or culture other than his own. Yet, under trance conditions, the child communicated freely in Zulu, a language he could not have even heard. Watson only recognized it because he had spent his early life in Africa (cited by Lazarus, 1993: 84).

Peter Ramster, an Australian psychotherapist, has documented several thoroughly investigated cases. In his book *The Search for Lives Past* (Ramster, 1990: 227), he describes the case of Cynthia Henderson. Her only contact with the French language had been a few months of very basic instruction in Year 7 of high school. Yet, under hypnosis, she was able to carry on a long and detailed conversation in French with a native speaker who commented that she spoke without any English accent and in the manner of the 18th century.

In some cases, subjects under trance have communicated in languages no longer in use or known only to a handful of experts. Dr. Joel Whitton cites the case of Harold Jaworski who under hypnosis wrote down 22 words and phrases which he 'heard' himself speaking in a past Viking life. Working independently, linguists identified and translated ten of these words as Old Norse and several of the others as Russian, Serbian or Slavic. All were words associated with the sea (Whitton and Fisher, 1987: 210).

In 1931, a young English girl from Blackpool, known as Rosemary in the files of the Society for Psychical Research, began to speak in an ancient Egyptian dialect under the influence of the personality of Telika-Ventiu who had lived in approximately 1400 BC. In the presence of Egyptologist Howard Hume, she wrote down 66 accurate phrases in the Ancient Egyptian language of hieroglyphs, and spoke in a tongue unheard of outside academic circles for thousands of years (Lazarus, 1993: 85).

Pearl Curran, a medium from Saint Louis who was barely literate, began to write in astonishingly accurate Middle English. Under the guidance of a spirit entity she produced 60 novels, plays and poems, including a 60,000-word epic poem (Lazarus, 1993: 119).

In addition to fraud and cryptomnesia, two other 'explanations' are sometimes given by skeptics for xenoglossy. The first is 'telepathy'. Yet there has never been, anywhere in the world, one documented case of a person being able to speak a foreign language they learned by telepathy.

The other so-called explanation, 'genetic memory', is equally difficult to take seriously. The claim that somehow an Ancient Chinese language became embedded in the genes of an 11-year-old Caucasian American enabling him to speak the language is risible.

There are hundreds of cases of xenoglossy which have been documented. They involve modern and ancient languages from all over the world. Psychic investigators, such as the highly credible Dr. Ian Stevenson, used scientific method to investigate them and claim that there are only two possible explanations – either spirit contact or past life memory. In either case, they provide evidence for the afterlife. The onus shifts onto the skeptic to provide an alternative credible explanation. Thus far, no one has been able to do so.

Chapter 26

CHILDREN WHO REMEMBER PAST LIVES

These children supply names of towns and relatives, occupations and relationships, attitudes and emotions that, in hundreds of cases around the world, are unique to a single dead individual, often apparently unknown to their present families.

Tom Shroder
AUTHOR, *Old Souls*

There have been many cases of children from the age when they can first talk saying that they can remember another life. They talk about another house, other parents and families and about how they died. Sometimes, they become so unhappy that their parents arrange for them to go to the place where they say they lived before. In many cases, they are able to identify their previous relatives. Usually, the memories start to fade by the time the child is six or seven.

Shanti Devi

At the age of four in 1930 in Delhi, India, Shanti Devi began to mention certain details about clothes, food, people, incidents and places which surprised her parents. She mentioned the following which were later verified to be true. She:

- said she was Lugdi who used to live in Muttra, 128 kilometers away
- spoke some words in the dialect of that area without having learned it
- claimed to have given birth to a son and died ten days later, events which it was later found did happen to Lugdi
- recognized her husband of her former life, Kedar Nath, and spoke of many things they had done together (when she was taken to Muttra)
- was able to identify with accuracy a number of landmarks where she used to live, in her previous life in Muttra
- was able to correctly state how the furniture used to be placed when she used to live there in her home
- knew where, in her former life, she had hidden 150 rupees in an underground corner of a room for safe-keeping in the house. The husband of the previous life, Kedar Nath, confirmed that although the money was not there then, he had indeed found it there
- correctly identified Lugdi's parents in her former life, from a large crowd.

A committee of respected people from the town was organized to investigate her claim. It included a well-known politician, a lawyer and a managing director of a newspaper. None of the members of the committee knew Shanti or had any connection with her in any way. They were satisfied that Shanti knew things that she could not have obtained knowledge about by cheating, fraud or in any illegitimate way.

The case became internationally known and attracted the attention of many sociologists and writers. For example, in the 1950s, a Swedish writer, Sture Lonnerstrand, travelled to India to meet Shanti Devi and to continue to investigate for himself. He too came to the conclusion that the Shanti Devi case is a foolproof case for reincarnation (Lonnerstrand, 1998).

James Leininger

A recent American case has been featured in the book *Soul Survivor: The Reincarnation of a World War II Fighter Pilot* (Leininger, 2009) and video. James (born in 1998) began having nightmares at the age of two. He remembered little known facts about WWII planes. He knew that Corsairs would veer to the left on take-off and blow tires on landings. He knew that Japanese fighters were called 'Zekes' and bombers were called 'Bettys'. He said that he had shot down a Japanese plane called a 'Tony' (not a 'Zero'). He said his name had been James, that his ship was the *Natoma*, that he had been killed at Iwo Jima, and that his friend was Jack Larsen. He also said that the names of the three people who welcomed him into heaven were Billy, Leon and Walter.

When his father did some research, he found that many of the things James mentioned were true. A James Huston, Jr., had been a pilot serving on the *Natoma Bay*. He was one of 18 who had been killed in action and the only one who died at Iwo Jima. A man named Jack Larsen (still living) had been a friend of James Huston. Billie Peeler, Leon Connor and Walter Devlin were all pilots from the *Natoma Bay* who had been killed before James Huston.

James' mother, Andrea Leininger, used census and other records to find the family of James Huston, Jr. She learned a surviving sister, Anne Huston Barron, was living in Los Gatos, California. Anne was 84 years old when Andrea contacted her. Andrea set up a phone call between Anne and little James. In this conversation, James knew many personal details of James Huston's life, which Anne confirmed as accurate. She accepted James Leininger as the reincarnation of her brother and sent him her brother's remaining possessions. Examples of details he remembered:

- that he was the only one who called her Annie
- that they had a sister named Ruth
- that Ruth was four years older than Anne
- that their father was an alcoholic who had to go into rehab

- that their mother's name was Daryl
- that he and Annie had matching portraits done by the same artist.

Dr. Ian Stevenson

Dr. Ian Stevenson, professor of psychiatry at the University of Virginia Medical School, spent many years investigating claims by children that they could remember a past life. He interviewed over 4,000 children from the United States, England, Thailand, Burma, Turkey, Lebanon, Canada, India and other places. He checked documents, letters, autopsy records, birth and death certificates, hospital records, photographs, newspaper reports and the like before publishing his cases. All of Stevenson's books have been published by the University of Virginia Press, and are all in print. They include *Twenty Cases Suggestive of Reincarnation* (1974) and *Cases of the Reincarnation Type*, in four volumes (1978).

Imad Elawar

In Lebanon, Dr. Ian Stevenson went unannounced into a Druse village. He asked the villagers if they knew of any cases where children talked of past lives. He was referred – again without any prior warning – to the home of five-year-old Imad Elawar. Since the age of one Imad had been talking all the time about a former life in a village 25 miles away. As a one-year-old, his first words had been the names 'Jamileh' and 'Mahmoud'. At the age of two, he had stopped a stranger in the street and identified him as a former neighbour.

Stevenson interviewed the child and the parents and recorded over 57 separate claims about his former life. Then Stevenson went with the boy and his father to the other village to investigate the boy's claims. It took them several days to locate the boy's former house. No contact with the relatives had been made before the visit. However, Imad:

- was able to make a total of 13 correct statements and identifications, about his former life, including photographs of himself and his brother
- recognized photographs of his former uncle, Mahmoud, and his former mistress, a prostitute named Jamileh
- was able to point out details of where he had kept his rifle – a secret known only to his mother – and of how his bed had been arranged during his last illness
- stopped a stranger and had a long talk with him about their experiences together in their army service.

In all, Stevenson calculates that of the 57 claims Imad had made about his former life, 51 could be verified (Stevenson, 1978).

Physical evidence

Stevenson found that, in cases of violent death, the child may show a birthmark where he was knifed, shot or whatever caused his death. An example of one of Dr. Stevenson's birthmark cases is that of Ravi Shankar. He recalled being horrifically decapitated as a child (in his former life) by a relative who was hoping that he would inherit the child's father's wealth. The reborn child was found to have a birthmark encircling his neck. When his claim was investigated, it was found that the person he claimed to have been, did, in fact, die by decapitation.

A second case involves a child in Turkey who recalled being a robber. When he was about to be captured by the police, he had committed suicide by shooting himself with a rifle placed against the right underside of his chin. The child who claimed to remember this life was born with a very distinct mark under his chin. On further investigation, he was found to have another birthmark on top of his head. It was exactly where the bullet would have exited. When Dr. Stevenson was investigating this particular case in Turkey, an old man informed Stevenson that he remembered the incident and testified as to the condition of the shot body.

Another boy in India remembered a past life in which some of his fingers were cut off by a fodder-chopping machine. This boy was born with stumps for fingers.

In order to show that reincarnation cases occur in European cultures where fewer people believe in reincarnation, Dr. Ian Stevenson wrote his last book *European Cases of the Reincarnation Type* (2003). This book focuses on 40 different reincarnation research case studies in a Western setting. The book describes behaviours or statements made by people, most frequently during childhood, that would be completely foreign to their upbringing or genetic factors.

For example, David Llewellyn, born in England in 1970 and raised as a Christian, possessed a significant knowledge of Jewish religious and dietary customs. He also experienced nightmares and phobias with themes of concentration camps. When Ian Stevenson interviewed him, David said that he had past life memories in which he was being put into a pit as a young boy. He remembered looking up to the top of the pit where he saw another boy looking at him. He thought the boy was a companion who might save him. There were other bodies in the pit. This image recurred many times and David told Stevenson that he remembered the terrible odour of the camp (Stevenson, 2003: 82).

Dr. Jim B. Tucker, M.D., a child psychiatrist at the University of Virginia, became Dr. Stevenson's assistant. Whereas Stevenson's books were written for an academic audience, Tucker's book *Life Before Life* (2005) was written for the general public. He presents an overview of more than 40 years of research at the University of Virginia's Division of Personality Studies into children's reports of past life memories. He describes some of the findings, including unusual play, behaviour patterns, specific phobias, and birthmarks or birth defects. He also discusses objections to reincarnation: the few persons who actually claim to remember a past life, the fragility of memories, the population explosion, the mind-body problem, fraud, and others.

Tom Shroder, was an editor for the *Washington Post* who investigated Dr. Ian Stevenson's work as a skeptic. He travelled with him on his two final research expeditions to Lebanon and India, and then in the American South. Tom Shroder published his findings in *Old Souls: The Scientific Evidence for Past Lives* (1999).

Shroder admitted he was convinced that Stevenson's findings were genuine, and concluded:

- Dr. Stevenson conducted very thorough and unbiased investigations
- he had seen for himself the evidence, and even this small sample was compelling. The evidence included birthmarks which were closely related to the circumstances of the previous life
- Dr. Stevenson's research has been replicated elsewhere by other scientists
- the use of children as investigational subjects sharply reduced the difficulty of establishing the credibility of a past life remembrance.

When critics are confronted with this most convincing evidence for reincarnation, they try to explain the results away. They usually come up with the following explanations:

Fraud

Initially, one has to take into consideration the qualifications, the professionalism, the caliber and the integrity of Dr. Ian Stevenson, a scientist with impeccable credentials. He had a long track record as a professional scientific investigator, psychiatrist and psychoanalyst. In addition, years of interviewing thousands of witnesses gave him enormous practical experience in detecting fraud. He himself wrote textbooks on psychiatric examination and diagnostic interviewing (Stevenson, 1977).

It would be an impossible task for anyone to fake Stevenson's 2,500 recorded cases which usually involved parents, relatives, friends, witnesses – sometimes over 50 people and more. Then, there would have to be the staging of the emotions when there is a reunion of the

203

child with the loved ones of his former life. The staging of the intense emotions of these situations is outside the human capacity to structure 'on site'. Having interviewed thousands of 'reborn' children, Dr. Stevenson adds that, "small children are not easy to coach for the assumptions of the roles that do not seem natural to them".

Dr. Stevenson was always aware that the scientific investigations he conducted would be scrutinized in the minutest detail by other scientists, by outsiders and by those hostile to the idea of reincarnation. This is why he was so thorough in all he did. He publicly stated that he did not give money to any of the people involved. He consistently applied his policy that no payment was to be made for any testimony. There was very little publicity given to the cases and 'fame' was not used as an incentive to cooperate; for many years his work was not known in the West outside of academic circles.

Cryptomnesia

One claim is that, consciously or unconsciously, the reborn child must have read the information, or heard about it, or been told about it, but had forgotten it. Dr. Stevenson explains that, in many cases, he investigated, the information the children came up with was not known to anyone around them. Some of the children were only two years old and had had very limited contact with others. He said he had found children who began to talk about a past life when they only knew a few words.

Inherited Memory/Collective Unconscious?

One of the arguments most frequently expressed by the critics of past life memory is that the child has 'inherited memories'. This argument has fundamental flaws. If a person was remembering the life of one of his or her ancestors, there would have to be both a racial and geographic link. However, many people remember past lives as members of totally different races. For example, in one of Stevenson's European cases, a young boy born in Hungary showed memories of a past life in Africa. He said: "My wife and children and other people there are not like people here; they are all black and completely half naked" (Stevenson, 2003: 116).

Extrasensory perception?

Anyone who suggests that these children are tapping into the memories of living people would have to concede the existence of extrasensory perception (ESP), also known as telepathy. But skeptics have been arguing, and still argue, that ESP and telepathy do not exist! Either ESP exists or it does not exist.

Stevenson claims these children would have to have 'super ESP' to remember the things that they come up with. This is because in some cases, the children give significant amounts of information, extending the existing boundaries of all presently known cases of ESP. And ESP does not explain the cases of birthmarks and deformities. These children, according to Dr. Stevenson, often point to a mark or marks on their body and explain that is where they were shot or mutilated. Parents attest that these marks were present from infancy. Other children born with deformities or missing limbs or missing fingers claim that these deformities indicate what caused their previous deaths.

Chapter 27

PAST LIFE MEMORIES
IN DREAMS

There are some dreams which are directly related to psychic phenomena.

Dr. Arthur Guirdham

PSYCHIATRIST

A number of people have had dreams or nightmares about past lives producing evidence which was later verifiable. An English case that convinced many experts, including psychiatrist Dr. Arthur Guirdham, was that of Mrs. Smith. She was a perfectly sane, healthy, ordinary English housewife. However, she had for years been suffering from nightmares of being burned at the stake. In 1962, Mrs. Smith went to Dr. Guirdham in a hospital's outpatient department, where Dr. Guirdham worked as a psychiatrist. She was seeking treatment for a recurring nightmare. She had experienced it occasionally since her teens, but it was now coming two or three times a week. In her dream, she was lying on her back on the floor while a man approached her from behind. She did not know what was going to happen, but was absolutely terrified.

Although Dr. Guirdham remained calm and professional, he had to hide his surprise while listening to his new patient. This was because he had been having the same nightmare for more than 30 years. The doctor did not tell his patient about this. But after this meeting neither the doctor nor the patient had the nightmare again. Their meetings continued, though. Dr. Guirdham was certain there was nothing mentally wrong with his patient. He tried to find out more about her knowledge of the past. She gave him a list of names of people she said had lived in the 13th century and described things that happened to them. As a psychiatrist, Dr. Guirdham knew about claims of reincarnation but never had much interest in the subject. However, he decided to investigate the information Mrs. Smith gave him.

He found that the names given to him by his patient were accurate, though they were only mentioned in rare history records of the Middle Ages. Those records had been written in French and had never been translated into English. The people Dr. Guirdham's patient described were all members of the Cathar sect, a group that had flourished in southern France and northern Italy in the Middle Ages. Among other things, the Cathars believed in reincarnation.

Over time, Dr. Guirdham met more and more individuals, 11 in total, who had memories of their past lives living together in a Cathar group. None of the subjects were drugged or hypnotized. Past names and incidents simply appeared in their minds, said Dr. Guirdham.

Mrs. Smith also gave Dr. Guirdham copies of drawings and verses of songs she had written as a schoolgirl. Experts in Mediaeval French confirmed that she was writing in 'langue doc', the language of Southern France in the 12th and 13th centuries. She went on to astonish experts with her knowledge of the Cathars in Toulouse who had been persecuted by the forces of the Inquisition. She reproduced word for word in 1944 old French songs which were only discovered in French archives in 1967. She knew historical details which only came to light later, upon the most painstaking investigation such as:

- correct drawings of old French coins, jewellery, and the layout of buildings
- correct details of the family and social relationships of people who do not appear in textbooks but who were ultimately traced though the records of the Inquisition

- that an underground room of a certain church was used to hold religious prisoners
- details of rituals and religious dress.

Professor Nellie, the greatest living authority on the period, was very impressed. He advised Dr. Guirdham that in future when there was conflict between the accepted historical view and the memories of his patient, he should "Go by the patient" (Guirdham, 1978).

Dr. Guirdham later went on to discover several other people close to him who all shared the same memories. He documented them all in his book *The Cathars and Reincarnation*. He went on to lecture his colleagues in the British medical profession about 'Reincarnation and the Practice of Medicine' (Guirdham, 1969).

Nightmares are often the triggers that lead parents to investigate the possibility of a past life memory with children. Six-year-old James Leininger began having nightmares as often as four times a week when he would kick and scream with his feet up in the air. It appeared as though he was fighting with something trying to get out. The only way he could escape the nightmares was for his parents to shake him awake. "He would say, 'Airplane crash on fire, little man can't get out'," says his mother Andrea. It was his parents' efforts to resolve the nightmares that led them to therapist Carol Bowman.

Andrea took her advice and began to talk to James about his nightmares right after they happened. As a result, Andrea says, the nightmares decreased drastically and James began to consciously remember details of a past life and death as a World War II fighter pilot (B. and A. Leininger and K. Gross, 2009).

Chapter 28

PAST LIFE
REGRESSIONS

So as through a glass and darkly
The age long strife I see
Where I fought in many guises,
Many names – but always me.

GENERAL GEORGE S. PATTON
AMERICAN WORLD WAR II GENERAL

Past life regression simply involves placing a person under hypnosis and asking them to go back through their childhood to a time before they were born. In many cases, the person begins talking about his or her life or lives before the present lifetime, about their previous death, and about the time between lives including the planning of the present lifetime.

The main reason why at least some of these claims must be considered as evidence are:

- the regression frequently leads to a cure of a physical illness
- in some cases, the person regressed begins to speak an unlearned foreign language
- in some cases, the person being regressed remembers details of astonishing accuracy which, when checked out, are verified by the leading historians

209

- the emotional intensity of the experience is such that it convinces many formerly skeptical psychiatrists who are used to dealing with fantasy and imagined regressions
- in some cases, the alleged cause of death in an immediate past life is reflected by a birthmark in the present life.

Past life regressions are nothing new. Lieutenant Colonel Albert de Rochas (1837–1914) had been conducting regressions for many years before he published his book *Successive Lives* in 1911. In one interesting case, he regressed a subject, Marie Mayo, to her life as the wife of a French nobleman 12 months after the first detailed regression. He found that she gave exactly the same details as in the first regression.

By the 1930s, past life regression was being accepted by doctors who had previously been total skeptics, because it worked. As psychiatrist Dr. Alexander Cannon wrote:

> For years, the theory of reincarnation was a nightmare to me and I did my best to disprove it… Yet, as the years went by, one subject after another told me the same story in spite of different and varied conscious beliefs. Now, well over a thousand cases have been investigated and I have to admit that there is such a thing as reincarnation (Cannon, 1937).

Psychiatrists all over the world have found that regression works.

Dr. Gerald Edelstein, psychologist, writes:

> These experiences [past life regressions], for reasons I cannot explain, almost always lead to rapid improvements in the patient (Edelstein, 1981).

Well known clinical psychologist, Dr. Edith Fiore of the United States, says:

If someone's phobia is eliminated instantly and permanently by his remembrance of an event from the past [life], it makes logical sense that the event must have happened (Fiore, 1978).

Dr. Gerald Netherton, who was raised a fundamentalist Methodist, has successfully used the method on 8,000 patients. He was initially skeptical, but as a result of his experience, is now convinced of the effectiveness of past life regression. His patients, who included both priests and physicists, are almost always skeptical at first but this had no effect on the effectiveness of the treatment. He says:

Many people go away believing in reincarnation as a result of their experience... What is the logical answer? That it actually happened! (Netherton, 1978).

Dr. Arthur Guirdham, English psychiatrist, maintains that he has been a skeptic ever since he was nicknamed 'Doubting Thomas' as a boy. But after his experience of 44 years doing hypnotic regressions he claims:

If I didn't believe in reincarnation on the evidence I'd received I'd be mentally defective (Guirdham, 1978).

Dr. Helen Wambach was a skeptic who in 1975 undertook a major study of past life regressions in order to find out once and for all if there was any truth to reincarnation. By doing a scientific analysis on the past lives reported by her 10,000-plus volunteers, she came up with some startling evidence in favour of reincarnation:

- 50.6 per cent of the past lives reported were male and 49.4 per cent, female – this is exactly in accordance with biological fact
- the number of people reporting upper class or comfortable lives was in exactly the same proportion to the estimates of historians of the class distribution of the period.

- the recall by subjects of clothing, footwear, type of food and utensils used was better than that in popular history books. She found over and over again that her subjects knew better than most historians – when she went to experts on obscure facts, her subjects were invariably correct.

Her conclusion was: "I don't believe in reincarnation – I know it!" (Wambach, 1978).

It may surprise the reader that Russian psychiatrists are also using past life regression. Dr. Varvara Ivanova, held in high esteem by Russian scientists and writers, is only one of a number of psychiatrists who are successfully using past life regression for therapy (Whitton and Fisher, 1987).

Peter Ramster

Of the research we have done over the years, the most impressive hypnotherapist we have come across in showing how past life regression is linked with reincarnation is psychologist and former skeptic Peter Ramster from Sydney, Australia. The following information is taken from one of Ramster's key works, *In Search of Lives Past* (1990), and from a speech he gave to the Australian Hypnotherapists ninth National Convention at the Sydney Sheraton Wentworth Hotel on 27 March, 1994, and from the films he made on reincarnation.

In 1983, he produced a stunning television documentary in which four women from Sydney, who had never been out of Australia, gave details under hypnosis of their past lives. Then, accompanied by television cameras and independent witnesses, he took them to the other side of the world. One of the subjects involved was Gwen MacDonald, a staunch skeptic before her regression. She remembered a life in Somerset between 1765–82. When she was taken there, she confirmed many facts about her past life in Somerset that she would not have been able to get out of a book. When she was taken in a blindfold to the area, she:

212

- knew her way around perfectly although she had never been out of Australia
- was able to correctly point out in three directions the location of villages she had known
- was able to direct the film crew as to the best ways to go – far better than the maps
- knew the location of a waterfall and the place where stepping stones had been. The locals confirmed that the stepping stones had been removed about 40 years before
- pointed out an intersection where she claimed that there had been five houses. Enquiries proved that this was correct and that the houses had been torn down 30 years before and that one of the houses had been a 'cider house' as she claimed
- knew correctly names of villages as they had been 200 years ago even though on modern maps they do not exist or their names have been changed
- knew people who were found to have existed – one was listed in the records of the regiment she claimed he belonged to
- knew in detail of local legends which were confirmed by Somerset historians
- used correctly obscure, obsolete West Country words no longer in use, no longer even in dictionaries, words like 'tallet' meaning a loft
- knew that the local people called Glastonbury Abbey 'St Michaels' – a fact that was only proved by reading an obscure 200-year-old history book not available in Australia
- was able to correctly describe the way a group of druids filed up Glastonbury Hill in a spiral for their spring ritual, a fact unknown to most university historians
- knew that there were two pyramids in the grounds of Glastonbury Abbey which had long since disappeared
- correctly described in Sydney carvings that were found in an obscure old house 20 feet from a stream, in the middle of five houses about one and a half miles from Glastonbury Abbey

- had been able to draw in detail, in Sydney, the interior of her Glastonbury house which was found to be totally correct
- described an inn that was on the way to the house. It was found to be there
- was able to lead the team direct to the house which is now a chicken shed. No one knew what was on the floor until it was cleaned. However, once cleaned, the floor revealed the stone that she had drawn in Sydney
- knew the answers to all the questions that locals asked her such as the local problem with a big bog where cattle were often lost.

Cynthia Henderson, another subject of Peter Ramster, remembered a life during the French Revolution. When under trance, she:

- spoke in French without any trace of an accent
- understood and answered questions put to her in French
- used dialect of the time
- knew the names of streets which had changed and were only discoverable on old maps.

Peter Ramster and other regressionists have many other documented cases of past life regression which, in very clear terms, constitute technical evidence for the existence of the afterlife.

The drowned submariner

Miles Edward Allen, the founder of the Association for Evaluation and Communication of Evidence for Survival (AECES), has compiled a list of the Top 40 most convincing cases of evidence of Survival. He assigns each case a weighting (out of 100) based on the reliability of the report and the credibility of the witnesses. He then gives it a score (out of 200) on how likely it is that the information could only have come from the afterlife. These cases make compelling reading (see http://www.aeces.info/Top40/top40-main.shtml).

214

Case number three on his list with a score of 281 out of 300 is that of Bruce Kelly. He was cured of a fear of water and enclosed spaces when he had a past life regression with hypnotherapist Rick Brown. Under hypnosis, Kelly relived his death as a submariner named James Edward Johnston who had drowned in 1942 on board the USS *Shark*. Three full names of crewmen, the ship's name and number, the date of the sinking, and scores of other details were given and confirmed. As well, the client went through extreme discomfort while reliving Kelly's death and afterwards was cured of all symptoms. This case and many others are discussed in Allen's two books *The Survival Files* and *The Afterlife Confirmed*.

Between lives

Dr. Joel Whitton, a professor of psychiatry at the University of Toronto medical school, spent thousands of hours hypnotizing a group of 30 people, many of whom did not believe in reincarnation. Every person in the group reported numerous past lives, some as many as 20. All reported that people live lives of both genders and that the purpose of life is to evolve and learn.

In his book *Life Between Life* (1986), he described what happened when he regressed his subjects to the period between lives. All described it as a dazzling, light-filled realm in which there was no time or space. They claimed that they reviewed their past life and planned their future lives. One subject, a man suffering with a serious, life-threatening kidney disease, learned that he had chosen the illness before being born. This, he said, was to punish himself for a past-life moral violation. However, dying from this illness was not part of his plan. He described arranging an encounter with someone or something, before coming into this life, which would trigger his memory and enable him to heal both his guilt and his body. Soon after starting his sessions with Dr. Whitton, he experienced a miraculous complete recovery (Whitton and Fisher, 1986).

Dr. Brian Weiss

Dr. Brian Weiss was a traditional psychotherapist and, at the age of 35, was a professor at the University of Miami medical school. He was publishing papers and becoming a nationally recognized expert on psychopharmacology and was not interested in anything mystical, philosophical or spiritual.

One patient changed all that. Weiss calls her 'Catherine' in his first bestselling book, *Many Lives, Many Masters* (1988). He had been using routine psychotherapy to treat her. After 18 months with little improvement, Weiss told her while she was under hypnosis: "Go back to the time from which your symptoms arise". She did. Back to the year 1863 BC when she was a 25-year-old named Aronda.

But Catherine also went to the space between lives and was able to give Dr. Weiss detailed information about his own family and his dead son. This was information that she could not have known by any normal means.

Dr. Michael Newton

When Dr. Michael Newton began regressing his clients back in time to access their memories of former lives, he became interested in seeing into the spirit world through the eyes of clients who are in a state of deep hypnosis. Around 7,000 clients over more than 20 years claimed to be able to tell him what their soul was doing between lives. This began when he was treating a middle-aged client for feelings of intense loneliness and told her to go back to the source of the problem. She burst into tears and said that she could see all the friends that she was missing in the spirit world which was her real home. His book, *Journey of Souls* (1994), presents ten years of his research and insights to help people understand the purpose behind their life choices.

Dr. Newton claimed that finding their place in the spirit world and their plan for their current life was far more meaningful to his patients than recounting their former lives. He claims that he learned

216

how to take patients to the superconscious mind, the highest centre of wisdom and perspective. His follow-up book, *Destiny of Souls* (2000), continues this work.

Edgar Cayce

Whereas Dr. Weiss and Dr. Newton hypnotized their clients to access the superconscious state, Edgar Cayce was able to hypnotize himself. He seemed to be able to consistently access information about rare and unusual holistic cures that was usually effective. For 43 years, he would go into a trance-like sleep by lying down, closing his eyes and putting his hands across his stomach. Then, provided with the name and location of anyone in the world, he would be able to give specific advice on their heath, healing and life circumstances. He also claimed to be able to access information on the individuals' past and future lives.

Today on file at the Association for Research and Enlightenment, Inc. (A.R.E.), in Virginia Beach, Virginia, are copies of more than 14,000 of Edgar Cayce's 'readings'. These are available to the public and have been filed along with any follow-up reports received from the individuals who had asked for the readings. The majority of the readings deal with holistic health and the treatment of illness. Others deal with dreams and dream interpretation, ESP and psychic phenomena, oneness, philosophy and reincarnation, spiritual growth, meditation and prayer. Further details about his life and work are explored in the classic works *There Is a River* (1942) by Thomas Sugrue, *The Sleeping Prophet* (1967) by Jess Stearn, *Many Mansions* (1950) by Gina Cerminara, and *Edgar Cayce: An American Prophet* (2000) by Sidney Kirkpatrick.

General agreement

Dr. Michael Newton, Dr. Joel Whitton, Peter Ramster, Dr. Brian Weiss, Helen Wambach, Ruth Montgomery, Roger Woolger, Dr. Hans Holzer and Edgar Cayce all have found consistent information about such topics as the death experience, being welcomed into the afterlife by relatives, undergoing a period of healing/rest/integration, the life review, learning with a group, planning a future life and previewing it.

Chapter 29

QUANTUM PHYSICS AND THE AFTERLIFE

Those who recognize that significant discoveries in science are very often prompted by observations that do not fit expectations will find a stimulating challenge in accumulating evidence that it is possible to elicit psychic functioning in experiments with ordinary volunteers acting as subjects. Even more convincing results occur with specially selected subjects.

NOBEL PRIZE WINNER *PROFESSOR BRIAN JOSEPHSON*
& PROFESSOR JESSICA UTTS

There is a revolution going on in science. Over the last few decades, there has been a significant increase in research into quantum physics. This is the study of the characteristics of and relationships between subatomic particles and energies. Innovative, unorthodox physicists tell us this important research has a strong bearing on the understanding of the paranormal and the afterlife.

These physicists are discovering no conflict at all between physics and belief in the paranormal and the afterlife. Indeed, they are showing that the phenomena we now call 'paranormal' are normal and consistent with the laws of science.

Professor Fred Alan Wolf sums up this view when he writes:

There is evidence that suggests the existence of a non-material, non-physical universe that has a reality even though it might not as yet be clearly perceptible to our senses and scientific instrumentation. When we consider out-of-body experiences, shamanic journeys and lucid dream states, though they cannot be replicated in the true scientific sense, they also point to the existence of non-material dimensions of reality (Alan Wolf, 1998: 245).

British scientist Ron Pearson, in his article "Survival Physics", argues that survival of death is a natural part of physics and efforts to discredit evidence of survival after death are misplaced:

Since survival can be shown an essential and integral part of physics, the hope must be that the efforts still being made to discredit all evidence of survival will soon come to an end. This theory has achieved publication in Russian conference Proceedings (1&2) of 1991 and 1993 respectively, and in the peer-reviewed scientific journal *Frontier Perspectives* (3) in 1997. Furthermore, Professor Peter Wadhams, professor of Ocean Physics at Cambridge University, supported the theory during a joint broadcast on the American radio shows in 2001 (Pearson, 2005).

For more than a hundred years, numerous physicists have been at the forefront of psychic research. They have seen no inconsistency between science and the existence of the paranormal and the afterlife.

Sir Oliver Lodge, one of the greatest physicists of all time, accepted life after death after using his scientific genius to prove it. He was a founder of the Society for Psychical Research. I have a lot of respect for Sir Oliver Lodge and would like to provide a short quote from his lecture Linking Life After Death To Subatomic Physics (Lodge, 1933):

If, then, we can adduce any evidence that life or mental activity exists in space, and only sporadically makes itself evident by some material activity, the state of our present knowledge of physics renders our acceptance of the fact entirely harmonious. We have to do no violence to our physical conceptions if we admit the fact of survival. Life and mind never were functions of the material body, they only displayed themselves by means of the material organism.

Other notable physicists who investigated survival or psychic phenomena include Sir William Barrett, Dr. Harold Puthoff, Professor Russell Targ, Professor Dr. Ernst Senkowski and Dr. Thomas Campbell.

Dr. Harold Puthoff is a physicist and was director of the Institute for Advanced Studies at Austin, Texas. He has made a significant contribution towards empirically establishing the validity of psi, particularly in the field of 'remote viewing'. This was a term he jointly coined to describe a form of psychic functioning historically known as clairvoyance.

Professor Russell Targ is a physicist and author who pioneered the development of the laser. He also co-founded the Stanford Research Institute's investigation into psychic abilities in the 1970s and 1980s. He authored numerous books suggesting that the mind itself reaches to the far ends of the universe and that it is this 'non-local' quality, rather than any particular mechanism, that accounts for the remarkable data of parapsychology.

Professor Dr. Ernst Senkowski is a professor of physics and electronics who conducted intensive paranormal and afterlife research for over 20 years. Dr. Senkowski repeatedly obtained positive paranormal and 'afterlife' results.

Several physicists have recently published books arguing that materialist science is incomplete and, therefore, unable to adequately account for positive paranormal evidence. They urge the acceptance of a new paradigm or worldview which includes psychic phenomena and the existence of multiple universes including the so-called afterlife.

Dr. Amit Goswami is a former professor of physics at the Institute of Theoretical Sciences at the University of Oregon. He is currently a senior resident researcher at the Institute of Noetic Sciences. His book *Physics of the Soul: The Quantum Book of Living, Dying, Reincarnation, and Immortality* (2001) defines consciousness, not materiality, as the primary reality.

Professor John Bokris in his book *The New Paradigm: A Confrontation Between Physics and the Paranormal Phenomena* (2005) discusses the evidence for the paranormal, including telepathy, near-death experiences, out-of-body travel, mediumship, reincarnation, apparitions, possession, distant healing, and other phenomena. He concludes that other concepts such as the paranormal, theories about consciousness, and interconnectedness must be integrated into science to enable a superior understanding of reality.

His central proposal is that we are living in a 'synchronized universe,' one layer of which we see and interact with and are synchronized with. This is what we identify as the 'real' universe. There are other universes alongside this, he argues, which are just as real as this one. This, he states, "begins to offer a way to understand how the soul, the centre of human consciousness, can exist in a permanent form, surviving human death. It offers a useful beginning to a deeper understanding of the universe and of ourselves" (Bokris, 2005).

Another physicist, Dr. Claude Swanson, has collated the 'best evidence' illustrating the inadequacy of our present scientific paradigm. In his book, *The Synchronized Universe* (2003), he describes scientifically controlled remote viewing and ESP experiments. He also includes demonstrations of long-range healing, psychokinesis (mind over matter), scientifically controlled experiments in levitation, teleportation and out-of-body phenomena (OBE). He outlines numerous examples of these strange forces being demonstrated under rigorous scientific conditions, with odds of millions or even billions to one against chance. Dr. Swanson argues that there is a need for a new, truly 'unified field theory' which can explain and understand both science and consciousness.

In his book *Entangled Minds* (2006), Dr. Dean Radin states that those who think that science has no place for the paranormal do not know what they are talking about. He writes:

... new discoveries in science are forcing an expansion to ideas of who and what we are, and that those who are most hostile to this topic know little or nothing about the evidence (Radin, 2006).

Many leading scientists are independently making discoveries in areas such as remote viewing, homoeopathy, bio-electrography and healing through prayer. These are all areas that challenge traditional reductionist scientific thinking. Their findings support the new view of a world in which everything is interconnected in a pulsating energy field (McTaggart, 2001).

Rather than being lifeless matter, subatomic particles are being revealed as having consciousness. Michael Talbot describes an experiment by Aspect, Dalibard and Roger in 1982 which he predicted will be seen as the most important experiment of the 20th century:

Aspect and his team discovered that under certain circumstances subatomic particles such as electrons are able to instantaneously communicate with each other regardless of the distance separating them. University of London physicist David Bohm believed Aspect's findings imply that objective reality does not exist and that despite its apparent solidity, the universe is fundamentally a phantasm, a gigantic and splendidly detailed hologram (Talbot, 2000: 196).

Many other physicists are converting to the view that rather than being made of inert matter and energy, the universe is essentially consciousness. As Professor Jacob D. Bekenstein puts it:

... a century of developments in physics has taught us that information is a crucial player in physical systems and processes. Indeed, a current trend, initiated by John A. Wheeler of Princeton University, is to regard the physical world as made of information, with energy and matter as incidentals (Bekenstein, 2003: 61).

Global consciousness

Many scientists, like Dr. Llewellyn Vaughan-Lee, have claimed a connection between these discoveries and growing movements toward global consciousness such as ecology. Dr. Ervin Laszlo is the recipient of the highest degree in philosophy and human sciences from the Sorbonne, as well as of the Artist Diploma of the Franz Liszt Academy of Budapest. His numerous prizes and awards include four honorary doctorates. The author of 69 books and over 400 articles and research papers, his paper "New Concepts of Matter, Life and Mind" talks about the impact of the new sciences on global consciousness.

One of the leading organizations in the world which is exploring the evidence and the implications for unity consciousness is the Institute of Noetic Sciences. It claims that systematic inquiries into consciousness will help birth a new worldview that recognizes our basic interconnectedness and interdependence and promotes the flourishing of life in all its magnificent forms.

Science is not static. During the 19th century, it was generally accepted that atoms were solid substantial particles that could not be broken down any further. Quantum physics is demonstrating that what we think of as solid is mostly empty space. 'Matter' is, to use Einstein's term, 'frozen energy' (Ash and Hewett, 1994: 16–26) and we are all living in a universe that is essentially consciousness.

Professor Jessica Utts and Nobel Laureate Dr. Brian Josephson state that science needs to adapt to accommodate the evidence. They write:

What are the implications for science of the fact that psychic functioning appears to be a real effect? These phenomena seem mysterious, but no more mysterious perhaps than strange phenomena of the past which science has now happily incorporated within its scope (Utts and Josephson, 1996).

These physicists and other scientists – some of the most inspired and probing minds working in their fields – are stating that there is an overwhelming amount of evidence to support the paranormal and the afterlife.

The record confirms that those orthodox, negatively entrenched, materialist reductionist scientists who fail to explore quantum physics, have been unable to rebut the existing empirical evidence for the paranormal and the afterlife.

As established above, there are now many physicists around the world who have demonstrated clear verification of psi and the afterlife. When added to other overwhelming evidence presented in this work, quantum physics is a powerful tool in proving that consciousness survives physical death. I predict, that in years to come, quantum physics will be the revolutionary method of absolutely demonstrating survival after death.

Those who think they can rely on outdated science to support a materialist view of a universe without an afterlife and psychic phenomena are clearly misinformed.

Chapter 30

CLOSING STATEMENT: SUMMING UP THE EVIDENCE

Very shortly, we will be giving scientific explanations for every known psychic phenomenon.

A PROMISE MADE BY SKEPTICS IN AD 1900. WE ARE STILL WAITING

As of AD 2013, closed-minded skeptics:
- have failed to scientifically rebut the argument for the existence of just one psychic phenomenon
- have failed to prove that life after death does not exist
- have failed to show that skepticism itself is not subject to complete invalidation.

Their successes?
- they have been able to delay – but not stop – knowledge of psychic phenomena
- because of vested interests and huge monetary profits, they have been able to find enormously wealthy sponsors – orthodoxy and the materialists – to finance anti-psychic lobbyists at universities and in the media
- they have been able to unfairly and savagely censor publication of information about successful investigation of psychic phenomena

- some have lied, misrepresented, used vicious propaganda and malicious tactics to try to unfairly denigrate, defame and discredit the characters of some of the leading lights of science and literature, who have investigated and accepted psychic phenomena
- they have been able to obtain allies in the conservative establishment to protect taxpayers' funding in dead-end jobs, dead-end university research projects, dead-end materialist programsmes
- some have been able to infiltrate organized psychic research societies to deliberately neutralize any genuine psychic finding.

On the other hand, genuine psychic researchers:
- have obtained repeatable physical scientific evidence for psychic phenomena and the afterlife
- have attained unprecedented success in the dissemination of information about psychic phenomena throughout the world, particularly via the Internet
- are using high technology to show through EVP and ITC the existence of the afterlife and other psychic phenomena
- have been able to continuously refine the objective evidence for the afterlife, especially in the areas of EVP, ITC, laboratory induced phenomenon, the aura, poltergeists and in direct communication
- can attest that throughout the world more direct personal revelations from the afterlife are being made to millions about the existence of the afterlife.

There is dramatic growth in the acceptance of psychic phenomena and the afterlife. It is estimated that at least 90 per cent of the world's population accept the existence of some form of afterlife. We read that in Western countries more people are seeking the services of mediums and psychics than are going to church on Sundays.

The evidence presented in the previous chapters including EVP, ITC, computer analysis of voice prints, the psychic laboratory experiments, mediums, Frederic Myers Correspondences, proxy sittings, near-death experiences, out-of-body experiences, apparitions, materialization and mental mediumship, xenoglossy, poltergeists and reincarnation show conclusively that there is overwhelming proof for the existence of the afterlife.

All these phenomena can be explained by the participation of intelligences from the afterlife, or in the cases of the OBE and the NDE, by the fact that we do have an invisible etheric body within our physical body that becomes our true 'body' once we physically die.

The afterlife has nothing to do with religion or with beliefs or superstition. The afterlife is now scientifically established. Those who refuse to investigate or rebut the voluminous available evidence have no technical right or authority to deny its existence or to make any valid comments about it.

When materialists and closed-minded skeptics refuse to accept the evidence for the afterlife, I am reminded of a courtroom scene. Imagine that the police prosecutor in a case of murder has brought in a hundred witnesses. All of these witnesses are highly accredited scientists, doctors, lawyers, writers, psychiatrists, psychologists, physicists and many others. All of the witnesses state that they actually saw the accused pull the trigger and shoot the victim five times in the chest.

Then the defence lawyer stands up and argues the debunkers' argument:

- all the prosecution witnesses are hallucinating
- they were all hypnotized
- they are all in collusion with the prosecutor
- alternatively, all of these witness are projecting their own guilt onto the accused
- these witnesses exteriorized their own extra energy collectively which really killed the victim
- (and, if all else fails) it was super ESP.

From my experience, I find that the closed-minded skeptics are applying to evidence for the 'paranormal' a totally unrealistic standard which is different from the tests applied by the courts and by science in other areas.

1. The impossible-to-pass test

Over the last 150 years, psychic history has shown that there is a core group of critics who will not accept that psychic phenomena can exist. These closed-minded materialists apply a test that will guarantee the psychic phenomena being investigated will not be accepted under any circumstances.

The test, also called the "I will not believe in the afterlife even if you can prove it to me" test, is applied by those materialists working for the establishment who investigate psychic phenomena. As 'investigators' they become the prosecutors, judge and jury who make sure that those who are producing genuine psychic phenomena are accused of fraud or cheating.

2. Cartesian logic test

From the Catholic Jesuit, René Descartes, today ignored in many quarters. The Cartesian test is, "Doubt anything which can be doubted". The courts do not apply this test, the churches do not apply this test, and the materialists do not apply this test when testing their own beliefs.

3. Beyond-reasonable-doubt test

This is the test used by the courts to establish the guilt of a person charged with a criminal offence. The testimony of one reliable witness is enough to find someone guilty of murder.

4. On the balance of probabilities

This is another test used by the courts to establish the liability of parties in a non-criminal, civil matter. It is obviously a much less strict test than the criminal test of beyond reasonable doubt. The Church sometimes uses this test for its own beliefs since theology is subjective and personal. No one can test theology on the basis of beyond reasonable doubt. It is also the test usually used in medical research to test the safety of new drugs and in most areas of science.

5. *Prima facie* test

The 'on the face of it' test. This is a very weak test. Circumstantial evidence is permitted to pass this test. Courts use it in criminal committal proceedings – the court decides whether a *prima facie* case has been established for the matter to be sent to a full hearing. Indirect evidence, sometimes even hearsay evidence, will be allowed. This is the test being used by some disciplines, such as psychology. All introspective psychology is accepted on the basis that it can establish *prima facie* that it may be correct.

Many materialists keep on applying test number one – the impossible to pass test – to evidence for the afterlife while applying far lower levels of proof in the courts and in medical research.

In fact, there were those accused of murder who were executed on the testimony of just one credible independent witness – much less evidence than we have for the afterlife.

There is so much evidence for the afterlife which is objective, stunning in its consistency, and which taken as a whole amounts to technical, irrefutable proof. Materialists, debunkers, and closed-minded skeptics have NOT given a credible alternative explanation for any of the above-demonstrated afterlife phenomena.

In the absence of a credible alternative explanation, society has no alternative but to accept that the afterlife exists and that we will all inevitably experience it.

'Courtroom Science' and the Afterlife

It may shock some people to learn that litigation – court procedure – especially in cross-examinations, is just as important as physical science when it comes to proving the existence of the afterlife.

Cross-examination is more than just an 'art'. It has certain defined principles the way scientific method has. Normally, scientists conduct experiments and indicate what the results are. Then the scientist interprets the results and writes a paper which sometimes is peer-reviewed. But in controversial areas of science, the credibility and the prejudices of the scientists working in the field and the credibility of those who oppose their results become an urgent, critical issue. Testing the credibility, the prejudices and degree of expertise of an expert witness is a standard task for attorneys. They know that the outcome of many trials depends on the testimony of one expert witness.

When it comes to the issue of the evidence for the afterlife, the skeptical 'physical scientists' would be the so-called expert witnesses. They would be cross-examined on the extent of their knowledge and prejudices.

Critical to the legal procedure and something which is not disclosed in scientific reports, is whether the scientist refuses to answer critical testing questions. This is most vital because in the courtroom the scientist witness is sworn to tell the truth – and if the witness is caught lying or refuses to answer a question, the witness could go to prison. Here is a very brief example of a part of a hypothetical cross-examination of an anti-afterlife 'closed-minded' skeptic-scientist:

Attorney: Do you accept there is an afterlife, Yes or No…

Skeptic: No, there is no afterlife …

Attorney: That is your own personal opinion …

Skeptic: Yes …

Attorney: What evidence do you have, to prove that there is no afterlife?

Skeptic: I don't think there is any evidence for the afterlife.

Attorney: I did not ask if there was any evidence for the afterlife. I asked what evidence do YOU have to say the afterlife does not exist?

Skeptic (very quietly): I do not have any evidence saying the afterlife does not exist …

Attorney: Could you repeat that louder so that the members of the jury can hear you?

Skeptic (more loudly): I do not have any evidence saying the afterlife does not exist…

Attorney: That's much better. Are you aware that there has NEVER been a book written by a scientist or anyone that there is no or cannot be an afterlife?

Skeptic (hesitating): …. Yes, I'm aware of that. But…

Attorney: NO BUTS … that called for a Yes–No answer. Have you ever read books by highly credible scientists confirming that there is an afterlife?

Skeptic: There are no real books by scientists about the afterlife …

Attorney: Have you ever investigated the afterlife evidence yourself?

Skeptic: No, never …. I say there is no evidence…

Attorney: Have you read books by that brilliant scientist Sir Oliver Lodge on why he, after investigating the afterlife, accepted the evidence for the afterlife? Yes or no.

Skeptic: No, I have not…

Attorney: Have you read any of the books – mostly by scientists – which clearly explain the afterlife evidence: Professor Fontana's *Is There an Afterlife?*, and the books by Sir William Crookes, Sir William Barrett, Arthur Findlay (and some 50 other titles mentioned)?

Skeptic: (hesitating): No … I have not read any of the books you mentioned.

Attorney: NO, YOU HAVE NOT? Why then would you come to a conclusion about something of critical importance BEFORE you investigated?

Skeptic: (Not answering).

Attorney (looking at the judge): Could you tell this witness your Honor he has to answer the question…

Judge: Yes, yes … (to the skeptic). You must answer the question.…

Skeptic: (Still refuses to answer the question).

Judge: If you do not answer the question, I will hold you in contempt … which means you could be locked up until you decide to answer the question.…

I have put on my website three highly informative, entertaining and interesting hypothetical cross-examinations of two internationally known scientists and one flamboyant skeptic to show that cross-examination flushes out the truth about the afterlife evidence in a way conventional science cannot. I have added a qualification that I would be more than happy to hear from any attorney to show where, when, how and why the cross-examination is unfair. In some twelve months since I put these cross-examinations on my website, I received many positive responses from lawyers but not one negative response. To view, go to the left-hand column of my website: www.victorzammit.com

Chapter 31

VICTOR ANSWERS CLOSED-MINDED SKEPTICS

I have failed to find that a single person who ridicules the evidence for the Afterlife has given to the subject any serious and patient consideration.

SIR WILLIAM BARRETT
PHYSICIST

In sharing the results of our research into the afterlife, I have come across many reactions – from those who readily accept the afterlife as a belief to others who are skeptics and debunkers. An open-minded skeptic is someone who generally will not accept superstition or beliefs to explain physical or psychical phenomena. He or she will, however, accept scientifically and other objectively based results. As has been explained, all of the most famous psychic researchers began their investigations as open-minded skeptics.

I am on record for being a skeptic. I was not prepared to accept on 'blind faith' things I was told. I doubted, I questioned, I read, researched and investigated. I still consider myself an open-minded skeptic – but not in the specific and the particular issue of the afterlife because I thoroughly investigated it.

Like the many scientists who bothered to systematically investigate the afterlife, I too came to the irreversible conclusion that we do survive physical death. The evidence I was able to obtain myself for the existence of the afterlife is for me definitive, absolute, irrefutable and positively conclusive.

However, there is a small but powerful class of what are known as 'closed-minded skeptics.' They are also known as 'materialist debunkers'. These individuals have already made up their minds that everything is matter. Anything which suggests that their current view of the world is flawed gives them enormous anxiety. And, like the clergy in Galileo's time, they will refuse to consider even scientific information that contradicts their personal beliefs. They have changed the definition of 'skeptic' from 'one who doubts' to 'one who will never accept'. The term 'closed-minded skeptic' as used in this book refers to this group. They have fewer personal experiences of the paranormal because of the proved 'expectation effect'. Laboratory experiements show that subjects who say that they don't believe in psychic phenomena repeatedly get fewer positive results than those who say they do (Schmeidler and McConnell, 1958).

Experimenters who are hostile to psychic phenomena get negative results due to the 'experimenter effect'. This happens even when they use the same subjects and the same procedures as experimenters who are open-minded. The classic 'experimenter effect' was demonstrated by Professor Marilyn Schlitz and Professor Richard Wiseman (1997 and 1999). In collaborative studies into whether or not a person can detect when someone is looking at them from behind, the more objective Marilyn Schlitz obtained positive results whereas negatively inclined Richard Wiseman consistently obtained negative results. This could be due to deliberate or unconscious influencing of the subjects, a reluctance to do extensive trials, or a deliberate or unconscious misrepresentation of the results.

Dr. Rupert Sheldrake has written a number of papers on it and comments:

There is overwhelming experimental evidence that experimenters' attitudes and expectations can indeed influence the outcome of experiments (Sheldrake, 1999).

Afterlife and paranormal research is different from other areas of science where debate about a scientific principle is conducted between two groups of scientists who are each doing ongoing research. In afterlife research, we encounter opposition from 'armchair critics' who do little or no research themselves and do everything in their power to misrepresent the evidence. We have seen the growth of a small group of about 15 'professional' skeptics who have done little or no research themselves, but have been able to get attention in the media for ridiculing serious researchers.

Susan Blackmore Ph.D. claimed to have done "ten years of intensive research in parapsychology" without finding any evidence of the paranormal. Parapsychologist Rick Berger checked and found that she had done "a series of hastily conducted, executed and reported studies that were primarily conducted during a two-year period for her Ph.D. dissertation between October 1976 and December 1978. She published 21 papers over this period, seven of which showed statistically significant results in favour of Psi. The odds of being successful in seven out of 21 attempts by chance are one in 20,000" (Carter, 2012: 106–111).

Professor Richard Wiseman has been exposed by Rupert Sheldrake. Wiseman did a series of experiments to see if Rupert Sheldrake's work on Jaytee, a dog who knows when his owner is about to come home, could be replicated. Jaytee was at the window for 78 per cent of the time when his owner was on the way home. He was at the window four per cent of the time the owner was away. The sample size was small but the results were still significant. Wiseman had replicated Sheldrake's results.

However, much to Sheldrake's astonishment, in the summer of 1996 Wiseman went to a series of conferences announcing that he had refuted the 'psychic pet' phenomenon and later he appeared on a series of television shows claiming to have refuted Jaytee's abilities. How did he justify his conclusions? Simple: Wiseman used an arbitrary criterion for success in the experiment, a criterion that allowed him to ignore most of the data he gathered. If Jaytee went to the window 'for no apparent reason' at any time during the experiment, Wiseman simply ignored all the rest of the data and declared the experiment a failure (Carter, 2012: 116–117).

James Randi's ridiculous million-dollar challenge has also been exposed as a hoax, a pure publicity stunt (McLuhan, 2010). Before anyone can attempt the challenge, they have to 'pass' his own preliminary test. However, when Dr. Dick Bierman took up the challenge with an offer to demonstrate tests of precognition, Randi wrote back, "I will stay in touch as we consider your proposal". Dr. Bierman says that, apart from a few irrelevant emails, he never heard anything from him again (Carter, 2012: 124). The same thing happened when psychic Chris Robinson responded to the challenge and when homoeopath John Benneth applied.

Even arch-skeptic Ray Hyman admits that the challenge is meaningless by scientific standards which require multiple trials, complex statistical analysis, and replication – all of which would cost more than a million dollars.

Dr. Rupert Sheldrake claims that opposition to the existence of psychic phenomena is not based on healthy skepticism, but "from a belief that the existence of psychic phenomena is impossible; they contradict the established principles of science, and if they were to exist they would overthrow science as we know it, causing chaos and confusion" (Carter, 2012: p. ix).

Seven reasons why skeptics and cynics refuse to accept the powerful evidence for the afterlife and the paranormal

My experience also tells me that these closed-minded skeptics and cynics do not have the skills, competence and the ability to perceive the paranormal with true empirical equanimity in an objective, scientific balanced way. Here are seven reasons why this is so:

1. Rationalization through cognitive dissonance

'Cognitive dissonance' is a term used by psychologists to describe the discomfort that arises when people are confronted with information fundamentally inconsistent with their cherished beliefs. Evidence that contradicts beliefs raises anxiety, increases blood pressure, sweating, etc. Denial will follow. The materialist will become angry, hostile, and even aggressive. He/she will try to reduce anxiety by rationalizing beliefs and going into extreme *denial*.

2. Cathexis

Some people have a very powerful, usually unconscious, 'superglued' connection to an idea or a thing. There is a class of skeptics who are 'cathexed' to closed-minded skepticism. Because the connection is powerful and unconscious, they will attack their source of anxiety – the person who puts forward the evidence for the paranormal. So, one cannot use logic, intelligence, science or repeatable and objective evidence to try to reverse their cathexis.

3. Neurolinguistic Programming (NLP)

This states that when these skeptics are confronted with information which is fundamentally inconsistent with their own deeply cherished beliefs, the mind of the skeptic will *delete* that information. This is because the new information will give a great deal of anxiety to the skeptic. As with 'cognitive dissonance' above, the skeptic will experience anxiety, disturbance of his 'comfort zone'. This accounts for the skeptic going into complete *denial*. The more aggressive skeptics will even cheat, mislead and lie about the real situation.

4. Environmental programming

Environment determines perception. Usually the environment you were born in will shape how you see the world. If a Western skeptic from New York was born in India, more likely than not the skeptic would be a Hindu. If born to a radical, extremist Islamic family, the skeptic would be a Moslem. If born to an Orthodox Jewish family, the skeptic would be an Orthodox Jew. One needs to have special skills to rise above environmental conditioning and programming.

5. Established neural pathways

When you have a rigid belief system, the neurons in the brain fire in a certain defined network. So, if information (e.g., afterlife evidence) comes into the brain, those neural pathways will fire in the same old way and will not decode the new information. It's just like a filter. It's only when the skeptic has a dramatic experience that a new neural pathway is established and the old one gradually falls into disuse. Belief systems are fundamental to filtering reality.

6. Money, power and status

There is also a very tiny minority who choose to be closed-minded skeptics for career advancement. Some may even make money, attain influence and celebrity. For example, you may get a scientist who will reject the paranormal because he or she can get funding for opposing the paranormal. These people will never listen to logic, to science, to rational reasoning, to common sense. They cannot move from their position because they would lose money, power and status.

7. The smorgasbord argument

Professor Stephen Hawking, the physicist, and Professor Richard Dawkins are most notorious for using this 'smorgasbord' argument. They choose only the information that supports their own prejudices. These closed-minded skeptical professors do not know that in a court-room situation their 'smorgasbord argument' would be torn to shreds. Why? Because they would be cross-examined on the critical, most vital evidence that they try to delete. These closed-minded skeptical scientists make a huge error thinking that they are experts in law as well. A litigation lawyer has exclusive technical knowledge of what is relevant, what is admissible evidence – certainly not an astronomer or a biologist. (See hypothetical cross-examinations of Professor Stephen Hawking and Professor Richard Dawkins on www.victorzammit.com).

The evidence has never been rebutted

For the purpose of the record, no genius materialist, no skeptic, no disbeliever, no scoffer scientist has ever written a book explaining why there is not and cannot be an afterlife. No closed-minded skeptic has ever rebutted the afterlife evidence showing where, when, how and why the afterlife evidence cannot be valid. Whereas hundreds of eminent scientists accepted the existence for the afterlife after they investigated it for themselves.

Some unreasonably closed-minded skeptics have made most cowardly attacks on the lives and reputations of great men and women involved in psychic science. They have been responsible for holding back knowledge of the afterlife for several decades. Many are still operating today, accepting large salaries and grants from the materialists to 'debunk' all things relating to the afterlife and psychic phenomena.

A classic comment which illustrates the inflexibility and the determination of the closed-minded skeptic to block any inconsistent new information was made at one of my meetings at a symposium of Humanists in Sydney. One hard-core, closed-minded skeptic burst out after I presented the objective evidence for the afterlife: "I would not believe in the afterlife even if you could prove it to me, Victor!"

Because of conscious and unconscious deletion, closed-minded skeptics only have some pieces of the jigsaw puzzle. They are *not* seeing the overall picture. Yet some of them are very loud and stubborn in their claim that the afterlife does not exist.

I agree with other psychic researchers that even if the perfect demonstration of evidence for the existence of the afterlife – say, materialization of a loved one – was witnessed by closed-minded skeptics, they would refuse to believe the evidence.

240

Historically, closed-minded skeptics and debunkers have opposed every invention and discovery:

- Sir William Preece, former chief engineer of Britain's Post Office, will be remembered for making one of the most 'idiotic' comments in history about Edison's inventions. Sir William stated that Edison's lamp (parallel circuit) was a "completely idiotic idea"

- Professors, including Professor Henry Morton who knew Edison, stated immediately before Edison demonstrated the electric light globe: "On behalf of science... Edison's experiments are a... fraud upon the public"

- The *Scientific American*, the *New York Times*, the *New York Herald*, the US Army, academics – including professor of mathematics and astronomy Simon Newcomb from Johns Hopkins University – and many other American scientists all heaped derision, ridicule and denigration on the Wright brothers, claiming that it was: "scientifically impossible for machines to fly!"

- One of the leading scientists from the French Academy of Sciences stated that hypnosis is a fraud and stated after seeing a hypnotized subject with a four-inch needle in the top of his arm: "This subject has been paid for not showing he's in pain"

- Another scientist from the French Academy of Sciences, after listening to a record made by Edison, stated: "... clearly that is a case of ventriloquism"

- John Logie Baird, the inventor of television, was attacked by closed-minded skeptics who stated it was: "absolute rubbish that television waves could produce a picture"!

241

The rational and informed searcher will reject the world conspiracy theory – that all those highly accredited scientists in different countries who have worked to show that the afterlife exists got together over the last one hundred years or so to fool the rest of the world. The afterlife is inevitable and the consequences of it are enormous.

Chapter 32

WHAT HAPPENS
WHEN WE DIE?

We have flowers such as you have never seen, we have colours
such as your eye has never beheld, we have scenes and forests,
we have birds and plants, we have streams and mountains. You
have nothing to compare them with.

SILVER BIRCH
TRANSMITTED FROM THE AFTERLIFE

Whilst I respect religious beliefs, what you will read in
this book has nothing to do with religion. It is based on
information gathered by hundreds of courageous open-
minded investigators over the last 150 years who used careful empirical observation and analysis. Why does the scientific information
have more authority than the descriptions of the afterlife given by
the Christian, Hindu, Jewish, Islamic, Buddhist and other religions?

First, beliefs about the afterlife in religions that rely on a 'holy
book' were written down by people who lived thousands of years
ago. One big problem is that the original documents do *not* exist any
more. We have copies of copies which we know have been changed
without authority a number of times.

Those who do want to believe what was written centuries ago by
people about whom we know very little have to balance those beliefs against the documented recent afterlife experiences of known

individuals. For example, those who want to believe that the dead lie in unawareness until the sounding of the trumpet on the day-of-judgment have to balance that belief against the experience of millions who have seen and spoken to their loved ones after their death.

Not too many people in the world today accept that some people will be punished in 'hell for eternity' in the afterlife. But some religions still teach that.

So why should you accept the 'scientific' explanation as to what is going to happen to you when you die and the conditions that exist in the afterlife when you inevitably cross over?

Where can we get the accurate information about the afterlife?

There are at least seven major areas of evidence for what happens when you die. These kinds of experience were the source of all religious beliefs but today can be subjected to close examination to look for consistency and and cross confirmation.

First, there are Near-Death Experiences or NDEs.

Second, there are out-of-body journeys and the experiences of shamans and remote viewers.

Third, there is direct experience through apparitions, clairvoyance, clairaudience, and deathbed visions.

Fourth, there are revelations through other-than-conscious states of awareness such as hypnosis, dreams, and holotropic states (the word Holotropic is from the Greek *Holos* meaning whole and Trepein meaning moving or oriented towards. It relates to a powerful method of self-exploration, personal transformation, and healing created by Christina and Stanislav Grof, MD).

Fifth, there are revelations through mental, trance, direct voice, and materialization mediums from loved ones who have died.

Sixth, there are revelations through electronic voice phenomena (EVP) and instrumental trans-communication.

Seventh, there are revelations through channellers and automatic writers from spirit teachers of high degree and from living masters.

244

SOURCES

Just some of the voluminous sources on which the following information is based include: Silver Birch (Ortzen, 1988, 1989, 1990, 1991), Arthur Findlay, White Eagle (Grace Cook), Anthony Borgia, Lord Dowding, Sir William Crookes, Sir Oliver Lodge, Leslie Flint, Ivan Cooke, George Meek, Dr. Carl Wickland, Sir William Crookes, Dr. Robert Crookall, Sir William Barrett, the Rev. C. Drayton Thomas, Geraldine Cummins, Frederic Myers, Raymond Bayliss, Arthur Ford, Johannes Greber, George Anderson, Charles Hapgood, Allan Kardec, Dr. Ian Stevenson, Emanuel Swedenborg, Robert James Lees, Ruth Montgomery, Stainton Moses, Ursula Roberts, Elisabeth Kübler-Ross, Jane Roberts, Helen Greaves, the *Proceedings* of the Society for Psychical Research, Professor James Hyslop, Mark Macy, The American Association for EVP, Edith Fiore, Dr. Raymond Moody, Edward C. Randall.

Some highly recommended recent collections of material from many reliable sources are contained in the following – for details, see Bibliography:

- Michael Tymn: *The Afterlife Revealed: What Happens After We Die* (White Crow Books, 2011)

- Professor Stafford Betty: *The Afterlife Unveiled: What the Dead Are Telling Us About Their World* (O-Books, 2011)

- Professor David Fontana: *Life Beyond Death: What Should We Expect?* (Watkins, 2009)

- Steve Beckow: "New Maps of Heaven: The Conditions of Life on the Spirit Planes" (Online 2103: http://www.angelfire.com/space2/light11/nmh/nmh-index1.html)

Once you are on this planet Earth, it is extremely important to know what is going to happen to you when you die. But how can you find out?

Vital messages from afterlife intelligences transmitted in different countries to us humans on this earth in the last few decades *repeatedly* inform us that:

- All humans survive physical death, no matter what they believe

- 'Hell for eternity' and 'eternal damnation' were invented by men to manipulate the hearts and the minds of the unaware – they do *not* exist. Whilst there *are* lower spheres in the afterlife which are particularly dark, unpleasant, and even horrific – some call them 'hell' – ending up there is *not* for eternity. The universal Law of Progress ensures that, at some time in the future, those with lower vibrations will eventually, even if it takes eons of time – centuries, even thousands of years – obtain higher vibrations and graduate to the higher spheres

- Shortly before they die, people often become aware of a loved one waiting to help them on the journey. They say that they can see glimpses of beautiful scenes, colours and hear music

- At the point of death, we take our mind with all its experiences, our character, and our etheric (spirit) body. This is a copy of the earth body which comes out of the physical body at the point of death and is connected to the earth body by a 'silver cord'. When the silver cord that joins the two together is broken, death occurs

- Spiritual people at the point of death find it easy to lift out of the dead physical body. Some very materialistic people have a very heavy duplicate body and it will be more difficult for the helpers to separate them from their dead physical body

- The state of mind at the point of death is very important. Some pass over consciously and are fully aware of the loved ones who come to welcome them. Others are unconscious and are taken

246

to a special place of rest like a hospital and given treatment Once they recover, there is a grand reunion with loved ones

- People who die suddenly may go through a period of confusion not knowing that they are dead. Sending prayers (positive energy) and love to these people can help them find their way to the light

- Any physical disabilities people had on earth will disappear. Once people have adjusted mentally, there will be no such thing as deformity, sickness, blindness or any other thing which adversely affected them on earth

- In our first stages in the afterlife, the spirit body and our surroundings will seem just as solid as our world seems to us now. You will find yourself in a very natural world, where there are flowers, parks, trees, gardens, rivers, mountains, and buildings. People often find themselves in a home exactly the same as they had in life

- The mind has enormous power in the afterlife and can influence the kind of environment you find yourself in. If you imagine you are at any place, you are there instantly

- There is no such thing as heaven 'up in the sky' or hell 'down below': the location of the afterlife is exactly where we are now – just on a different 'vibrational frequency'. There are many different areas in the afterlife called 'spheres'. Many say that there are at least seven main ones from the lowest level to the highest

- People will be attracted to an area that matches the level of spirituality they reached in their lifetime. 'Like attracts like' in the afterlife. You will be with people who share your interests and beliefs. Most reasonable, decent people find themselves on the 'third level' which is also called 'Summerland'

- Atheists, agnostics, and others will not be prevented from passing on to the higher spheres – what they did in their lifetime and the motivation for what they did will be important, not what they believed in

- Ordinary reasonable people are met by their loved ones – soulmates are reunited. Higher Intelligences inform us that in the afterlife our appearance can return to our best age – for most people from the early to mid-twenties

- The kind of life to be lived in the afterlife – the beauty, peace, light and love which await most people are unimaginable. People talk about a feeling of lightness compared to being in a 'heavy' physical body

- You can continue to learn spiritual lessons in the afterlife and progress to higher, even more beautiful spheres. There will be many opportunities to give spiritual service and to continue learning

- Those who die as children grow to adulthood in the afterlife. They are surrounded with love and special care

- Those in the afterlife have the power to visit loved ones still living on earth. Children who die are usually taken to visit their families and are aware of everything that is happening there

- People in the afterlife communicate with telepathy. When a living person thinks about someone in the afterlife, the message is received telepathically

- Those in the afterlife can send evidence that they are still alive. The most frequent way is through dreams. They appear younger and healthier than when they died

- Those with stubborn fixed ideas about what to expect immediately after death are likely to experience serious problems because the mind has enormous power to create what they expect. Some find themselves in a deep sleep for centuries because that is what they expected

- Like attracts like in the afterlife. Unlike on the earth plane, those with lower vibrations cannot mix freely with those in the higher spheres

- Those who commit suicide are met with love and compassion when they find themselves in the afterlife. Most are disappointed in themselves and regret their decision to leave early

- Those who were consistently cruel are either left alone or are met by those others of the same very low vibrations, with the same very low spirituality to be attracted to the darker lower spheres

- At some time people go through at least one life-review. Nobody judges you, but in your life-review you will re-experience the effects of all of your thoughts, words and actions

- Self responsibility – ultimately, you yourself are responsible for all acts and omissions during your time on the earth plane

- After some time on the 'third level', some people find themselves wanting to move to a more spiritual level. They can progress through spiritual service and go through what is called 'the second death'. The etheric body is discarded just as the physical body was. They find themselves in the fourth level which is much more beautiful but more detached from earth

- In the higher spheres, you will be able to recall and see any event in any period of your existence three dimensionally

- Energy – positive or negative – is a 'boomerang'. When you send out good energy towards someone, that good energy is returned sooner or later. If you send out negative energy by unfairly being dishonest or by cheating or lying or harassing or discrediting or causing harm to someone, that kind of negative energy will inevitably return to you

- Cruelty – mental or physical against humans or animals – is highly karmic and is never justified

- You will reap what you 'sow' is the recognized universal spiritual law of cause and effect. Karma works with mathematical precision which means no one will 'get away with it'. All negative deeds against others have to be experienced for the purpose of 'continuous spiritual refinement'

- It is guaranteed that those who consistently abuse and harass others will have to face their victims in the afterlife

- Those who deliberately violated people's rights will have to apologize and seek forgiveness by the victims before they are allowed to make any progress

- Deathbed conversion? Immediately after we die, our vibrations do not change – not even if one repents shortly before death. We take with us our accumulated vibrations (level of spirituality)

- Being religious does not necessarily mean being spiritual. Not participating in religious rituals, e.g., baptism, confessions, and non-belief in creeds and dogmas does *not* stop anyone from gaining higher spiritually

- Baptism, repentance, and 'the last rites' are absolutely meaningless as a way of getting 'a better deal' immediately after death

- If you help just one person to attain the true knowledge, you would have justified your existence on earth – Silver Birch

- You do not come into this world to have a dream run – without pain, suffering, without problems. The more varied your experience, the more learning from many mistakes, the more valuable your lifetime

- The universal laws operate whether or not you are aware of them.

BIBLIOGRAPHY

The following books have been cited in this book.

Aksakov, A. (1896). *A Case of Partial Dematerialization*. Boston.

Alexander, E. (2012). *Proof of Heaven: A Neurosurgeon's Journey into the Afterlife*. New York: Simon & Schuster.

Allen, M.E. (2007). *The Survival Files*. Hanover, PA: Momentpoint Media.

Allen, M.E. (2012). *The Afterlife Confirmed*. Charleston, VA: CreateSpace.

Almeder, R. (1992). *Death and Personal Survival: The Evidence for Life After Death*. Maryland: Littlefield Adams.

Arcangel, D. and Schwartz, G. E. (2005). *Afterlife Encounters: Ordinary People, Extraordinary Experiences*. Charlottesville, VA: Hampton Roads.

Aries, P. (1982). *The Hour of Our Death: The Classic History of Western Attitudes Toward Death over the Last One Thousand Years*. New York: Vintage Books (2nd edition).

Assante, J. (2012). *The Last Frontier: Exploring the Afterlife and Transforming Our Fear of Death*. Novato: New World Library.

Atwater, P. M. H. (1994). *Beyond the Light: What Isn't Being Said About Near-Death Experience*. New York: Carol Pub Group.

Atwater, P. M. H. (1988). *Coming Back to Life: The After-Effects of the Near-Death Experience*. New York: Ballantine Books.

Atwater, P. M. H. (2007). *The Big Book of Near-Death Experiences*. Charlottesville, VA: Hampton Roads.

252

Baird, J. L. (1988). *Sermons, Soap and Television: Autobiographical Notes.* London: Royal Television Society.

Bander, P. (1973). *Voices from the Tapes.* New York: Drake.

Barbanell, M. (1945). *The Case of Helen Duncan.* London: Psychic Press.

Barrett,W. (1926). *Deathbed Visions.* London: Methuen.

Beard, P. (1970). "How to Guard Against Possession". *Spiritual Frontiers,* Autumn 1970.

Beckenstein, J. D. (2003). "Information in the Holographic Universe". *Scientific America,* Vol. 289, 2 August 2003.

Beckow, S. (undated). *New Maps of Heaven: The Conditions of Life on the Spirit Planes.* Online <www.angelfire.com/space2/light11/nmh/nmh-index1.html> Accessed 15/04/2013.

Benedict, M.T. (1996). "Through the Light and Beyond" in Bailey, L. W. and Yates, J. L. *Near-Death Experience: A Reader.* New York: Routledge 39–52.

Beischel, J. (2007/2008). "Contemporary methods used in laboratory-based mediumship research". *Journal of Parapsychology,* 71, 37–68.

Beischel, J., & Rock, A. J. (2009). "Addressing the survival *vs.* psi debate through process-focused mediumship research". *Journal of Parapsychology,* 73, 71–90.

Beischel, J. (2010). "The Reincarnation of Mediumship Research". *EdgeScience* 3, April–June 2010.

Beischel, J. (2013). *Among Mediums: A Scientist's Quest for Answers.* [kindle edition]. Tucson: Windbridge Institute.

Betty, S. (2011). *The Afterlife Unveiled: What the Dead are Telling Us About Their World.* Reprint edition. London: O-Books.

Borgia, A. (1997). *Life in the World Unseen.* First Published 1954. London: Two Worlds Publishing Co.

Bokris, J. O. (2005). *The New Paradigm: A Confrontation Between Physics and the Paranormal Phenomena.* Normangee, Texas: D&M Enterprises.

Botkin, A. and Hogan, C. (2005). *Induced After-Death Communication: A New Therapy for Healing Grief and Trauma.* Charlottesville, VA: Hampton Roads.

Bourguignon, E. (1972). "Dreams and Altered States of Consciousness in Anthropological Research". *Psychological Anthropology*, ed. F. L. K. Hsu, Cambridge, MA: Schenkman, 403–434.

Bowman, C. (1997). *Children's Past Lives*. New York: Bantam.

Bowman, C. (2001). *Return from Heaven*. New York: HarperColl.

Braude, S. (2003). *Immortal Remains: The Evidence for Life After Death*. Lanham, Maryland: Rowman & Littlefield.

Brinkley, D. and Perry, P. (1994). *Saved by the Light*. London: Piatkus.

Buhlman, W. (1996). *Adventures Beyond the Body: How to Experience Out-of-Body Travel*. San Francisco: Harper.

Buhlman, W. (2001). *The Secret of the Soul: Using Out-of-Body Experiences to Understand Our True Nature*. New York: HarperOne.

Bushman, R. (2009). "Bibliography of Out-of-Body Experiences". Online: <obebibliography.info/index.htm> Accessed 15/03/2013

Butler, J. (1947). *Exploring the Psychic World*. London and Melbourne: Oak Tree Books.

Butler, T. and L. (2003). *There is No Death and There are No Dead*. Reno, NV: AA-EVP Publishing.

Byrne, G. (1994). *Russel*, London: Janus.

Callanan, M. and Kelley, P. (1997). *Final Gifts: Understanding the Special Awareness, Needs, and Communications of the Dying*. New York: Bantam Books.

Campbell, T. (2007). *My Big TOE: A Trilogy Unifying Philosophy, Physics, and Metaphysics*. Huntsville. AL: Lightning Strike Books.

Cardoso, A. (2010). *Electronic Voices: Contact with Another Dimension?* Winchester, UK: John Hunt Publishing.

Carrington, H. (1973). *The World of Psychic Research*. New Jersey: A. S. Barns & Co.

Cassirer, M. (1996). *Medium on Trial: The Story of Helen Duncan and the Witchcraft Act*. Stanstead, Essex: PN Publishing.

Carter, C. (2012). *Science and Psychic Phenomena: The Fall of the House of Skeptics*. Rochester, Vermont: Inner Traditions.

Cayce, H. (1964). *Venture Inward*. Virginia Beach: Association for Research and Enlightenment.

Cerminara, G. (1950). *Many Mansions: The Edgar Cayce Story on Reincarnation.* Reprinted 1988. New York: Paperback.

Chapman, G. (1984). *Surgeon from Another World: The Story of George Chapman and Dr. William Lang.* Revised and expanded. Wellingborough: Aquarian.

Cineflix Productions (2006–2009) *Psychic Investigators.* TV Show. Canada.

Collier, J. (2002). *Quit Kissing My Ashes: A Mother's Journey Through Grief.* Anchorage, AK: Forty-two Publishing.

Cocks, M. (2011). *Afterlife Teaching From Stephen the Martyr.* Guildford, UK: White Crow.

Continuing Life Research. (1996). *Contact Volume 1* #96/01. P.O. Box 11036, Boulder Colorado 80301 USA.

Continuing Life Research. (1997). [Audiotape] *The Miracle of ITC.* [Videotape] *ITC Today.* P.O. Box 11036, Boulder Colorado 80301 USA.

Cooper, C. (2012). *Telephone Calls from the Dead.* Portsmouth: Tricorn Books.

Copeland, M. (2005). *I'm Still Here.* Reno, NV: AAEVP Publishing.

Crawford, W.J. (1919). *Experiments in Psychical Science: Levitation, contact, and the direct voice.* New York: E. P. Dutton & Co.

Crawford, W.J. (1916). *The Reality of Psychic Phenomena.* London: John M. Watkins.

Crawford, W. J. (1921). *The Psychic Structures in the Goligher Circle.* New York : E. P. Dutton & Co.

Crookall, R. (1961). *The Supreme Adventure.* London: James Clarke & Co.

Crookall, R. (1970) *Out-of-the-Body Experiences: A Fourth Analysis.* Reprint. New York 1992: Citadel Press.

Crookall, R. (1973). "Out-of-the-Body Experiences and Survival." in Pearce, J. D. and Higgens, S. W.(eds) *Life, Death and Psychical Research: Studies on Behalf of the Churches Fellowship for Psychical and Spiritual Studies.* London: Rider and Company, 66–68.

Crookes, W. (1871). "Some Further Experiments with Psychic Force." *The Quarterly Journal of Science.* 1 October 1871. London: John Churchill and Sons.

Crookes, W. (1874). *Researches in the Phenomena of Spiritualism.* London: Burns.

Crossley, A. E. (1975). *The Story of Helen Duncan: Materialization Medium.* Devon: Arthur H. Stockwell Ltd.

Cummins, G. (1932). *The Road to Immortality.* Republished 2012. Guildford, UK: White Crow.

Cummins, G. (1956). *Mind in Life and Death.* London: Aquarian Press.

Cummins, G. (1965). *Swan on a Black Sea.* London: Routledge and Kegan Paul.

Currie, I. (1998). *Visions of Immortality: The Incredible Findings of a Century of Research on Death.* First published as *You Cannot Die,* 1978. Shaftsbury: Element Books.

Currier, J., & Neimeyer, R. (2008). "The Effectiveness of Psychotherapeutic Interventions for the Bereaved: A Comprehensive Quantitative Review." Paper presented at the 30th Annual Association for Death Education and Counselling (ADEC) Conference in Montreal, Canada, 30 April–3 May, 2008.

da Rosa Borges, V. (2010). "Polêmica do além" in *Brasília Em Dia* – published em 20 May 2010.

DeRochas, A. (1911). *Les Vies successives, documents pour l'étude de cette question* ("Successive lives, documents for the study of this question"). Paris: Bibliothèque Chacornac:

Dong, P., Raffill, T. E. (1997). *China's Super Psychics.* Cambridge, MA: Marlowe & Company.

Dowding, H. C. T.(1943). *Many Mansions.* London: Rider and Co.

Dunne, B. and Jahn, R. (2003). "Informations and Uncertainty in Remote Perception Research." *Journal of Scientific Exploration,* Vol. 17, No. 2, 207–241.

Eadie, B. (1992). *Embraced by the Light.* London: Aquarian.

Ebon, M. (1976). *The Satan Trap: Dangers of the Occult.* New York: Lombard Associates.

Edelstein, M. G. (1981). *Trauma, Trance and Transformation.* New York: Brunner/Mazel.

Edwards, H. (1962). *The Mediumship of Jack Webber.* Burrows Lea Surrey: The Healer Publishing Co. Ltd.

Estep, S. (1997). *American Association Electronic Voice Phenomena, Inc. Newsletter*, Vol. 16, No. 2.

Estep, S. (2005). *Roads to Eternity*. Lakeville MN: Galde Press.

Extra Dimensions. (1987). Episode 5: *Accounts of Near-Death Experiences*. Online: <youtube.com/watch?v=rQZefyIIbus&feature=youtube> Accessed 15/04/2013.

Fenwick, P. and E. (1995). Interview – "All the questions are essentially simple but the answers remain elusive." *The Daily Mail* (London) 2 March 1995, p. 47.

Fenwick, P. and E. (1996). *The Truth in the Light: An investigation of Over 300 Near-Death Experiences.* London: Headline.

Fenwick, P. and E. (2008). *The Art of Dying: Journey to Elsewhere.* London, New York: Continuum.

Findlay, A. (1931). *On the Edge of the Etheric: The Afterlife Scientifically Explained.* London: Psychic Press Limited, 1970 (66th Impression).

Findlay, A. (1933). *The Rock of Truth.* London: Psychic Press Limited, 1986 (22nd Impression).

Findlay, A. (1947) *The Curse of Ignorance. A History of Mankind from Primitive Times to the End of the Second World War* (in two volumes). London: Spiritualists' National Union, 1993 (Seventh Impression).

Findlay, A. (1955). *Looking Back.* London: Psychic Press Limited.

Fiore, E. (1978). *You Have Been Here Before.* New York: Coward, McCann and Geoghegan.

Fisher, J. (1986). *The Case for Reincarnation.* London: Grafton Books.

Fisher, J. and Wilson, C. (2001). *The Siren Call of Hungry Ghosts: A Riveting Investigation into Channelling and Spirit Guides.* New York: Paraview.

Flammarion, C. (1900). *The Unknown.* London and New York: Harper and Brothers.

Flammarion, C. (1920–23) *Death and Its Mystery.* (3 vol., 1920–21; tr. 1921–23). London and New York: Harper and Brothers.

Flint, L. (1971). *Voices in the Dark.* London: Psychic Press.

Fodor, N. (1934). *The Encyclopedia of Psychic Science.* London: Arthurs Press.

Fontana, D. (2005). *Is There an Afterlife: A Comprehensive Overview of the Evidence.* London: O-Books.

Fontana, D. (2009). *Life Beyond Death: What Should We Expect?* London: Watkins.

Fox, O. (1920). *Astral Projection: A Record of Out-of-the Body Experiences.* Reprinted 1926. New York: University Books.

Foy, R. (2008). *Witnessing the Impossible.* Diss, Norfolk: Torcal Publications.

Fuller, J. G. (1987). *The Ghost of 29 Megacycles.* London: Grafton Books.

Gabbard, G. W. and Twemlow, S. W. (1981). "Explanatory Hypotheses for Near-Death Experiences." *ReVision,* 4: 2, 68–71.

Funk, I. (1907). *The Psychic Riddle.* New York: Funk and Wagnalls.

Gallup, G. (1982). *Adventures in Immortality.* New York: McGraw-Hill.

Garcia-Garcia J., Landa Patralanda V., Grandes Odriozola G., Mauriz Etxabe A., Andollo Hervas I. (2005). "A Randomized, Controlled Bereavement Intervention Study in Primary Care: Preliminary Results." Presented at the 7th International Conference on Grief and Bereavement in Contemporary Society, Kings College, London, 12–15 July, 2005.

Gauld, A. (1971). "A series of 'Drop-in' Communicators." *Proceedings of the Society for Psychical Research* 55, 273–340.

Gauld, A. and Cornell, A. D. (1979). *Poltergeists.* London: Routledge and Kegan Paul.

Gauld, A. (1983). *Mediumship and Survival: A Century of Investigations.* London: David & Charles.

Geley, G. (1927). *Clairvoyance and Materialization: A Record of Experiments.* London: T. Fisher Unwin Limited.

Gibson, A. (1999). *The Fingerprints of God: Evidences from Near-Death Studies, Scientific Research on Creation & Mormon Theology.* Bountiful, Utah: Horizon Pub & Dist.

Giovetti, P. (1982). "Near-Death and Deathbed Experiences: An Italian Survey." *Theta,* 10: 1, 10–13.

Goss, M. (1979). *Poltergeists: An Annotated Bibliography of Works in English 1880–1975.* Metuchen NJ and London: The Scarecrow Press.

Goswami, A. (2001). *Physics of the Soul: The Quantum Book Of Living, Dying, Reincarnation And Immortality.* Charlottesville, VA: Hampton Roads.

Greaves, H. (1969). *Testimony of Light.* London: Neville Spearman Publishers, the C. W. Daniel Company.

Greaves, H. (1974). *The Wheel of Eternity.* London: Saffron Walden, The C. W. Daniel Company.

Greber, J. (1970). *Communication with the Spirit World of God: Personal Experiences of a Catholic Priest.* Teaneck, NJ: Johannes Greber Memorial Foundation 139 Hillside Avenue USA 07666.

Green, C. (1967). "Ecsomatic Experiences and Related Phenomena." *Journal Society for Psychical Research* 44: 111–130.

Green, C. (1973). *Out-of-Body Experiences.* New York: Ballantine.

Greeley, A. M. (1975). *The Sociology of the Paranormal: A Reconnaissance.* Beverly Hills and London: Sage Publications.

Greenhouse, H. (1976). *The Astral Journey.* New York: Avon Books.

Grey, M. (1985) *Return from Death.* London: Arkana.

Greyson, B. and Stevenson, I. (1980) "The Phenomenology of Near –Death Experiences." *American Journal of Psychiatry* 137: 10, 1193–1196.

Greyson, B. (1989). "Can Science Explain the Near-Death Experience?" *Journal of Near-Death Studies,* 8:2, 77–92.

Greyson, B. (1998). "Near-Death Experiences Survival of Bodily Death". *An Esalen Invitational Conference.* 6–11 December.

Greyson, B. (2008). "Is Postmortem Survival A Scientific Hypothesis?" A Talk given for the Society for Scientific Exploration. Online <www.youtube.com/watch?v=sdqRzmXQE78> Accessed 15 April 2013.

Greyson, B. (2010). "Seeing Dead People Not Known to Have Died: 'Peak in Darien' Experiences." *Anthropology and Humanism,* Vol. 35, Issue 2, 159–171.

Gross, M. (1979). *Poltergeists: An Annotated Bibliography of Works in English*, circa 1880–1975. Methuchen, NJ and London: The Scarecrow Press, Inc.

Grosso, M. (1981). "Towards an Explanation of Near-Death Phenomena". *The Journal of the American Society for Psychical Research*, 75: 1, 37–60.

Guirdham, A. (1969). Lecture. "Reincarnation and the Practice of Medicine", delivered on 25 March 1969, before the College of Psychic Science, London.

Guggenheim, B. and J. (1997). *Hello from Heaven: A New Field of Research-After-Death Communication Confirms That Life and Love Are Eternal*. New York: Bantam.

Guirdham, A. (1970). *The Cathars and Reincarnation*. London: Spearman.

Guirdham, A. (1978). *The Psyche in Medicine*. Jersey: Neville Spearman.

Hamilton, T. G. (1942). *Intention and Survival: Research Studies and the Bearing of Intentional Actions by Trance Personalities on the Problem of Human Survival*. Reprinted 1977. London and Toronto: Regency Press.

Hapgood, C. H. (1975). *Voices of Spirit*. New York: Nordon Publications.

Haraldsson, E. *et al.* (1977). "National survey of psychical experiences and attitudes towards the paranormal in Iceland." *Research In Parapsychology* 1976 (182–186). Metuchen, NJ: Scarecrow Press.

Haraldsson, E. (2008). "Ian Stevenson's Contribution to the Study of Mediumship." *Journal of Scientific Exploration*, Vol. 22: 1, 64–72.

Harris, L. (2009). *Alec Harris: The Full Story of His Remarkable Physical Mediumship*. York: Saturday Night Press Publications.

Hart, H. (1959). *The Enigma of Survival: The Case For and Against an After Life*. London: Rider.

Hastings, A. *et al.* (2002). "Psychomanteum Research: Experiences and Effects on Bereavement." *Omega: Journal of Death and Dying*, Volume 43, Number 3, 2002, 211–228.

Heagerty, N. R. (ed.) (1995). *The French Revelation*. Kearney: Morris Publishing.

Hogan, R. C. (2008). *Your Eternal Self.* New York: Greater Reality Publications.

Holbe, R. (1987). *Bilder aus dem Reich der Toten.* Munich: Knaur.

Holzer, H. (1963). *Ghost Hunter.* New York: Bobbs Merril Co.

Holzer, H. (1965). *Ghosts I've Met.* New York: Bobbs Merril Co.

Holzer, H. (1975). *Born Again: The Truth about Reincarnation.* London: Bailey Bros. & Swinfen.

Honorton, C. and Ferrari, D. (1989). "A meta-analysis of forced-choice precognition experiments 1935–87." *Journal of Parapsychology* 53, 281–308.

Hunt, S. (1985). *Ouija: The Most Dangerous Game.* New York: Harper and Rowe.

Hyman, R. (1996). "Evaluation of a program on anomalous mental phenomena." *Journal of Scientific Exploration*, 10: 31–58.

Hyslop, J. H. (1918). *Life after death, problems of the future life and its nature.* New York: E. P. Dutton and Company.

Hyslop, J. H. (1919). *Contact with the Other World: The Latest Evidence As to Communication With the Dead.* New York: Century Co.

Inglis, B. (1977). *Natural and Supernatural: A History of the Paranormal until 1914.* London: Abacus.

Inglis, B. (1984). *Science and Parascience: A History of the Paranormal 1914–1939.* London: Hodder and Stroughton.

Ireland, M. (2008). *Soul Shift: Finding Where the Dead Go.* Mumbai: Frog Books.

Ireland, M. (2009). *Richard Ireland Finds Minerals, Using his Psychic Ability.* Video. Online: <youtube.com/watch?v=lhFXP4_opOQ> Accessed 15 April 2013.

Johnson, R. C. (1971). *The Imprisoned Splendour.* Illinois: Quest Books.

Jones-Hunt, J. (2011). *Moses and Jesus: The Shamans.* Alresford UK: John Hunt Publishing.

Jordan, J. & Neimeyer, R. (2003). "Does Grief Counselling Work?" *Death Studies*, 27, 765–786.

Josephson, B. (1975). "Possible Relations Between Psychic Fields and Conventional Physics," and "Possible Connections between Psychic Phenomena and Quantum Mechanics," *New Horizons,* 1(5), January.

Kardec, A. (1989). *The Spirits Book.* Albuquerque, New Mexico: Brotherhood of Life Incorporated (First Published 1859).

Kardec, A. (1989). *The Book on Mediums.* Albuquerque, New Mexico: Brotherhood of Life Incorporated (First Published 1861).

Keen, M. and Ellison, A. (1999). "Scole: A Response to the Critics." in "The Scole Report." *Proceedings of the Society for Psychical Research.* Vol. 58 Part 220. November 1999.

Kirkpatrick, S. (2000). *Edgar Cayce: An American Prophet.* New York: Riverhead.

Kübler-Ross, E. (1997). *On Death and Dying.* New York: Scribner.

Kübler-Ross, E. (1983). *On Children and Death.* New York: Collier.

Kübler-Ross, E. (1991). *On Life After Death.* New York: Celestial Arts.

Kübler-Ross, E. (1992). *The Facts on Life After Death.* New York: Harvest House.

Kübler-Ross, E. (1995). *Death is of Vital Importance: On Life, Death and Life After-Death.* New York: Talman Company.

Kübler-Ross, E. (1997). *The Wheel of Life.* London: Transworld Publishers (Bantam).

Kübler-Ross, E. (2005). *Is There Life After Death?* Boulder, CO: Sounds True.

Kubris, P. and Macy, M. (1995). *Conversations Beyond the Light with Departed Friends and Colleagues by Electronic Means.* Boulder, CO: Griffin Publishing. (Available from Continuing Life Research, Box 11036, Boulder, Colorado 80301, USA.)

Lamont, P. (2005). *The First Psychic: The Extraordinary Mystery of a Notorious Victorian Wizard.* London: Little, Brown.

Landau, L. (1963). "An Unusual Out-of-Body Experience." *Journal of the Society for Psychical Research* 42: 126–128.

Lazarus, R. (1993). *The Case Against Death.* London: Warner Books.

Laszlo, E. (undated) "New Concepts of Matter, Life and Mind".

Online:<www.physlink.com/education/essay_laszlo.htm> Accessed 15 April 2013.

Leininger, B. and A. and Gross, K. (2009). *Soul Survivor: The Reincarnation of a World War II Fighter Pilot.* New York: Grand Central Publishing.

Locher, T. and Harsch-Fischbach, M. (1997). *Breakthroughs in Technical Spirit Communication.* Available from Continuing Life Research, Box 11036 Boulder Colorado 80301 USA.

Lodge, O. (1916). *Raymond or Life After Death.* London: Cassell & Co.

Lodge, O. (1928). *Why I believe in Personal Immortality.* London: Cassell & Co.

Lodge, O. (1933) "The Mode of Future Existence". Lecture at The Queen's Hospital Annual: Birmingham.

Long, J. and Perry, P. (2010). *Evidence of the Afterlife: The Science of Near-Death Experiences.* New York: HarperOne.

Lonnerstrand, S. (1998). *I Have Lived Before: The True Story of the Reincarnation of Shanti Devi.* Huntsville, AR: Ozark Mountain Publishers.

Lowental, U. (1981). "Dying, Regression, and the Death Instinct" in *Psychoanalytic Review* 68: 3, 363–370.

Lundahl, C. (1981/82). "The Perceived Other World in Mormon Near-death Experiences: A Social and Physical Description." *Omega: Journal of Death and Dying* 12: 4, 319–327.

MacGregor, G. (1978). *Reincarnation in Christianity.* Wheaton Illinois: Quest Books.

McCloy, Nicola, Ninox Television (2008). *Sensing Murder: What You Didn't Know.* Auckland, N.Z. : Hodder Moa.

McKenzie, A. (1971). *Apparitions and Ghosts: A Modern Study.* London: Arthur Baker Ltd.

McLuhan, R (2010). *Randi's Prize: What Sceptics Say About the Paranormal, Why They Are Wrong, and Why It Matters.* Kibworth: Troubador Publishing Limited.

McMoneagle, J. (1997). *Mind Trek: Exploring Consciousness, Time, and Space Through Remote Viewing.* Charlottesville Virginia: Hampton Roads.

McMoneagle, J. (2000). *Remote Viewing Secrets.* Charlottesville Virginia: Hampton Roads.

McTaggart, L. (2008). *The Field: The Quest for the Secret Force of the Universe.* New York: Harper Perennial.

Macy, M.H. (n.d). *The Phenomenal History and Future of ITC Research* . Online: <worlditc.com> Accessed 15/04/2013.

Malone, D. (2010). *Never Alone.* North Sydney: William Heinemann.

Marris P. (1958). *Widows and their Families.* London: Routledge and Kegan Paul.

Martin, J. and Romanowski, P. (1989) . *We Don't Die: George Anderson's Conversations with the Other Side.* New York: Berkley.

Maynard, N.C. (1917). *Was Abraham Lincoln a Spiritualist?* Revised edition, 1956. London: Psychic Book Club.

Meek, G. (1973). *From Séance to Science.* Columbus Ohio: Ariel Press. (Contact Continuing Life Research PO. Box 11036 Boulder Colorado 80301 USA.)

Meek, G. (1987). *After We Die What Then?* Columbus Ohio: Ariel Press. (Contact Continuing Life Research PO. Box 11036 Boulder Colorado 80301 USA.)

Merrill, J. (1982). *The Changing Light at Sandover.* New York: Atheneum.

Miller, P. (1943). *Faces of the Living Dead: The Amazing Psychic Art of Frank Leah.* Republished 2010. York: Saturday Night Press.

Miron. S. (1973). *The Return of Dr. Lang.* Aylesbury: Lang Publishing Co. Ltd.

Mitchell, J. L. (1981). *Out-of-Body Experiences: A Handbook.* New York : Ballantine Books. (Contains an excellent bibliography on out-of-body experiences).

Moen, B. (2005). *Afterlife Knowledge Guidebook: A Manual for the Art of Retrieval and Afterlife Exploration.* Charlottesville Virginia: Hampton Roads Publishing.

Monroe, R. (1971). *Journeys Out of the Body.* New York: Doubleday.

Monroe, R. (1985). *Far Journeys.* New York: Doubleday.

Monroe, R. (1994). *Ultimate Journey.* New York: Three Rivers Press.

Moody R.A. (1975). *Life After Life.* New York: Bantam Books.

Moody, R.A. and Perry, P. (1993). *Visionary Encounters with Departed Loved Ones.* New York: Ballantine Books.

Moody, R.A. and Perry, P. (2010). *Glimpses of Eternity.* New York: Guideposts.

Moorehouse, D. (1996). *Psychic Warrior: The True Story of the CIA's Paranormal Espionage Program.* London and New York: Penguin Books.

Moore, W. (1913). *The Voices.* London: Watts and Co.

Moorjani, A. (2012). *Dying to Be Me: My Journey from Cancer, to Near-Death, to True Healing.* London and New York: Hay House.

Morris, J. D., Roll, W. G. and Morris, R. L. eds. (1976). *Research in Parapsychology.* Metuchen, NJ: Scarecrow Press.

Morris R. *et al.* (1978). "Studies of Communication During Out-of-Body Experiences." *Journal of the American Society For Psychical Research;* Vol. 72, N. 1.

Morse, M. (undated). "Are Near-Death Experiences Real?" Online: <http://spiritualscientific.com/yahoo_site_admin/assets/docs/Are_Near_Death_Experiences_Real.65201445.pdf> Accessed 15 April 2013/

Morse, M. and Perry, P. (1992). *Transformed by the Light.* New York: Piatkus.

Morse, M. and Perry, P. (1993). *Closer to the Light: Learning From the Near-Death Experiences of Children.* London: Bantam Books.

Morse, M. and Perry, P. (1994). *Parting Visions: An Exploration of pre-Death Psychic and Spiritual Experiences.* New York: Piatkus.

Moses, W. S. (1878). *Direct Spirit Writing, Psychography: A Treatise on One of the Objective Forms of Psychic or Spiritual Phenomena.* Reprinted 2006 Whitefish, Montana: Kessinger Publishing.

Muldoon, S. and Carrington, H. (1951). *The Phenomenon of Astral Projection.* London: Rider and Company.

Myers, F.W. H. (1903). *The Human Personality and its Survival of Bodily Death.* Reprinted 1992 . Pelgrin Trust in association with Pilgrim Books.

Neech, W. (1957). *Death Is Her Life. A Biography of Lilian Bailey.* Psychic: Spiritualist Press.

Netherton, M. and Schiffrin, N. (1978). *Past Lives Therapy.* New York: William Morrow.

Newton, M. (1994). *Journey of Souls: Case Studies of Life Between Lives.* Minnesota: Llewellyn.

Newton, M. (2000). *Destiny of Souls: New Case Studies of Life Between Lives.* Minnesota: Llewellyn.

Nicholls, D.J. (undated). *The Mediumship of Helen Duncan.* London: The Noah's Ark Society for Physical Mediumship. Online: <homepage.ntlworld.com/annetts/ark/mediums/helen_duncan_physical_medium.htm> Accessed 15 April 2013.

Ninox Televsion, David Baldock producer. (2006–2010) *Sensing Murder.* TV Series. Auckland.

Nowatzki, N., & Kalischuk, R. (2009). "Post-Death Encounters: Grieving, Mourning, and Healing." *Omega: Journal of Death and Dying* 59(2), 91–111.

Ortzen, T. ed. (1988). *Silver Birch Companion.* London: Psychic Press.

Ortzen, T. ed. (1989). *The Seed of Truth: More Teachings from Silver Birch.* London: Psychic Press.

Ortzen, T. ed. (1991). *A Voice in the Wilderness:Further Teachings from Silver Birch.* London: Psychic Press.

Ortzen, T. ed. (1991). *Lift Up Your Hearts: Teachings from Silver Birch.* London: Psychic Press.

Osis, K. (1961). *Deathbed Observations by Physicians & Nurses.* New York: Parapsychology Foundation.

Osis, K. and Haralddsen, E. (1977). *At the Hour of Death.* New York: Hastings House.

Osty, E. (1923). *Supernormal Faculties In Man.* London: Methuen.

Ostrander, S. and Schroeder, L. (1973). *Psi Psychic Discoveries Behind the Iron Curtain.* London: Sphere Books.

Ostrander, S. and Schroeder, L. (1977). *Handbook of Psi Discoveries.* London: Abacus, Sphere Books.

Owen, A.R.G. (1974). "A Preliminary Report on Matthew Manning's Physical Phenomena." *New Horizons,* 1(4), July 1974, 172–3.

Palmer, J. (1975). "The Influence of Psychological Set on ESP and Out-of-Body Experiences." *Journal ASPR* 69: 193–213.

Pasricha, S. and Stevenson, I. (1986). "Near-Death Experiences in India." *The Journal of Nervous and Mental Disease,* 174, 3: 165–170.

Pearson, R. (1990). *Intelligence Behind the Universe.* Headquarters Publishing Company.

Pearson, R. (2005). *Survival Physics* Online: <http://survivalafterdeath.info/articles/pearson/survival.htm> Accessed 15 April 2013.

Pemberton, A. (1995). Video. *The Science of Eternity,* by Alan Pemberton with Ronald Pearson, Michael Roll. Online: <www.youtube.com/watch?v=yr-xBTipxos> Accessed 15 April 2013.

Peterson, R. (1997). *Out-of-body experiences: How to Have Them and What to Expect.* Charlottesville, VI: Hampton Roads Pub. Co.

Pike, J. (1968). *The Other Side.* New York: Doubleday & Co.

Playfair, G. (1975). *The Flying Cow: Research into Paranormal Phenomena in the World's Most Psychic Country.* London: Souvenir Press.

Playfair, G. (1980). *This House Is Haunted: An Investigation of the Enfield Poltergeist.* London: Souvenir Press.

Podmore, F. (1887). *On Poltergeists.* Reprinted 2010. Whitefish, Montana: Kessinger Publishing, LLC.

Polge, C. and Hunter, K. (1997). *Living Images: The Story of a Psychic Artist.* London: HarperCollins.

Psychic News. Weekly newspaper based in England: Clock Cottage, Stansted Hall, Stansted, Sussex CM24 8UD, UK.

Psychic Press Ltd. (1979). *The Church of England and Spiritualism: The full text of the Church of England Committee appointed by Archbishop Lang and Archbishop Temple to investigate Spiritualism.* London.

Psychic World. Monthly newspaper based in England: 22 Kingsley Ave., Southall, Middlesex UB1 2NA, UK.

Puthoff, H.E. and Targ, R (1976). "A Perceptual Channel for Information over Kilometer Distances." *Proceedings of the IEE.* 64: 3, 329–354.

Puthoff, H.E. (1996). "CIA-Initiated Remote Viewing Program at Stanford Research Institute." *Journal of Scientific Exploration,* 10: 1, 63–76.

Puthoff, H. E. (1984). "ARV (Associational Remote Viewing) Applications" in White, R.A. & Solfvin, J. (1984). *Research in Parapsychology.* Metuchen, NJ: Scarecross Press.

Puthoff, H. E. and Targ, R. (1979). "Direct Perception of Remote Geographical Locations." in Puharich, A. (ed.) (1979). *The Iceland Papers: Select Papers on Experimental and Theoretical Research on the Physics of Consciousness.* Amherst, MA: Essential Research Associates, 17–48.

Quintero, K. (2008). "Psychic detective used to crack Oregon's unsolved murders." *KVAL News.* Nov 19, 2008.

Radin, D. (1997). *The Conscious Universe: The Scientific Truth of Psychic Phenomena.* New York: HarperCollins Publishers.

Radin, D. (2006). *Entangled Minds: Extrasensory Experiences in a Quantum Reality.* New York: Pocket Books.

Ramster, P. (1990). *In Search of Lives Past.* Sydney: Somerset Film and Publishing, P.O. Box 967 Bowral, NSW 2576

Randall, N. (1975). *Life After Death.* Republished 2001. London: Robert Hale and Co.

Randles J. and Hough P. (1996). *Life After Death and the World Beyond.* London, Piatkus.

Raudive, K. (1971). *Breakthrough.* London: Colin Smyth.

Rawlings, M. (1978). *Beyond Death's Door.* Nashville, Tennessee: Thomas Nelson Inc.

Rees, W. D. (1971). "The Hallucinations of Widowhood". *British Medical Journal* Vol. 4, 37–41.

Rhine, J. B., Pratt, J. G., Smith, Burke M., Stuart, Charles E., and Greenwood, J.A. (1940). *Extra-Sensory Perception After Sixty Years.* Holt: New York. Republished 1966. Humphries: Boston.

Richet, C. (1927). *Our Sixth Sense.* Paris: 1927 London: 1930. Reprinted 1957 London and Henley: Routledge and Kegan Paul.

Richet, C. (1923). *Traité de Métapsychique.1922.* (English ed.: *Thirty Years of Psychical Research.*) New York: Macmillan.

Rifat, T. (1999). *Remote Viewing: The History and Science of Psychic Warfare and Spying.* London: Century.

Rinaldi, S. (1996). "Sound Tests Show Spirit Voices are Unique, Non-human" in *Contact*, a publication of Continuing Life Research Issue #96/03 pp.6–7 (available from P.O. Box 11036, Boulder, CO 80301, USA).

Ring, K. (1980). *Life at Death.* New York: Quill.

Ring, K. (1984). *Heading Towards Omega.* New York: William Morrow and Co.

Ring K. and Valarino, E. (1998). *Lessons from the Light: What We Can Learn from the Near-Death Experience.* New York: Insight Books.

Ring, K. and Cooper, S. (1999). *Mindsight.* Palo Alto, CA: Institute of Transpersonal Psychology.

Roberts, J. (1972). *Seth Speaks.* Toronto and New York: Bantam Books.

Roberts, J. (1994). *The Nature of Personal Reality.* New York: New World Library. Reprint Edition.

Roberts, J. (1997a). *How to Develop Your ESP Power: The First Published Encounter with Seth.* New York: Lifetime Books. Reissue Edition.

Roberts, J. (1997b). *Unknown Reality Volume 1.* Reissue Edition. New York: Amber-Allen.

Robertson, T. J. & Roy, A. E. (2001a). "A preliminary study of the acceptance by non-recipients of medium's statement to recipients." *Journal of the Society for Psychical Research* 65: 91–106.

Robertson, T. J. and Roy, A. E. (2001b) . "A Double-Blind Procedure for Assessing the Relevance of a Medium's Statements to a Recipient", *Journal of the Society for Psychical Research.* 65.3: 864, 161–174.

Rogo, D. S. (1974). *An Experience of Phantoms.* New York: Taplinger Publishing Company.

Rogo, D. S. (1983). *Leaving the Body: A Complete Guide to Astral Projection.* New York: Fireside/Simon & Schuster (reprinted 1993).

Rogo, D. S. and Bayless, R.(1955). *Phone Calls from the Dead.* New York: Berkley Books.

Roll, M. (1996a). "The Physicists and Rationalists Case for Survival after the death of our physical bodies." [Booklet]. 28 Westerleigh Road, Downend, Bristol BS 16 6AH.

Roll, M. (1996b). "The Scientific Proof of Survival After Death." [Booklet]. 28 Westerleigh Road, Downend, Bristol, BS16 6AH.

Roll, M. (1996c). "Interview with Michael Roll, Gwen and Alf Bryne and Tom Harrison" in Pemberton, A. (1995). *The Science of Eternity* [60-minute video presented by Alan Pemberton]. Online: <https://www.youtube.com/watch?v=yr-xBTipxos> Accessed 15 April 2013.

Roll, W. (1972). *The Poltergeist.* Garden City NY: Nelson Doubleday.

Rose, A.C. (2005). *The Rainbow Never Ends: The Autobiography of Aubrey Rose.* London: Virgin Books.

Roy, A. (1996). *The Archives of the Mind.* London: SNU Publications.

Roy, A. E. & Robertson, T. J. (2004). "Results of the application of the Robertson-Roy protocol to a series of experiments with mediums and participants". *Journal of the Society for Psychical Research,* 68: 18–34.

Rudy, L. (2011) *Interview* by Dr. Mike Milligan at the 2011 AAOSH Scientific Session. Online: <http://www.youtube.com/watch?v=JLloDuvQR08&feature=related> Accessed 15 April 2013.

Sabom, M. and Kreutziger, S. (1976) "The Experience of Near-death." *Death Education* 1: 2, 195–203.

Sabom, M. (1980). *Recollections of Death.* New York: Harper and Rowe.

Sabom, M. (1998). *Light and Death: One Doctor's Fascinating Account of Near-Death Experiences.* Grand Rapids, Michigan: Zondervan.

Schmeidler, G. R., and McConnell, R. A. (1958). *ESP and Personality Patterns.* Westport, CT: Greenwood Press.

Schmid, L. (1976). *When the Dead Speak.* Zurich (publisher not known).

Schnabel, J. (2011). *Psychic Spies: Whatever happened to America's remote viewers?* Online:<http://www.forteantimes.com/features/articles/5164/psychic_spies.html> Accessed: 15 April 2013.

Schnabel, J. (1997). *Remote Viewers: The Secret History of America's Psychic Spies.* New York: Dell Publishing.

Schroder, T. (1999). *Old Souls: The Scientific Evidence for Past Lives.* New York: Simon & Schuster.

Schwartz, G. (2001). "Accuracy and Replicability of Anomolous After-Death Communication Across Highly Skilled Mediums". *Journal of the Society of Psychical Research*, London, January 2001.

Schwartz, G. and Russek, L. (1999). *The Living Energy Universe.* Virginia: Hampton Roads.

Schwartz, G. Simon, W. and Chopra, D. (2002). *The Afterlife Experiments: Breakthrough Scientific Evidence of Life After Death.* New York: Atria Books.

Schwartz, S. A. (2001). *Mind Rover: Explorations with Remote Viewing.* Alexandria, VA: Nemoseen.

Schwartz, S. A. (2001). *The Alexandria Project.* Bloomington, IN: iUniverse

Schwartz, S. A. (2005). *The Secret Vaults of Time: Psychic Archaeology and the Quest for Man's Beginnings.* Bloomington, IN: iUniverse.

Schwartz, S. A. (2007). *Opening to the Infinite.* Alexandria, VA: Nemoseen (3rd Edition.)

Senkowski, E. (1990). "Instrumental Trans-communication" *TransKommunikation.* Vol. 1.I, No. 1, 1990. Internet Version of 3rd edition of 1995 translated by Heidemarie Hallmann, Germany. Online: <www.worlditc.org> Accessed: 15 April 2013.

Sheldrake, R. (2013) *Rupert Sheldrake Online Experiments.* Online: <http://www.sheldrake.org/Onlineexp/portal/> Accessed 15 April 2013.

Sidgwick, H., Johnson, A., Myers, A. T., Podmore, F. and Sidgwick, E. (1894). Report on the Census of Hallucinations. *Proceedings of the Society for Psychical Research.* 26: 10, 25–422.

Smith, S. (1964). *The Mediumship of Mrs. Leonard.* New Hyde Park, N.Y: University Books.

Smith, S. (1971). *Confessions of a Psychic.* New York: New American Library.

Society for Psychical Research. (1894). *Proceedings* Vol. 10 H 10, London.

Society for Psychical Research. (1898). *Proceedings* Vol. 13 H 10, London.

Society for Psychical Research. (1951). *Proceedings* Vol. 66 July 1951, Number 3.

Society for Psychical Research. (1999). *Proceedings* Vol. 58 Part 220 November 1999. *The Scole Report*, Society for Psychical Research London.

Society for Psychical Research. (1913). *Combined Index* Part III.

Society for Psychical Research. (1913). *Combined Index* Part IV.

Solomon, G. and J. (1999). *The Scole Experiment: Scientific Evidence and Life After Death.* London: Piatkus.

Souter, M. (2004). *As Vidas de Chico Xavier 2 edição revista e ampliada.* São Paulo: Editora Planeta Brazil.

Spottiswoode, J. and May, E. (2003). 'Skin Conductance Prestimulus Response: Analyses, Artifacts and a Pilot Study'. *Journal of Scientific Exploration*, 17: 4, pp. 617–641.

Spraggett, A. (1975). *The Case for Immortality.* Scarborough, Ontario: New American Library of Canada.

Stevenson, I. (1959). "The uncomfortable Facts about Extrasensory Perception." *Harper's Magazine*, 291: 19–25.

Stevenson, I. (1970). 'The case of Uttar Huddar'. *Journal of the American Society for Psychical Research* July.

Stevenson, I. (1972). "Are Poltergeists Living or Are they Dead?" *J. Am. Soc. Psychical Research* 66: 233–252.

Stevenson, I. (1974a). *Xenoglossy.* Charlottesville: University of Virginia Press.

Stevenson, I. (1974b). *Twenty Cases Suggestive of Reincarnation.* Charlottesville: University Press of Virginia. (2nd Revised edition.)

Stevenson, I. (1977). "Reincarnation: Field Studies and Theoretical Issues" in *Handbook of Parapsychology.* Benjamin B., Wolman E. V. N. New York: Reinhold Co. 631–63.

Stevenson, I. (1978). *Cases of the Reincarnation Type Volume 3: Fifteen cases in Thailand, Lebanon and Turkey.* Charlottesville: University of Virginia Press.

Stevenson, I. (2003). *European Cases of the Reincarnation Type.* Charlottesville: University of Virginia Press.

Stearn, J. (1967). *The Sleeping Prophet.* Virginia Beach: A.R.E.

Sugrue, T. (1967). *Story of Edgar Cayce: There is a River.* Reprinted 1997. Virginia Beach: A.R.E.

Superfine Films (2004–2008) *Psychic Detectives.* Television Series. New York.

Sutherland, C. (1992). *Transformed by the Light.* Sydney: Bantam.

Swaffer, H. (1945). *My Greatest Story.* London: W. H. Allen.

Swanson, C. (2003). *The Synchronized Universe: New Science of the Paranormal.* Tucson, AZ: Poseidia Press.

Swedenborg, E. (1758). *Heaven and Hell.* Revised Dole translation. New York 1979: Swedenborg Foundation.

Sylvia, C. and Novak, W. (1998). *A Change of Heart: A Memoir.* Boston: Mass Market Paperback, Grand Central Publishing.

Tabori, P. and Raphael, P. (1971). *Beyond the Senses.* London: Souvenir Press.

Tabori, P. (1972). *Pioneers of the Unseen.* London: Souvenir Press.

Talbot, M. (1991). *The Holographic Universe.* New York, NY: HarperCollins,

Targ, R. (1996). "Remote Viewing at Stanford Research Institute in the 1970s: A Memoir". *Journal of Scientific Exploration,* 10: 77–88.

Targ, R. (1999). "Comments on Parapsychology" in "Intelligence: A Personal Review and Conclusions". *Journal of Scientific Exploration,* 13: 87–90.

Targ, R. (2012). *The Reality of ESP.* Wheaton Illinois: Quest Books.

Targ, R. and Harary, K. (1984). *Mind Race: Understanding and Using Psychic Abilities.* New York: Villard Books.

Targ, R, Puthoff, H.E. (1977). *Mind Reach.* New York: Delacorte Press.

Tart, C.T. (1968). "A psychophysiological study of out-of-the-body experiences with a gifted subject". *Journal of the American Society for Psychical Research* 6: 43–44.

Tart, C.T. (2009). *The End of Materialism: How Evidence of the Paranormal Is Bringing Science and Spirit Together.* Oakland, CA: New Harbinger Publications/Noetic Books.

Tart, C. T., Puthoff, H. and Targ, R. (eds.) (2002). *Mind at Large: IEEE Symposia on the Nature of Extrasensory Perception (Studies in Consciousness)* Charlottesville, VA: Hampton Roads.

Thomas, C. D. (1928). *Life Beyond Death with Evidence.* London: W. Collins Sons and Co. Ltd.

Tucker, J. (2005) *Life Before Life.* New York: St Martins Press.

Twemlow *et al.* (1980). "The Out-of-body Experience: Phenomenology". Paper presented at the annual meeting of the American Psychiatric Association.

Twigg, E. and Brod, R. (1972). *Ena Twigg: Medium.* New York: Hawthorn Books.

Tymn, M. (2008). *The Articulate Dead: They Brought the Spirit World Alive.* Minnesota: Galde Press.

Tymn, M. (2011a). "Was Etta Wriedt the Best Medium Ever?" Blog 31 October 2011<http://whitecrowbooks.com/michaeltymn/entry/was_etta_wriedt_the_best_medium_ever/> Accessed 15 April 2013.

Tymn, M. (2011b). *The Afterlife Revealed: What Happens After We Die.* Guildford, UK: White Crow.

Tymn, M. (2012). *The Afterlife Explorers: Vol. 1: The Pioneers of Psychical Research.* Guildford, UK: White Crow.

Tymn, M. (2012). *Resurrecting Leonora Piper: How Science Discovered the Afterlife.* Guildford, UK: White Crow.

Tyrrell G. (1963). *Apparitions.* Collier Books: New York.

Utts, J. (1996). "An Assessment of the Evidence for Psychic Functioning". *Journal of Scientific Exploration,* 10: 1, 3–30 Online: <http://www.scientificexploration.org/journal/jse_10_1_utts.pdf> Accessed 15 April 2013.

Utts, J. and Josephson, B. (1996). "The Paranormal: The Evidence and its Implications for Consciousnes" in *Times Higher Education Supplement*'s Special section on Consciousness linked to the Tucson II conference *Toward a Science of Consciousness,* 5 April 1996, page (v).

Vandersande, J. (2008). *Life After Death: Some of the Best Evidence.* Parker, CO: Outskirts Press.

Van Lommel, P., Van Wees, R. , Meyers,V . and Elfferich, I.(2001). "Near-death experience in survivors of cardiac arrest: A prospective study in the Netherlands". *Lancet* 358: 2039–2045.

van Lommel, W. (1995). "Doctor Convinced of Survival by New Study." Interview: *Psychic News,* 11 March 1995, Page 1.

Vieira, Waldo (2007*)*. *Projections of the Consciousness.* New York: International Academy of Consciousness. (3ʳᵈ edition.)

Wambach, H. (1978). *Reliving Past Lives.* New York: Hutchinson.

Walker, E. H. (2000). *The Physics of Consciousness: Quantum minds and the Meaning of Life.* Cambridge Massachusetts: Perseus Books.

Westwood, H. (1949). *There is a Psychic World.* New York: Crown Publishing.

White Eagle: The following books were dictated by the Spirit Being White Eagle through the mediumship of Grace Cooke. They have been published and republished many times by The White Eagle Publishing Trust. Liss, Hampshire, England: *The Gentle Brother, Golden Harvest, Heal Thyself, Jesus Teacher and Healer, The Living Word of St. John, Morning Light, The Path of the Soul, Prayer in the New Age, The Quiet Mind, Spiritual Unfoldment 1, 2, 3 and 4, The Still Voice, Sunrise, The Way of the Sun, Wisdom from White Eagle.*

Whiteman, J. (1961). *The Mystical Life.* London: Faber and Faber.

Wickland, C. (1924). *Thirty Years Among the Dead.* Van Nuys, CA: reprinted 1974. Newcastle Publishing Co.

Wilson, C. (2009). *Poltergeist: A Classic Study in Destructive Hauntings.* Llewellyn Publications.

Wilson, C. (1987). *Afterlife.* London: Grafton Books.

Wilson, C. (1981). *Poltergeist.* London: New English Library.

Wilson, I. (1984). *The After-Death Experience.* Harmondsworth Middlesex England: Penguin.

Williams, G. (1989). *A Life Beyond Death.* London: Robert Hale.

Williams, K. (undated) *Near-Death Experiences and the Afterlife.* Online: <www.Near-death.com> Accessed 15 April 2013.

Williams, K. (2002). *Nothing Better than Death.* Bloomington, IN: Xlibris.

Wills-Brandon, C. (2000). *One Last Hug Before I Go.* Deerfield Beach, FL: HCI Publishing.

Wills-Brandon, C. (2012). *Heavenly Hugs Comfort, Support, and Hope from the Afterlife.* Pompton Plains, NJ: New Page Books.

Wiseman, R. & Schlitz, M. (1997). "Experimenter effects and the re-mote detection of staring." *Journal of Parapsychology*, 61: 197–08.

Wiseman, R. & Schlitz, M. (1999). "Experimenter effects and the remote detection of staring: An attempted replication". *Proceedings of Presented Papers: The 42nd Annual Convention of the Parapsychological Association* (pp. 471–479). The Parapsychological Association.

Wolf, F. A. (1985). *Mind and the New Physics*. New York: Simon and Schuster.

Wolf, F. A. (1998). *The Spiritual Universe: One Physicists Vision of Spirit, Soul, Matter, and Self.* Portsmouth, NH: Moment Point Press.

Wright, R. and Hogan, R. C (2011). *Guided Afterlife Connections.* New York: Greater Reality Publications.

Wright, S. H. (2001). *When Spirits Come Calling: The Open-Minded Skeptics' Guide to After-Death Contacts.* Nevada City, CA: Blue Dolphin Publications.

Whymant, N. (1931). *Psychic Adventures in New York*. Reprinted 2012. Guildford, UK: White Crow.

Yogananda, P. (1946). *Autobiography of a Yogi.* Los Angeles: Self-Realization Fellowship.

Yram (1974). *Practical Astral Projection.* New York: Weiser.

Zaleski, C. (1987). *Otherworldly Journeys: Accounts of near-death experiences in medieval and modern times.* Oxford, UK: Oxford University Press.

Zeitschrift fuer Parapsychologie (1927). *O Medium Mirabelli.* (A copy of this book is held in the British Library in London).

Zammit, V. and W. (2010–13). *Afterlife Evidence.* Online: http://victorzammit.com (Accessed 15 April 2013)

Ziewe, J. (2008). *Multidimensional Man.* Lulu.

INDEX

B

C

P

ABOUT VICTOR AND WENDY

Victor James Zammit, B.A.Grad. Dip.Ed. M.A. LL.B. Ph.D worked as an attorney in the Local Courts, District and Supreme Courts in Sydney Australia. For many years his main interest was in human rights and social justice. Around 1990 he began to experience spontaneous clairvoyance and clairaudience which led him to begin a systematic investigation of the afterlife. He was astonished to discover a hidden world of research that he felt provided overwhelming evidence for life after death. Since that time his priority has been sharing his discoveries on his website victorzammit. com where an earlier version of this book has been viewed by more than a million people.

Wendy Zammit B.A. Dip Ed. M.A. is Victor's long-time partner in afterlife research and in life. She worked for a number of years as a professional psychologist/college-school counselor before transferring to adult education. With Victor she has been researching the evidence for the afterlife for more than twenty years. She is the co-author of the Friday Afterlife Report that is sent weekly free of charge to thousands of subscribers all over the world.

Paperbacks also available from White Crow Books

Elsa Barker—*Letters from a Living Dead Man*
ISBN 978-1-907355-83-7

Elsa Barker—*War Letters from the Living Dead Man*
ISBN 978-1-907355-85-1

Elsa Barker—*Last Letters from the Living Dead Man*
ISBN 978-1-907355-87-5

Richard Maurice Bucke—
Cosmic Consciousness
ISBN 978-1-907355-10-3

Arthur Conan Doyle—
The Edge of the Unknown
ISBN 978-1-907355-14-1

Arthur Conan Doyle—
The New Revelation
ISBN 978-1-907355-12-7

Arthur Conan Doyle—
The Vital Message
ISBN 978-1-907355-13-4

Arthur Conan Doyle with
Simon Parke—*Conversations with Arthur Conan Doyle*
ISBN 978-1-907355-80-6

Meister Eckhart with Simon Parke—
Conversations with Meister Eckhart
ISBN 978-1-907355-18-9

D. D. Home—*Incidents in my Life Part 1*
ISBN 978-1-907355-15-8

Mme. Dunglas Home; edited, with an Introduction, by Sir Arthur Conan Doyle—*D. D. Home: His Life and Mission*
ISBN 978-1-907355-16-5

Edward C. Randall—
Frontiers of the Afterlife
ISBN 978-1-907355-30-1

Rebecca Ruter Springer—
Intra Muros: My Dream of Heaven
ISBN 978-1-907355-11-0

Leo Tolstoy, edited by Simon Parke—*Forbidden Words*
ISBN 978-1-907355-00-4

Leo Tolstoy—*A Confession*
ISBN 978-1-907355-24-0

Leo Tolstoy—*The Gospel in Brief*
ISBN 978-1-907355-22-6

Leo Tolstoy—*The Kingdom of God is Within You*
ISBN 978-1-907355-27-1

Leo Tolstoy—*My Religion: What I Believe*
ISBN 978-1-907355-23-3

Leo Tolstoy—*On Life*
ISBN 978-1-907355-91-2

Leo Tolstoy—*Twenty-three Tales*
ISBN 978-1-907355-29-5

Leo Tolstoy—*What is Religion and other writings*
ISBN 978-1-907355-28-8

Leo Tolstoy—*Work While Ye Have the Light*
ISBN 978-1-907355-26-4

Leo Tolstoy—*The Death of Ivan Ilyich*
ISBN 978-1-907661-10-5

Leo Tolstoy—*Resurrection*
ISBN 978-1-907661-09-9

Leo Tolstoy with Simon Parke—
Conversations with Tolstoy
ISBN 978-1-907355-25-7

Howard Williams with an Introduction by Leo Tolstoy—*The Ethics of Diet: An Anthology of Vegetarian Thought*
ISBN 978-1-907355-21-9

Vincent Van Gogh with Simon Parke—
Conversations with Van Gogh
ISBN 978-1-907355-95-0

Wolfgang Amadeus Mozart with Simon Parke—*Conversations with Mozart*
ISBN 978-1-907661-38-9

Jesus of Nazareth with Simon Parke—
Conversations with Jesus of Nazareth
ISBN 978-1-907661-41-9

Thomas à Kempis with Simon
Parke—*The Imitation of Christ*
ISBN 978-1-907661-58-7

Julian of Norwich with Simon
Parke—*Revelations of Divine Love*
ISBN 978-1-907661-88-4

Allan Kardec—*The Spirits Book*
ISBN 978-1-907355-98-1

Allan Kardec—*The Book on Mediums*
ISBN 978-1-907661-75-4

Emanuel Swedenborg—*Heaven and Hell*
ISBN 978-1-907661-55-6

P.D. Ouspensky—*Tertium Organum:
The Third Canon of Thought*
ISBN 978-1-907661-47-1

Dwight Goddard—*A Buddhist Bible*
ISBN 978-1-907661-44-0

Michael Tymn—*The Afterlife Revealed*
ISBN 978-1-970661-90-7

Michael Tymn—*Transcending the
Titanic: Beyond Death's Door*
ISBN 978-1-908733-02-3

Guy L. Playfair—*If This Be Magic*
ISBN 978-1-907661-84-6

Guy L. Playfair—*The Flying Cow*
ISBN 978-1-907661-94-5

Guy L. Playfair —*This House is Haunted*
ISBN 978-1-907661-78-5

Carl Wickland, M.D.—
Thirty Years Among the Dead
ISBN 978-1-907661-72-3

John E. Mack—*Passport to the Cosmos*
ISBN 978-1-907661-81-5

Peter & Elizabeth Fenwick—
The Truth in the Light
ISBN 978-1-908733-08-5

Erlendur Haraldsson—
Modern Miracles
ISBN 978-1-908733-25-2

Erlendur Haraldsson—
At the Hour of Death
ISBN 978-1-908733-27-6

Erlendur Haraldsson—
The Departed Among the Living
ISBN 978-1-908733-29-0

Brian Inglis—*Science and Parascience*
ISBN 978-1-908733-18-4

Brian Inglis—*Natural and Supernatural:
A History of the Paranormal*
ISBN 978-1-908733-20-7

Ernest Holmes—*The Science of Mind*
ISBN 978-1-908733-10-8

Victor Zammit—*Afterlife: A
Lawyer Presents the Evidence.*
ISBN 978-1-908733-22-1

Casper S. Yost—*Patience
Worth: A Psychic Mystery*
ISBN 978-1-908733-06-1

William Usborne Moore—
Glimpses of the Next State
ISBN 978-1-907661-01-3

William Usborne Moore—
The Voices
ISBN 978-1-908733-04-7

John W. White—
The Highest State of Consciousness
ISBN 978-1-908733-31-3

Stafford Betty—
The Imprisoned Splendor
ISBN 978-1-907661-98-3

Paul Pearsall, Ph.D. —
Super Joy
ISBN 978-1-908733-16-0

**All titles available as eBooks, and selected titles available in Hardback and
Audiobook formats from www.whitecrowbooks.com**